MONEY FOR MINORS

MONEY FOR MINORS

A Student's Guide to Economics

MARIE BUSSING-BURKS

GREENWOOD PRESS
Westport, Connecticut • London

Library of Congress Cataloging-in-Publication Data

Bussing-Burks, Marie, 1958–
 Money for minors : a student's guide to economics / Marie Bussing-Burks.
  p. cm.
 Includes bibliographical references and index.
 ISBN-13: 978-0-313-34757-3 (alk. paper)
 1. Economics—Textbooks. 2. Economics—Terminology. 3. Economics—Outlines,
syllabi, etc. 4. Economics—United States. I. Title. II. Title: Student's guide to economics.
 HB171.5.B974 2008
 330—dc22   2008004496

British Library Cataloguing in Publication Data is available.

Library of Congress Catalog Card Number: 2008004496
ISBN-13: 978-0-313-34757-3

First published in 2008

Greenwood Press, 88 Post Road West, Westport, CT 06881
An imprint of Greenwood Publishing Group, Inc.
www.greenwood.com

Printed in the United States of America

The paper used in this book complies with the
Permanent Paper Standard issued by the National
Information Standards Organization (Z39.48–1984).

10 9 8 7 6 5 4 3 2 1

Dedicated to—

Marilyn and Norb Stone,
for years of encouragement.

A word after a word after a word is power.
—Margaret Atwood, poet and novelist (1939–)

Contents

Preface

After teaching college economics for over a decade at the University of Southern Indiana, I was asked to teach economics to a high school class. These students wanted to gain an upper edge in preparation for the competitive field of college micro- and macroeconomics. But I quickly discovered the college-level economics reference dictionaries for this jargon-filled discipline were too technical for them. In an effort to clarify and simplify the economics language, I began making a list of reference words that would aid in understanding the high school material. Soon my list totaled over 400 illuminating terms, and thus began the development of *Money for Minors: The Student's Guide to Economics.*

The words you will find here build a basic foundation for those interested in succeeding in middle school and high school consumer and general economic theory classes. There are many influential economists—even your economics teacher is influencing your economic understanding of the world. However, due to space constraints, only the economists that have influenced major economic theories have been included here. The book provides basic terminology for students just beginning to understand how economies work and function. The entries included cover the vocabulary in macro and micro theory, along with key business terms to build the whole picture of our extensive economic system. This book is unique and will provide the reader with a systematic overview of how economies work. Once you have mastered these terms, I encourage you to extend your economic knowledge by reading more advanced economics books, magazines, and articles.

As you read, remember you are an important part of our economic system. Every day you participate and influence the $13 trillion U.S. economy. Even as a student, you likely have a part-time job, which makes you part of the employed population. You are earning wages and contributing to the economic production of the U.S. economy, the largest and most powerful economy in the world. You may have a savings or checking account and are concerned about the ever-changing interest rates. If you own savings bonds, you are participating in the economy by lending the U.S. government money to finance the $9 trillion national debt. And chances are you are a big spender—the average person in the United States spends just over $45,000 per year on food, housing, health care, cars, clothing, entertainment, and more. Teenagers alone spend over $176 billion a year and influence everything from clothing styles to music to food and more. The key terms in this book provide more in-depth knowledge of the world around you and how your decisions influence this amazing system.

And for students interested in a more in-depth analysis of how our economy works and functions, see Part II: Money 101, for six lessons on our ever-changing economy. Lesson 1, America's Central Bank, details how the Federal Reserve affects the economic actions of every American. Lesson 2, Big Production, examines gross domestic product, an impressive indicator that provides a gauge on both the size and health of the U.S. economy. Lesson 3, Government in Action, examines the federal government's $2.9 trillion spending patterns. Lesson 4, The National Credit Card, examines the rising national debt, now standing at $29,000 per person. Lesson 5, Money, Money, Everywhere, looks at the different kinds of money and how it has evolved over time. And finally, Lesson 6, The Big Bouncing Economy, checks out the business cycle extremes, the good times and the bad times in the economy.

The purpose of *Money for Minors: The Student's Guide to Economics* is twofold. First, the explanation of the economics words will help you understand the fascinating and ever-changing economy. Secondly, the knowledge in Money 101 will prepare you for success in your economics course.

What other steps can you take to succeed in economics? Having now taught college economics for 20 years, along with teaching numerous high school economics courses over the years, I have developed *Ten Steps to Succeed in Economics*. Use these tips and you will not only know the economic jargon, but will understand how the economic system works.

TEN STEPS TO SUCCEED IN ECONOMICS

1. Attend class regularly. Make it your policy always to attend class. If you are ill, contact your instructor as soon as possible for make-up work or to get class notes. This will show your interest. Instructors have a tendency to remember students who attend class regularly, which will work in your favor. Some instructors also count attendance as part of your grade. The study of economics builds upon itself, so any class you miss will limit your ability to understand upcoming economics lessons.

2. Pay attention to your instructor. Always listen closely to the instructor. Write notes and assignments down right away. Don't daydream or talk during class. It is essential that you remain alert. Classroom lessons and lectures will contain terminology that's often new to you and filled with economics jargon.

3. Take great class notes. Keep your attention focused on what the teacher is saying. Listen for clues, such as "this is important" or "you may want to pay close attention to this." Reread notes after class and rewrite any illegible notations.

4. Read your textbook. Stop occasionally as you are reading the economics textbook and put into your own words what you have just read. Economics is technical and it will be beneficial to you if you can make sense of what you have read. At the end of each chapter, write down the main economic points. Also, as you are reading be sure to highlight key phrases and terminology.

5. Ask questions in class. If you have any trouble or concerns, ask your instructor for help. Economists, by very nature, understand the "opportunity cost" of your time and effort in class and want you to succeed. Insightful questions are always appreciated, and your peers may thank you for asking a question they were too shy to ask.

6. Review all special terms and concepts listed in each chapter. Remember, these terms are defined within the economics textbook and/or at the end of the chapter, so be sure to consult them for a complete recap.

7. Use your study guide. Economics texts often come with a study guide. So practice the problems and take advantage of the review and graphing opportunities. Economics makes intense use of graphing to illustrate points and concepts. Practice, practice, and practice.

8. Study often and don't cram. It is essential to keep a regular study schedule. Study often and have uninterrupted study time. Regular study habits will allow you to gradually learn the economic terminology and skills, which build on one another.

9. Use wise test-taking strategy. Read your economics test very carefully, starting with the test directions. If there is anything about the directions you do not understand, ask your instructor. Next, scan the test in its entirety. Then be sure to read each test question astutely. Use your time wisely. Allow time to complete the entire test, but plan to spend the time necessary on the questions that carry the most points. Often in economics this happens to be the essay portion of the exam. (That's why knowing all the terminology is very important.) So scope out the exam before beginning—have a strategy in place.

10. Read and understand *Money for Minors: The Student's Guide to Economics*. Economics has its own technical language and jargon. Used in conjunction with your textbook or as a review for tests, this book will help you learn the language of economics. You are on your way to good grades.

Acknowledgments

I would like to thank Jeff Olson, Senior Acquisitions Editor at Greenwood Publishing Group, for allowing me this exciting opportunity to have fun with economics. It has truly been a pleasure writing this reference book for students who are just embarking on their economic journey through society. My gratitude is also extended to Cathy Bowman for her editorial assistance.

A group of highly skilled economic and business professionals shared their time and expertise in the development of this text. I owe them all a debt of gratitude. Dawn Conner, Senior Economic Education Specialist at the Federal Reserve Bank of St. Louis; Shelly Smith, Senior Economist, Bureau of Economic Analysis; Brian M. Riedl, Grover M. Hermann Fellow in Federal Budgetary Affairs, Heritage Foundation; Peter Hollenbach, Director of Public Affairs, Bureau of Public Debt; Donna Zerwitz, Public Relations Director, National Bureau of Economic Research. Without the input from these and other helpful experts in the field, this book would not have been complete.

Lastly, my thanks go to my husband, Barry; my children, Amie and Katie; and my parents, Connie and Bud, who always encourage my writing.

PART I

DICTIONARY OF ECONOMICS

ABILITY-TO-PAY PRINCIPLE

A taxation principle that states the burden of taxes should be given to those who can afford to pay. Taxing income may reduce one's incentive to work. Nevertheless, in contrast to the benefit principle (those who receive the benefits are taxed), the ability to pay is widespread for modern economies. The U.S. system of federal taxation is based on the ability-to-pay principle, specifically employing a progressive tax, where those with a higher income are taxed a larger fraction of their income than lower-income earners.

ABSOLUTE ADVANTAGE

When a country is able to produce a certain good—like cars, clothing, or microchips—with fewer resources than another country, or is more efficient at production. An absolute advantage may exist because of expertise, educational level, technical dominance, or control of resources. For example, because of technical dominance, Japan makes television sets more efficiently, and at a lower-per-unit cost, than Mexico.

ACCOUNTING PROFIT

The difference between a firm's total revenue and explicit costs.

ACQUISITION

A takeover or buyout of one firm by another. Often used as an entry barrier to ward off potential competitors. Corporate expansion is often accomplished with the purchase of other businesses.

ADAPTIVE EXPECTATIONS

A theory of how people form their expectations about future values based on previous and present values of the variable in question. For example, if the inflation rate is higher than in previous years people will, gradually, and over time, adjust their expectations for inflation upward.

AGGREGATE DEMAND

The total spent on final goods and services within an economy. It is the sum of consumption (consumer spending), investment, government spending, and net exports (exports less imports). An increase in aggregate demand is a necessary condition for an increase in real output, but such economic policies are a matter of debate among economists. John Maynard Keynes cited a lack of aggregate demand as the major cause of the depression. The private sector was not spending enough to keep people employed, so the government needed to increase output by spending, and spending big.

AGGREGATE SUPPLY

The total of all goods and services produced within an economy. Supply side economists, prevalent during the early 1980s Ronald Regan presidency, concentrated on economic policies designed to increase aggregate supply. They believe the best way to stimulate the economy is to raise aggregate supply—the amount of goods and services we produce. They think the economy can be stimulated by creating incentives for people and businesses to produce and work. An example would be to cut taxes, which would create an incentive for people to work harder, and output would go up.

AGRICULTURAL POLICY

Government programs designed to support commodity prices and farm incomes. Such programs have played a key role in U.S. agricultural policy since the 1930s.

News Flash!

Less Than Half of Farms Receive Government Payments
In 2005, less than half of all farms in the United States—42.7%—received government payments through a host of programs providing income support to farmers. For the farms that received a government payment, the average payment was $17,944. But, while the average payment for a rural-residence farm was a mere $5,672, the average payment for a commercial farm was a staggering $64,644.

ALLOCATIVE EFFICIENCY

Making the most efficient use of inputs. A market is efficient when it is highly competitive and produces goods at the lowest possible cost. When a market is efficient, it will coordinate the desires of both consumers and businesses. Firms will become highly competitive, producing the goods and services desired most at a low price. The excessive profits for firms will disappear.

AMERICAN STOCK EXCHANGE (AMEX)

A stock exchange located at 86 Trinity Place in New York City. Companies traded on the AMEX tend to be smaller than those listed on the New York Stock Exchange. AMEX trades 1,598 issues, and it is known for trading corporate bonds, exchange traded funds, and options.

The American Stock Exchange began in the 1800s as an outdoor market. Brokers who could not afford a NYSE seat began to meet outside on a curb on Broad Street in New York City to sell stock. The market moved indoors in 1921. It was originally called the New York Curb Exchange because of the initial street trading, and the nickname "The Curb" has survived.

ANNUAL PERCENTAGE RATE (APR)

The total cost of credit, often referred to as the APR, expressed as a yearly percentage. The APR must account for interest charges plus any other associated charges, such as the membership fees for using a credit card. This allows consumers to compare rates. For example, if a consumer is being charged a 14% APR, while his best friend is being charged a rate of 9% for a credit card, the best friend certainly has the most advantageous deal.

ANTITRUST

U.S. legislation designed to prevent monopoly control. The Sherman Anti-Trust Act of 1890 prohibited acts, including mergers, acquisitions, and contracts, which create a monopoly. The Clayton Anti-Trust Act of 1914 was passed to clarify the Sherman Act, prohibiting price discrimination, certain dealing agreements, and interlocking board of directors among firms selling similar products. The Federal

Trade Commission Act of 1914 created the Federal Trade Commission (FTC), a federal government agency, which oversees antitrust polices.

ARTICLES OF INCORPORATION

A document filed within a state where the corporation will be headquartered. Although often similar, each state has its own laws governing the formation of a corporation. These articles will generally include: name, address, and purpose of the corporation; number and identity of directors; number of stock shares to be issued; and the amount of capital that is to be raised through issuing stock. After approving these articles, the state issues a certificate of incorporation. These two documents together become the corporate charter that gives the corporation its legal existence—in essence, a license to operate from that state.

ASIAN CRISIS

The crisis that threatened a number of East Asian countries during 1997–1998, most notably Indonesia, Thailand, and Korea. These countries found both their financial and economic systems threatened, with declines in currency, the stock markets, and their real economies. For many, severe poverty resulted. Not only was pressure put on the Asian economy, but the Asian crisis also negatively affected global financial markets. One main cause of the crisis was improper private sector financing—the inflow of foreign money used to finance unsound investment projects that ultimately collapsed. In light of the crisis, banking reforms and capital requirements have been initiated by many Asian countries.

ASYMMETRIC INFORMATION

A situation in which all economic agents do not have the same information. For example, imagine a situation in which only the seller knows how much an item costs to produce. The buyer is at a disadvantage and may get fleeced. Asymmetric information can make it hard for two people to conduct business. All the agents do not have full information, and so one or more must conduct negotiations understanding that another may have access to information he or she does not have.

AUCTION MARKET

An organized system whereby financial securities like stocks, bonds, and options are bought and sold. Buyers compete against each other and sellers compete against each other for the best price. Prices continually adjust based upon supply and demand shifts. Examples of auction markets include traditional securities exchanges like the New York Stock Exchange and the American Stock Exchange. (Also referred to as auction market trading.)

AUSTRIAN SCHOOL

Developed in the late nineteenth century by a group of Austrian economists, the thrust of the Austrian School's theories stress the importance of utility to the consumer in determining the value of a product. It is a controversial theory in mainstream economic theory, because it is associated with libertarian social and political views.

AUTHORITARIAN SOCIALISM

An economic system in which the government owns or controls nearly all the factors of production; also known as communism. There is virtually no free enterprise in authoritarian socialism.

AUTOMATIC STABILIZERS

Federal expenditures or receipts that tend to automatically counteract shifts in the business cycle. Automatic stabilizers are built in and do not require any specific changes to legislation by Congress or the President. Taxes and transfer payments are automatic stabilizers of the economy. As an example, an economic downturn causes unemployment benefits to rise. The automatic action of receiving unemployment means Americans have more disposable income to spend and thus stimulate the economy.

AUTOMATION

Production or delivery of goods and services using machines to do the work. Automation may eliminate the need for immediate human intervention, although the setting up of the equipment generally involves a great deal of skilled human labor, and the additional safeguards of monitoring by people is often beneficial. Automation is highly common in our society—look around at such things as traffic signals, escalators, unattended tollbooths, and vending machines. Automation may result in fewer jobs for people, but more opportunities for better-paying, skilled employment.

AVERAGE

The arithmetic mean. It is calculated by summing the numbers in the list and the dividing by the total quantity of numbers in the group. Example:

$$15 + 78 + 60 = 153$$
$$153 \div 3 = 51$$

The average is thus 51.

BALANCED BUDGET

When the funds a government collects is equal to the funds it spends for a year. While this is common at the municipal or state level, it is not so common at the federal level.

BALANCE OF PAYMENTS

A summary record of financial transactions between nations over a 1-year period. These transactions include exports, imports, international investments, international grants and loans, and all other sources of capital inflows and outflows. Technically, the balance of payments should measure all the transactions between residents of the domestic country and residents of the foreign country. In reality, this measurement is very much a ballpark estimate. Many of the numbers are difficult to locate and approximations must be made. But this statistic does provide countries an idea of their financial strengths and weaknesses and allows them to evaluate the relative strength of their domestic currency.

BALANCE OF TRADE

The difference between the value of a nation's imports and the value of its exports. When a country imports more than it exports, like the United States, this number will be negative and is referred to as a trade deficit. When a country exports more goods than it imports it is referred to as a trade surplus.

BALANCE SHEET

An accounting statement that summarizes the total assets, liabilities, and stockholders' equity of an organization, usually on the last day of a quarter or year. Following is the balance sheet formula:

ASSETS = LIABILITIES + STOCKHOLDERS' EQUITY

Assets include current assets, cash, or things that can be easily converted to cash within 1 year (such as marketable securities and inventories), and fixed assets (such as buildings, equipment, and land). Liabilities include current liabilities that must be paid within 1 year (such as accounts payable, taxes payable, and short-term notes) and long-term debt (such as banks loans and bonds payable). The difference between the assets and liabilities is the stockholders' equity, or the net worth of the organization.

BANK

One of several different types of financial institutions whose main job is to accept deposits from customers, and in turn, loan this money out. Commercial banks may be state chartered or federally chartered, and are sometimes referred to as retail banks. Commercial banks attract deposits from the general public and invest these funds in loans. Historically, commercial banks operated from their main offices and branch offices, but many have now made use of the Internet to conduct business. A savings bank, formerly known as a savings and loan, offers services similar to commercial banks but generally concentrates on mortgage loans. Investment banks raise money for firms from private investors or in the financial markets, by finding buyers for their equity and bonds.

BANK HOLDING COMPANY

A company owning one or more banks. According to the Bank Holding Company Act of 1956, companies forming a bank holding company must register with the Federal Reserve System and keep their activities limited to those that are regulated.

BANKRUPTCY

A situation in which a debtor is unable to make payments owed to creditors. Debtors may go to court and file for bankruptcy. In the United States there are two basic types of bankruptcy proceedings. A filing under Chapter 7 is called liquidation. It is the most common type of bankruptcy proceeding and involves a court appointed trustee who takes possession and sells certain nonexempt property of the debtor and then gives the proceeds of the sales to the creditors. Bankruptcy proceedings under Chapters 11 (usually business related), 12 (for family farms), and 13 (for wage-earners), are friendlier for the debtors and even allow them to borrow additional funds. The goal is to work out the debtor's financial problems so he or she can use future earnings to pay off creditors.

BARRIERS TO ENTRY

Obstacles that make it difficult or impossible for firms to enter a market and compete with existing suppliers. Sources of entry barriers commonly include ownership of a key resource, economies of scale (the ability to churn out more and more goods with per unit cost declining), patents, technical superiority, or when a government grants a single producer the right to produce some good or service.

BARTER

A simple exchange of one good or service for another without the use of money. Early societies used barter to take advantage of the division of labor and the gains from specialization. In modern society, money, and the price system—goods and services produced in exchange for a specific amount of standard currency—have largely replaced bartering. Limited arrangements of barter, such as in a small town or among business associates, are still utilized.

BEAR MARKET

Prices are falling or anticipated to fall. A market where investors are selling due to a feeling of gloom about worsening economic conditions.

BECKER, GARY (1930–)

An American economist and winner of the Nobel Prize in Economic Sciences in 1992 "for having extended the domain of microeconomic analysis to a wide range of human behaviour and interaction, including nonmarket behaviour." Becker earned an undergraduate degree from Princeton University and both a master's and a Ph.D. from the University of Chicago. He taught at Columbia University from 1957 to 1968 and then returned to the University of Chicago where he has spent his academic career. At Chicago he is a University Professor in Economics, Sociology, and the Graduate School of Business. Becker is the Rose-Marie and Jack R. Anderson Senior Fellow at the Hoover Institution, a public policy research center. His wide range of research interests includes human capital, economics of the family, economic analysis of crime, influence of social forces on the economy, and population change and economic growth. He is the author of numerous books including *Accounting for Tastes* (Harvard University Press, 1996); *A Treatise on the Family* (Harvard University Press, 1981; expanded edition, 1991); *The Economic Approach to Human Behavior* (University of Chicago Press, 1976); and *Economic Theory* (A. Knopf, 1971). Brief writings are available at the well-known Becker-Posner Blog at www.becker-posner-blog.com—a Web log he writes with judge and legal scholar Richard Posner.

BEHAVIORAL ECONOMICS

An intellectual discipline that combines psychology and economics to study nonrational behavior by economic agents. Psychologist Daniel Kahneman from Princeton University, a leader in the field of behavioral economics, won the 2002 Nobel Prize in Economic Sciences (along with corecipient Vernon Smith from George Mason University, who is notable in the field of experimental economics) "for having integrated insights from psychological research into economic science, especially concerning human judgment and decision-making under uncertainty." Behavioral economics attempts to explain why people engage in behaviors that appear not to be rational. Example: deciding not to engage in physical exercise when its benefits are clear and well known. Yet people may choose not to exercise because they devalue the future, and discount the future benefit of exercising.

BENEFITS PRINCIPLE

A principle of taxation that states the people who benefit from public expenditures should be the people who pay the taxes for these services. For example, gasoline taxes that go to pay for roads are supported by drivers and those using the roads every time they fill up their tanks. In reality, this principle of taxation is extremely difficult to apply. Often the individuals in need of certain public services are the individuals least likely to be able to pay. For example, people who are out of work and in need of unemployment insurance cannot realistically be taxed for this service. The ability-to-pay principle, taxing those who can afford to pay, is the predominant method of taxation in modern economies.

BERNANKE, BEN (1953–)

American macroeconomist and chairman of the Federal Reserve System (2006–). During 2005 he briefly served as chairman of the White House Council of Economic Advisors, and previously spent 3 years as a member of the Board of Governors of the Federal Reserve. Bernanke's research specialties include causes of the Great Depression, measuring the effects of monetary policy on the economy, and inflation targeting. He is the author of *The Great Depression* (2000) and *Inflation Targeting: Lessons from the International Experience* (with coauthors, 1999), as well as several economics textbooks. He has written over fifty scholarly publications and is one of the most cited economists in the world. Bernanke received his B.A. in economics from Harvard University and his Ph.D. in economics from Massachusetts Institute of Technology. He taught at Stanford Graduate School of Business from 1979 to 1985, and Princeton University from 1985 to 1996. He served as chair of Princeton University's economics department from 1996 to 2002.

BLUE-CHIP STOCK

Stocks of strong, well-established companies. Blue-chip companies have a long record of earnings profits and paying dividends to stockholders. Examples: IBM, General Electric, and Citibank.

BOARD OF GOVERNORS

The Board of Governors, located in Washington, DC, oversees the operations of the Federal Reserve System—making supervisory and regulatory decisions, setting reserve requirements, and approving the discount rate. The Board is composed of seven members who serve staggered 14-year terms. Each member is appointed by the President and confirmed by the Senate. The Board Chairman and Vice Chairman positions are named by the President and confirmed by the Senate for 4-year terms and can be reappointed for additional 4-year terms as long as their Board terms have not expired.

BOND

An IOU issued by a company or government. Bonds generally carry a fixed rate of interest, pay the bondholder at regular intervals (generally every 6 months), and have a fixed maturity date. At the redemption date, the bondholder will receive the par value of the bond, generally $1,000. This asset is negotiable (that is, it can be sold) at any time prior to its maturity. Consequently, the price (and hence yield) on the bond fluctuates drastically depending on market conditions.

Bond Basics

Bonds are securities just like stocks, but while stockholders own part of a corporation, bondholders are loaning money to the issuer. The main issuers of bonds include corporations, municipalities, and the federal government. Bonds are essentially an IOU to the bondholder. Bonds generally promise to pay a fixed rate of interest at regular time periods (usually every 6 months), and at the end of a stated time period the bondholder will receive the full amount of the loan, referred to as the principal payment, back. So while stocks may be outstanding indefinitely, bonds have a stated time frame in which they will be redeemed. Although bonds are generally viewed as safer investments than stocks because you receive a principal payment at maturity, you still need to do your homework. All bonds are not of the same quality; some may be safe, others highly risky. Getting repaid is not a sure thing as companies and occasionally municipalities can default on the bond. But don't be concerned about the Treasury obligations you may hold. The Federal Government is considered risk-free by the investment community.

Two major cautions to keep in mind when considering buying bonds:

1. Bond prices can be volatile. Bond prices are inversely related to interest rates. When interest rates fall, bond prices rise. Conversely, when rates rise, bond prices will fall. If you are a long-term investor, holding a bond until its redemption date, the price fluctuations are not a concern. You still get the interest payments promised at the time of issuance and the principal payment at maturity.

But if you are an investor who buys and sells bonds, volatility is definitely an issue. Let's say you purchased a 5% bond—called the coupon rate—and you will receive $50 a year (0.05 × $1,000 face value) in interest for the life of the bond. If interest rates on similar quality and term bonds rise to 6%, these bondholders would receive $60 a year in interest. Of course, $60 sounds better than $50, so what would need to happen in order to get investors interested in purchasing your bond on the secondary market? That's right—in order to sell your bond, you must reduce the price to increase the yield to 6% and make it look more attractive. For this reason, bonds with longer maturity terms tend to be riskier than shorter-term bonds.

2. Bonds can be risky. Don't assume because it is a fixed income security that all bonds are safe. Issuers do occasionally default on their obligations. Corporations can go bankrupt and default on their bonds. Municipalities are

not immune and can occasionally default as well. There are rating systems that help you analyze the risk of particular issues and make educated bond purchases. Ranking assesses the borrower's capacity to meet financial obligations in a timely manner. The higher rated bonds carry less risk while lower rated bonds carry more risk. Moody's, Standard & Poor's, and Fitch all help you with your homework by ranking bonds. Moody's gives bond ratings from best quality to lowest quality—Aaa, Aa, A, Baa, Ba, B, Caa, Ca, and C. Standard & Poor's and Fitch assign bond credit ratings from best quality to default—AAA, AA, A, BBB, BB, B, CCC, CC, C, and D (payment default). Anything BBB (Bbb) and higher is considered investment grade.

Learn to Read a Bond Quote

The business section of newspapers will often display bond tables, although the display format may vary. Bond quotes list essential data about a company's bond prices, which is helpful to investors monitoring the marketability of their bonds. Here is a fictitious municipal bond quote for Zippy School District. The quote is representative of what you will find in the bond business section.

Bond Quotation

(1) Company	(2) Coupon	(3) Maturity	(4) Price	(5) Yield
Zippy Sch Dist	5.000	August 1, 2036	103	4.63

Bond Terminology

Column (1), Company. This is the abbreivated name of the municipality which issued the bond. The complete name is Zippy School District, which issued bonds to fund the districtwide repair and mantainence of school buildings.

Column (2), Coupon. The coupon refers to the annual fixed interest rate that the issuer pays to the bondholder. In this example, the coupon rate is 5.000 (or 0.05 times $1,000 par value=$50) or $50 a year.

Column (3), Maturity Date. This is the date the bond will mature and the bondholder will be paid back the par value, or the principal payment. Commonly this is $1,000. In this example, the Zippy bonds will mature on August 1, 2036.

Column (4), Price. This is the price the bond sold for the last time it was traded. It is quoted in as a percentage of its par value, $1,000. In this example, a last price of 103 means the price was 103% of $1,000 (1.03 times $1,000) or $1,030.

Column (5), Yield, or Yield to Maturity. The yield to maturity indicates the annual return based on the last traded price until the bond matures. Yields and prices are inversely related. In this example, the yield to matutity at 4.63% is lower than the coupon rate of 5%, because the bond is selling at a price over $1,000.

BOURGEOISIE

The property-owning ruling class in Marxist theory. In the era of the Industrial Revolution, the bourgeoisie owned the mass-producing factories where the proletariat, or working class, struggled to earn a living. In 1848, in the *Communist Manifesto*, Karl Marx and Friedrich Engels predicted the proletariat would overthrow the bourgeoisie in a Communist revolution.

BUCHANAN, JAMES MCGILL (1919–)

American economist who was awarded the 1986 Nobel Prize in Economic Science "for his development of the contractual and constitutional bases for the theory of economic and political decision making," commonly referred to as public choice theory. This theory centered on politicians' self-interested behavior and how it, along with other noneconomic forces, affects government economic policy.

Buchanan is the Holbert L. Harris University Professor at George Mason University (1983–). He was born in Murfreesboro, Tennessee, and began his education with a B.A. from Middle Tennessee State College in 1940, followed by a M.S. from the University of Tennessee in 1941. Prior to George Mason, he taught at the University of Tennessee, University of Virginia, Florida State, University of California, Los Angeles (UCLA), and the Virginia Polytechnic Institute.

Buchanan has written over twenty books, including *The Calculus of Consent: Logical Foundations of Constitutional Democracy* (1962); *Public Finance in a Democratic Process* (1966); *Cost and Choice: An Inquiry into Economic Theory* (1969); *Theory of Public Choice: Political Applications of Economics* (1972); *The Power to Tax* (1980); and his autobiography, *Better than Plowing and Other Personal Essays* (1992).

BUDGET

An itemized spending plan based on expected revenues for a given period of time. Budgets can be created for any number of entities, including individuals, businesses, governments, and countries. Budgets often include systematic proposals on how expenses will be met. In a balanced budget, revenues are expected to cover expenses.

BUDGET DEFICIT

A shortfall of revenues compared with spending. The government is said to run a deficit when government spending exceeds government revenue, or when government spending is greater than what the government collected in tax revenues. Since 1945, the United States has run a deficit almost every year. The deficit for fiscal 2007 was $163 billion.

BUDGET SURPLUS

An excess of revenue over spending. The government is said to run a surplus when government revenue exceeds government receipts, or when tax revenue is greater than government spending. The federal government typically runs a deficit almost every year; state and local governments typically run a surplus each year.

BULL MARKET

Prices are rising or anticipated to rise. A market in which investors are buying due to optimism about economic conditions.

BUREAU OF ENGRAVING AND PRINTING (BEP)

A bureau of the U.S. Treasury Department. The BEP furnishes a large variety of security products, including printing billions of Federal Reserve Notes (U.S. currency) for delivery to the Federal Reserve System, U.S. postage stamps for the Post Office, Treasury securities, identification cards, and naturalization certificates. The BEP also produces the hand-engraved invitations on behalf of the White House.

Monetary Trivia!

Dollar Details

• Of all the notes printed by the Bureau of Engraving and Printing, $1 notes make up about 45% of currency production.

• 95% of the notes printed each year are used to replace notes already in, or taken out of, circulation.

• During the Civil War period, the Bureau of Engraving and Printing was called upon to print paper notes in denominations of 3 cents, 5 cents, 10 cents, 25 cents, and 50 cents. The reason for this is that people hoarded coins because of their intrinsic value, which created a drastic shortage of circulating coins.

• The legend "In God We Trust" became part of the design of United States currency in 1957 and has appeared on all currency since 1963.

• During Fiscal Year 2007, it cost approximately 6.2 cents per note to produce 9.1 billion U.S. paper currency notes.

• The $100 note has been the largest denomination of currency in circulation since 1969.

Source: Bureau of Engraving and Printing.

BUSINESS

A business is a private producing unit of society that makes several economic decisions: what to produce, how to produce, and for whom to produce. A business is an organization that uses resources to produce goods and services that are sold to consumers, other firms, or the government.

Ten Steps to Starting a Business

Have you ever thought of starting your own business? Following are ten steps that will provide groundwork in the startup process. Being creative is an essential entrepreneurial skill for starting a business, along with careful planning, which will lay the foundation for success in your venture. Following your dream may not be as risky as you imagined. A total of 66% of new businesses endure at least 2 years, and 44% continue to survive at least 4 years, according to research cited in the *Monthly Labor Review*.

1. Get your business idea. There are nearly 30 million businesses in the United States, and each one began with a smart business idea. Start brainstorming ideas by making a list of things you like to do. If you have a passion for a business, you will devote more time and energy and thereby increase your chances for success. Couple your interests with your strengths and skills for a winning business idea. Can any of your interests or hobbies be transformed into a business? Be creative—Play-Doh, Monopoly, Hula-Hoop, and the Frisbee—fabulous ideas that have revolutionized fun in the world; television, laptops, and cell phones—technology that has transformed society; eBay, House Hunter, FedEx Corporation, Welcome Wagon—service businesses started by people with an entrepreneurial flair. Service businesses are great start-ups for young people. Pet sitting, lawn care, tutoring, and babysitting services are just a few of the businesses students can start that require minimal investment and work well around school schedules. Check out the U.S. Small Business Administration's Teen Business Link at www.sba.gov/teens for business tips specifically targeted to teens.

2. Write a business plan. A business plan is a blueprint of your business. It includes a description of the company, mission, objectives, strategies, plans, and financial requirements and forecasts. The business plan will contain your objectives, the goals to measure your level of success. A dual purpose is served by the business plan: It provides direction to the owner and employees, and it also is essential for bankers and investors who want to analyze the opportunity for success before investing.

3. Choose a business structure. The four main legal types of business structures are:

• *Sole proprietor:* a business owned and managed by one person.

• *Partnership:* a business owned by two or more partners, who share in the profits or losses.

• *Corporation:* a separate legal entity, which has a separate legal existence from its shareholders, and limited liability.

• *LLC:* a limited liablity company, offering personal liability protection to its owners, combined with the tax benefits of a partnership.

   Each of the above business structures has advantages and disadvantages. Consult an accountant or attorney to assist you in this decision to select the form of ownership which best suits your needs.

4. Pick a business name. Okay, here is the fun part. Choose a business name that is catchy and identifies the products and/or services provided by the firm. If the company domain name is available for use on the Internet, you may want to purchase it. If not, you may want to pick a different name. Check with the Secretary of State to make sure the name is not part of an existing corporation or LLC in your state. For unregistered names like sole

proprietorships or partnerships, you may start your search on available state databases or Internet search engines to see how names are being used. Some states will require sole proprietors and partnerships to use their own name as the business name unless they register the name, so be sure to look at your state rules.

5. Find funding. There is a multitude of different ways to finance a startup business. One way is to use your own funds. It is certainly the easiest if costs are minor. Obtaining a bank loan, a loan from friends or relatives, taking in investors, or using venture capital are other options. Check out the details before settling on a source, as each has different requirements for repayment. Of course, if you use your own money you have no debt to repay.

6. Select a location. Picking the right location for your business can make or break your company. Search for the best location you can afford, as it is a major factor in business survival. Be sure to investigate all the legal restrictions of the locale.

7. Obtain permits and licensing. Most states and some cities and counties require a business license for operation. If the item or service you sell is taxable, you will need a sales tax permit. Also, investigate federal requirements for your business, like obtaining an Employer Identification Number (EIN). Investigate necessary permits, licensing, and registration.

8. Organize bookkeeping. Be sure to be prepared to handle income and expense items. Good records, by hand or with the use of software, are essential for a successful business and will assist you in monitoring the financial success of your business. Keep track of documentation throughout the year—receipts, expenses, and deductibles—for an easier time preparing income taxes.

9. Open a bank account in your company's name. Be sure to check out banking institutions for the best deal on a company checking account. Bank fees and services vary a great deal, so look for a competitive offer.

10. Hire great employees. The success of your company lies in the hands of your employees. Hire a talented, energetic, and dynamic group and grow the company together as a team. Your employees will be your biggest asset—or stumbling block—to success.

BUSINESS CASE

A business case is a plan utilized as a tool in decision-making by management. A business case functions like a proposal, and details what the financial impact will be if a specific project is undertaken. If a new product line is being considered by a company, for example, the business case should contain such essentials as the rate of return on the investment, revenue streams, costs, and inherent risks involved with the new undertaking. Along with financial concerns, a business case should explain how the proposed project would enhance the overall vision of the business.

> ### News Flash!
>
> ### Wal-Mart Leads List of Largest Employers
> The retail chain Wal-Mart was founded in 1962 by Sam Walton with the opening of the first Wal-Mart store in Rogers, Arkansas. Wal-Mart Stores, the nation's largest company in 2007, had over $351 billion in revenues. Today, Wal-Mart Stores is an international company with more than 7,000 stores and wholesale clubs. It employs more than 1.9 million people worldwide.
>
> ### Ranking of America's Largest Corporations, by Employees
>
> | Rank | Company | 2006 Number of Employees |
> | --- | --- | --- |
> | 1. | Wal-Mart Stores | 1,900,000 |
> | 2. | McDonald's | 465,000 |
> | 3. | United Parcel Service | 428,000 |
> | 4. | Intl. Business Machines | 355,766 |
> | 5. | Sears Holdings | 352,000 |
> | 6. | Target | 352,000 |
> | 7. | Citigroup | 332,000 |
> | 8. | GE | 319,000 |
> | 9. | Home Depot | 305,760 |
> | 10. | A T & T | 302,770 |
>
> *Source: Fortune Magazine, 2007.*

BUSINESS CYCLE

The regular fluctuations in economic activity, namely Gross Domestic Product (GDP). Prolonged contractions in economic activity are referred to as recessions. Recurrence of periods of recovery, or strong levels of activity, are referred to as expansions. Although the typical cycle can vary greatly, the average U.S. recession runs about 1 year, while the typical expansion period is 5 years long. Business cycles are influenced by a multitude of factors in the economy, including seasonal spending, consumer confidence, inflation, employment, war or the threat of war, monetary policy, or fiscal policy.

BUYER

A person or business that purchases goods and services from a seller in the marketplace for a price.

CALL OPTION

A contract that gives the holder the right to buy a stock at a particular price, called a strike price, within a fixed period of time.

CAPITAL

Goods used in the production of other goods and services. These goods make up a nation's productive capacity because they are needed to turn out all the things and services a nation supplies. Capital goods are produced goods used as factor inputs for production of additional goods and services. These might include machinery, equipment, office buildings, computers, airplanes, and trucks.

In finance, the term often refers to money, specifically funds used by businesses for capital spending activities.

CAPITALISM

An economic system in which private businesses and individuals produce all goods and services. Decisions about what to produce, how to produce, and for whom to produce are made largely by businesses and individuals in the economy. The market forces of supply and demand, or fluctuations in prices, coordinate with individuals' wants. Capitalism is sometimes referred to as free enterprise, the free market, a market economy, or private enterprise. For capitalism to exist, private property rights must be defended by the government. Most developed economies are highly capitalistic.

CAPITAL SPENDING

Investment in new capital, such as machinery, equipment, and trucks. This spending provides the means for expanding production, which in turn generates growth in employment, income, and demand. Strong capital spending is needed for sustained economic growth.

CARTEL

A formal organization of oligopolists, designed to restrict competition or fix prices. Cartels are illegal in the United States. The most famous cartel is an international cartel, OPEC, the Organization of Petroleum Exporting Countries. OPEC, originally formed in 1960, today consists of thirteen oil-producing and exporting countries, from Africa, Asia, the Middle East, and South America.

CENTRAL BANK

A bank in charge of controlling a country's financial and banking system. Central banks typically control monetary policy, issue currency, provide banking services to the government, act as a lender of last resort to commercial banks, and transfer money from other central banks. Examples of central banks include the U.S. Federal Reserve, the Bank of Canada, the Bank of England, and Germany's Bundesbank.

CETERIS PARIBUS

A Latin phrase meaning "other things being equal." Economic models frequently use this phrase in order to make predictions. It gives models predictive value, assuming nothing else changes. All the variables, other than the specific ones being studied, are assumed to remain constant. As an example, an economic model that predicts students' responses to a price change at the soft drink machine assumes other things (like inflation, incomes, unemployment, and student population) remain equal or unchanged.

CHECK

A written order instructing a financial institution to pay a specified amount of money to a third party upon demand. Checks are negotiable instruments transferred by one person to another by endorsement.

> **Monetary Trivia!**
>
> **Loads of Checks**
>
> Do you have a checkbook? How many checks do you write in a year? Even if you are a big check writer, it pales in comparison to the checkwriting activity we do as a nation. Despite the proliferation of plastic, we are still big checkwriters. Can you imagine how many checks are written in the United States each year?
>
> a. 100,000
>
> b. 7 million
>
> c. 55 billion
>
> You guessed it! The correct answer is 55 billion checks are written in the United States each year.

CHIEF EXECUTIVE OFFICER (CEO)

The individual ultimately responsible for the overall strategy and daily activities of a firm. The CEO title is often a dual title given to a senior executive of the firm, such as the president or chairman of the board.

CIRCULAR FLOW

A model that shows the flow of income and expenditures between households and businesses. Income and expenditures will equal one another. Firms pay households for work. People will, in turn, spend the money they receive.

CIVILIAN LABOR FORCE

All people 16 years of age or over in the labor force, excluding those in the armed services. This is the total number of people in an economy willing and able to work.

CLASSICAL ECONOMICS

The dominant school of economics, dating from the publication of Adam Smith's *The Wealth of Nations* in 1776, to the late 1930s. Classical economists generally promote a laissez-faire philosophy, and oppose government intervention. Another predominant belief is that the economy self-regulates. In other words, downturns and recessions are not of great concern because the economy will eventually correct itself and get back on track toward growth and full employment. Along with Smith, other leading classical economists and their books include: Thomas Robert Malthus, *Essay on the Principle of Population as it Affects the Future Improvement of Society* (1798); David Ricardo, *The Principles of Political Economy and Taxation* (1817); Jean Baptiste Say, *A Treatise on Political Economy* (1803); and John Stuart Mill, *Principles of Political Economy with Some of Their Applications to Social Philosophy* (1848).

COASE, RONALD (1910–)

Britain economist who migrated to the United States in 1951, making Chicago his home. Coase taught at the Dundee School of Economics and Commerce (1932–1934), the University of Liverpool (1934–1935), the London School of Economics

(1935–1951), the University of Buffalo (1951–1958), and the University of Virginia (1958–1964). Since 1964, Coase has been affiliated with the University of Chicago. He is currently Clifton R. Musser Professor Emeritus of Economics at the University of Chicago Law School. Coase received the Nobel Prize in Economic Sciences in 1991 "for his discovery and clarification of the significance of transaction costs and property rights for the institutional structure and functioning of the economy."His main contribution to economics has been in the field of property rights. The so-named Coase Theorem appeared in a 1959 article in the *Journal of Law and Economics*, and proposed that many externalities can be solved by competitive bargaining among parties. He later became editor of the same journal from 1964 to 1982. He is currently the research advisor to the Ronald Coase Institute, whose mission is to better understand how real economic systems work so individuals and societies have greater opportunities to improve their well-being.

COASE THEOREM

A 1960 proposition by Ronald H. Coase that many externalities (third-party effects that impact a person not directly involved in the transaction) can be solved by competitive bargaining among parties. The product must have clearly defined property rights and parties must be able to bargain with very low transaction costs. The result will be an efficient use of resources with no taxation or government intervention. Parties have a market incentive to negotiate a mutually beneficial trade. For example, an efficient outcome for a barking dog, a negative externality for a next-door neighbor, might be the payment of a small fee, or bribe, to the owner of the dog to take her dog inside. Conversely, the owner of the dog may end up paying her next-door neighbor a small fee for allowing her dog to remain outside and bark. Either solution is mutually beneficial.

COINCIDENT INDEX

A monthly index released by The Conference Board, a private research group. The index is actually a compilation of four "coincident indicators" (see below) all rolled into one easy number to give a verification of current economic activity. The coincident index roughly coincides with the highs and lows in the economy, so on average, the coincident index turns upward when the whole economy hits an expansion period, and turns downward when the whole economy hits a recession. The indicators in the coincident index are: employees on nonagricultural payrolls, personal income less transfer payments (for example, unemployment, welfare, Social Security, etc.), industrial production, and manufacturing and trade sales.

COINCIDENT INDICATORS

Indicators that have a historical tendency to turn at about the same time the whole economy moves. Coincident indicators are high when economic activity is high, and low when economic activity is down. The most well known U.S. coincident indicator is actually a composite of four coincident indicators, the Coincident Index produced monthly by The Conference Board, a private research group.

COLLATERAL

A piece of valuable property or an asset used to secure a loan. Examples of collateral would be jewels, land, boats, stocks, and bonds.

COMMERCIAL PAPER

Short-term debt obligation issued by a business or bank to investors who have funds to lend. Typically, it is only the large creditworthy firms that sell commercial paper because it is an unsecured form of debt. Maturity terms can run up to 270 days, but 30 days is common.

COMMON STOCK

Stock is a share of ownership in an incorporated company. Owners are entitled to all the rewards as well as risks. Common stock carries with it a claim on the company's assets and earnings. A share certificate is generally issued that represents the ownership in the corporation. This piece of paper represents the number of shares one holds in the corporation. The value of these shares changes daily and may be traded on one of the three most well known exchanges—the New York Stock Exchange (NYSE), the American Stock Exchange (AMEX), and the National Association of Securities Dealers Automated Quotations (NASDAQ).

If you buy common stock, you may experience great reward—a huge increase in the market price of the stock or healthy quarterly dividend checks. Preferred stockholders are entitled to a specified level of dividends before any common stock dividends can be paid. Once the preferred stock payments are made, company profits are available for common stockholders. The good thing is that there is no limit on the amount of quarterly dividends that common stockholders can receive. So while preferred payments stay steady, common payments have the potential for significant upswing.

The downside with common stock is that a dividend may be reduced or eliminated. And in the event the company goes bankrupt, common stockholders are the last group to be paid back. Their claim on assets is inferior to bondholders and preferred stockholders. It is even possible in a bankruptcy situation to lose your entire investment. The upside to common stock is that you have limited liability. If the company goes bankrupt or gets into financial or legal difficulty, the maximum amount of money you can lose is your investment.

Being a shareholder in a company carries with it voting rights. Practically speaking, this means you are entitled to vote at the annual meeting (by proxy ballot or in person) for the board of directors of the company, which in turn appoints the management of the company, and other shareholder initiatives. Generally, each share of common stock carries with it one vote. Although this is generally the limit of power of common stock, if a significant number of shareholders become dissatisfied with the performance of the board of directors, a new group of people can be voted in—often called an overthrow. However, this is generally possible only if a major shareholder—a billionaire like Warren Buffet or a large pension fund— goes along with the revolt.

The term common stock is often used interchangeably with capital stock, if no other form of stock is available from the company.

COMMUNISM

An economic system in which all goods are owned collectively by the workers and placed in the hands of the government. Communism is a theory developed by Karl Marx, who envisioned a classless society where the people in the government represent the workers who control production, wages, and prices.

COMPARATIVE ADVANTAGE

When one country can produce a good at a lower opportunity cost, forgoing production of another good, than another country. Every country has a comparative advantage in some good, and this is the basis for specialization and trade among nations. Countries should produce what they have the greatest advantage in, or specialize in goods where they have the least disadvantage. For example, the United States could supply all its own clothing, yet the United States makes little of its own clothing and much of the population wears clothes made in Bangladesh. The United States has the greatest advantage in technical production, like semiconductors, civilian aircraft, and computer accessories. But third world countries like Bangladesh, even though they may not be as efficient as the United States in making clothing, do have a great deal of low-cost labor, giving them a comparative advantage in clothing manufacturing. It is best for the United States to devote time and resources to technical production and buy the clothing from Bangladesh. World output is maximized when each country produces goods in which they have a comparative advantage, and participates in free trade with other countries to obtain desired goods.

COMPETITION

Individuals and firms bidding against one another for customers and business sales. In a competitive economy, individuals and firms can freely enter into and exit business ventures. Competition provides an opportunity for a business profit, yet it provides no guarantees for success. Consequently, many new businesses will start each year, and an even greater number will go out of business. This competitive drive to win the sales dollars results in many new business services, products, and ventures coming on the market. The U.S. economic system promotes competition; yet the government also regulates and restricts sales.

COMPLEMENTARY GOODS

Goods that are typically used or consumed together. When the price of product "A" falls, the demand for product "B" rises. As an example, peanut butter and jelly are complementary goods. People typically use the two together making the standard fare, a PB&J sandwich. When the price of peanut butter falls, the demand for jelly will rise.

COMPLIANCE COSTS

The cost for firms to comply with government regulations. For example, the costs might include additional administrative staff needed to file reports with regulatory authorities, license payments, and helmets for worker safety protection.

COMPOUND INTEREST

Interest paid on principal and accumulated interest. Assume you deposited $1,000 in an account, which earns 3% compounded annually. At the end of 1 year you would have $1,030, $1,060.90 after 2 years, and $1,092.73 after 3 years. With compounding, your investment grows more quickly than through simple interest. Contrast the amount with simple interest on $1,000 at 3% for 3 years, which totals $1,090. The additional $2.73 is due to compounding.

CONCENTRATION RATIO

The percentage of total industry output produced by the four largest firms. The standard measure of market power depicting the degree to which the industry is centralized.

CONFERENCE BOARD

The Conference Board is a not-for-profit organization and has 501 (c) (3) tax-exempt status in the United States. The U.S. headquarters is located in New York with additional offices around the world. The organization started in 1916, when falling business confidence and labor unrest prompted a group of business leaders to organize The Conference Board. The organization centers on providing information to management in order to help businesses strengthen their performance and better serve society. The board conducts research, holds conferences, makes forecasts, assesses trends, publishes information, and brings executives together to learn from one another. For economists and those interested in economic data, The Conference Board publishes *Business Cycle Indicators*, composites of leading economic indicators (LEI), coincident, and lagging indexes designed to signal peaks and troughs in the business cycle, for nine countries around the world. The organization makes this data available to the public on a monthly basis on their Web site: www.conference-board.org.

CONSTANT RETURNS TO SCALE

This is the scale of operation in which the lowest point of the long-run average cost curve is attained. Put another way, the average long-run total cost stays the same as output changes. Because of the low average total cost, constant returns to scale is the optimum scale of operations.

CONSUMER

A person who buys goods and/or services for personal use, and not for manufacture or resale.

CONSUMER PRICE INDEX (CPI)

Published by the Bureau of Labor Statistics of the U.S. Department of Labor (www.bls.gov), the CPI program produces monthly data on changes in the prices paid by consumers for a representative basket of goods and services. The data is often referred to as a cost of living index because it measures inflation rates for typical households. Specifically, the CPI reflects spending patterns for two population groups: all urban consumers, and urban wage earners and clerical workers. The all-urban consumer group represents about 87% of the total U.S. population. It is based on the expenditures of almost all residents of urban or metropolitan areas. This includes professional business people, self-employed workers, the poor, unemployed, and retired persons, as well as urban wage earners and clerical workers. Some groups are not included in CPI calculations: people living in rural nonmetropolitan areas, on farms, and those in the armed forces, prisons, or mental institutions. About 30,000 families and individuals have provided spending information for use in determining the importance, or weight, of the more than 200 items in eight categories—food and beverage, transportation, medical care, recreation, education, communication, apparel, and other goods and services—in the CPI index structure.

Monetary Trivia!

Inflation Calculation

Inflation, a sustained rise in the prices of goods and services, means the value of your money decreases. The money you get from working, allowance, and even gifts from Grandma and Grandpa, buys fewer goods and services due to the inflation rate. The Bureau of Labor Statistics *CPI Inflation Calculator* allows you to plug in dollar amounts to see how inflation has affected purchasing power over the years. The data used represents changes in the prices of all goods and services purchased for consumption by urban consumers.

Let us assume Sally Spendalot made $200 in 1997, by babysitting 1 week. With that money she went to the mall and had a spending spree, buying a purse, shoes, and makeup. But 10 years later if she wanted to go on a similar spending spree, she would have to earn $259.09, because of inflation. In other words, $200 in 1997 has the same buying power as $259.09 in 2007. Call up the BLS Web page at www.bls.gov/cpi/ and see how inflation affects the value of your money.

CONSUMER SURPLUS

The measure of the benefit to a consumer from participating in the market. Simply stated, it is the difference between what a consumer is willing to pay for a good or service and the price the consumer actually pays. Consumer surplus plus producer surplus measures the total economic surplus, or economic benefit, generated for both consumers and producers.

News Flash!

Think Like an Economist

Eva Economist is working on a consumer surplus problem for the city of Econtown. The city budget director of Econtown is willing to pay $25,500 for a brand new city car. The current price for the new car is $17,500. Help Eva calculate the consumer surplus for the city of Econtown.

$25,500 − $17,500 = $8,000

That's correct. Eva can inform the city budget director there is a whopping $8,000 consumer surplus. But before Eva can deliver the good news to the budget director, she sees an ad in the morning paper. The car dealership is running a sale and the price of the car is now $16,750. How will this affect consumer surplus for the city of Econtown?

The city budget director, who always likes to feel he is getting a good deal for Econtown, will be pleased to learn of the sale and that consumer surplus has risen an additional $750!

$25,500 − $16,750 = $8,750

CONTRACT

A legal agreement between two parties specifying the actions to be taken and payments to be made between parties. A contract may be oral, written, or partially written; however, certain contracts are only valid by law in written form.

CORPORATION

One of the three major types of business organizations (the other two being a proprietorship and a partnership) in the United States. A corporation is a legal entity having an independent existence distinct from the owners. As such, it can enter into contracts in the name of the corporation, own property and other assets, sue, and be sued.

A corporation has several advantages over a proprietorship or partnership. It can raise large sums of money through the sale of stock. It has limited liability, which means the owners can lose only the money they invested in the business. It has a continuity of existence, since ownership is in the form of shares of stock, which can be transferred from one person to another without the corporation being dissolved.

A corporation also has a few disadvantages in comparison to a sole proprietorship or partnership. It is subject to double taxation, meaning the corporation itself must pay income tax on profits and then stockholders must pay income taxes on the dividends they receive from the corporate profits. States charge a fee to obtain a business charter and numerous reports must be filed in the state of incorporation, as well as other states where the corporation does business.

There are two other main choices to consider in lieu of a traditional corporation, or C-corporation, when organizing a business. Choosing to be established as an S-corporation, or limited liability company (LLC), allows you to avoid personal liability, while letting income pass directly onto the owners' income tax returns. LLCs, which are permitted by state statute, do not issue stock and are owned by the member/managers of the company. S-corporations issue stock but allow no more than seventy-five shareholders in total.

COST-BENEFIT ANALYSIS

A study utilized by government and private organizations, which compares the costs of a project with the benefit of providing the project. It is the best use of resources to pursue those projects that have the highest ratio of benefits to costs. The cut-off point for engaging in further projects is when the proposal shows the proposed project will yield no additional benefit over its costs. Government officials use cost-benefit approximations when making decisions on the benefits to society of projects like highway construction or development of a public park. Economists, accountants, or project managers may be enlisted to detail the rough cost-benefit approximations used by government officials to make such decisions. Private organizations engage in cost-benefit analysis when analyzing financial benefits of activities like purchasing equipment, selling products, or expanding production.

COST-PUSH INFLATION

A rise in the level of prices due to an increase in the cost of production inputs, such as wages and material costs. As an example, this type of inflationary spiral occurs when wages increase, causing firms to raise the price of their goods and services, which leads to pressure for further wage increases. This is referred to as the wage-price spiral.

COUPON RATE

The rate of interest paid by a bond until maturity. Coupon payments are typically paid every 6 months. A $1,000 bond which pays 5% means you will receive $50 a year, typically $25 every 6 months.

CREDIT BUREAU

A credit bureau acquires information about how individuals use and repay credit that has been extended (for example: credit cards, consumer loans.) The information, prepared in a credit report, helps lenders assess the creditworthiness of borrowers. A credit report includes such detailed information as current and past employers, credit lines, account and payment history, liens, collection agencies assigned to collect overdue bills, legal judgments, and bankruptcies for up to ten years.

News Flash!

Free Credit Check

Under the Fair and Accurate Credit Transactions Act of 2003 (FACT Act), an amendment of the Fair Credit Reporting Act, consumers have a right to inspect their credit reports annually free of charge. Be sure to link from the FTC's Web site, www.ftc.gov, or go directly to annualcreditreport.com to link to the authorized Web site. The three nationwide consumer reporting companies (Equifax, Experian, and TransUnion) have set up a central Web site, a toll-free telephone number (1-877-322-8228), or you may mail your completed Annual Credit Report Request Form to:

Annual Credit Report Request Service
P.O. Box 105281
Atlanta, GA 30348-5281

This opportunity allows you a chance to check for unauthorized activity, including activity that might be the result of identity theft. (Identity theft is when someone uses personal information—like your Social Security number, credit cards, or bank account number—to access your finances or make purchases.) Credit reporting companies, like the major three listed, sell credit reports to creditors, financial institutions, and other businesses. Your credit information provides credit, work, and residence history. It affects whether you get a loan, a job, or insurance. So be sure to check that your report is accurate and does not contain suspicious activity.

News Flash!

Record Consumer Credit

Consumer credit has reached an all-time high of approximately $2.469 trillion, increasing at a rate of 6% annually. That is a total of

$2,469,600,000,000! Borrowing is clearly big business in the United States. *Source*: The Federal Reserve, August 2007, preliminary data.

CREDIT CARD

A small plastic card issued by a bank or business, which allows the cardholder to make purchases on credit. With a credit card, the cardholder charges purchases of goods or services and reimburses the issuer later. Most credit cards, also called charge cards, have a limit on the dollar amount you can charge each month. The cardholder will receive a monthly statement of purchases, balance owed, fees, and finance charges. A cardholder who does not pay his or her credit card balance in full each month will be assessed a finance charge on the balance.

News Flash!

Credit Card Convenience

A credit card can be either a fabulous convenience that allows you to buy goods and services without cash, or a piece of plastic that makes it all too easy to overspend. Credit is definitely big business in America. A credit card study by the Government Accountability Office found consumers held more than 691 million credit cards. Consumers use credit cards to buy virtually everything, from items at the grocery store, mall, school, and over the Internet, to services at the hair salon, accountant, or doctor's office—to the tune of over $1.8 trillion a year, according to the GAO study. The issuer, typically a financial institution or business, lends the money to consumers. Consumers must pay the money back, but interest rates, fees, charges, and options can vary quite a bit. So be sure to shop around and read the fine print in order to find the best credit card for you. Make sure you fully comprehend the terms of the credit card. And remember, if you are under 18 years of age, you can't apply without your parent's cosignature. Check out these major clues to pump up your credit card knowledge.

Annual Percentage Rate (APR)—The APR states the effective cost of credit, accounting for interest, fees, and services charges, expressed as a yearly rate. Generally speaking, the lower the APR, the better. An APR of 12 means that 1% interest is charged each month. But read the details. Often credit card companies will offer a low introductory APR. So watch out—the rate may increase in a few short months. Your credit card may actually have different APRs. For example, one for purchases, another for cash advances, or overdrafts. To make it even more complicated, the APR can be fixed or it can be a variable rate, tied to an economic index like the prime rate.

Grace Period—This is the interest-free period. It is the period of time between the date of the credit card purchase and the date you must pay your bill in full before the company starts charging you interest on the purchase. Normally, the grace period applies only to new purchases and runs between 20 and 30 days.

Annual Fee—Many credit card companies will charge you an annual fee for giving you credit. Fees commonly range from $25 to $55 per year; gold or platinum cards commonly run from $65 to $75. But you can find some great no-fee cards if you are a good shopper. And remember, you must pay the annual fee even if you never use the card during the year.

Credit Limit—The credit limit is the maximum amount you are allowed to charge on your credit card. If you go over this limit, you may be charged a fee for exceeding the credit limit—an over-the-limit fee.

Finance Charge—The finance charge is the interest charge on your outstanding credit card balance. Companies vary on how they calculate the finance charge, so be sure to do some homework. Often the method that costs the least interest is the adjusted balance; the beginning balance is adjusted downward for payments and credits received during the current billing period.

For detailed information on choosing a credit card wisely, scan the many articles provided by the Better Business Bureau Web site at www.bbb.org or the Federal Trade Commission at www.ftc.gov.

CREDIT LINE

A credit line, or line of credit, is an amount a business or personal customer can borrow. Typically a credit line is extended by a financial institution. The advantage of a credit line, versus a traditional loan, is that the borrower will only pay interest on the amount of money drawn on the line. A possible disadvantage is that the line must be repaid in full every so often, like once a year.

CREDIT RATING

An evaluation of a business firm or individual's creditworthiness, analyzing such determinants as payment history, financial strength, and ability to repay a loan. A strong credit rating means a business or person is a good credit risk and is likely to repay a loan. Any past problems like a bankruptcy or failed loan payments will sharply reduce one's credit rating. The higher the credit rating, the easier it is to obtain a loan from a financial institution.

CREDIT UNION

A financial institution that is organized as a not-for-profit cooperative. Credit unions are organized for people who share a common bond, such as living in the same neighborhood, working at the same business, or going to the same church or school. Most credit unions permit members' family members to join. A credit union is owned by its members and operated by a volunteer board of directors, and thus tends to provide lower loan rates and higher savings rates than other financial institutions.

CROSS ELASTICITY OF DEMAND

A measure showing the relationship between the change in the price of one good, and its effect on the quantity demanded of another good. When two goods are substitutes, the cross elasticity measurement will be positive. For example, if the price of butter rises, consumers will demand more margarine. Likewise, when two goods are complementary, the cross elasticity measurement will be negative. For example, when the price of syrup falls, consumers will demand more pancake mix. When two goods are not related, the cross elasticity measurement will be zero.

CROWDING OUT

When the government borrows money, it occasionally crowds private borrowers out of the financial market. Here's the scenario: The government can pay any interest rate necessary in order to obtain money, but private borrowers like individuals and firms can't always do that. So to make bonds attractive to borrowers, the government may have to push up interest rates to a higher level. This makes it more expensive for individuals and businesses to compete for borrowed funds, so they reduce their borrowing and investment spending.

CURRENCY

The paper money and coins that circulate from person to person in an economy, acting as a medium of exchange to make trading goods and services possible without bartering. In the United States, the Fed issues paper money and the Treasury issues token coins (called "token" because the circulating value is now unrelated to their metal content).

Newly sworn-in Secretary of the Treasury, Henry M. Paulson, Jr., provides his signature to the Bureau of Engraving and Printing Director Larry Felix for use on U.S. paper currency (July 14, 2006). *Source:* The Department of the Treasury.

In 1914, the Federal Reserve began issuing notes, which is today the only paper currency manufactured by the Bureau of Engraving and Printing. *Source:* Federal Reserve Bank of Chicago.

News Flash!

Foreign Currencies
The Bureau of Engraving and Printing not only prints U.S. currency, but has also printed currency for the Philippines in 1928, the Republic of Cuba in 1934, Siam in 1945, and Korea in 1947.

News Flash!

Currency Conversion

Most countries have their own national currency, such as the U.S. dollar or the Swiss franc. These currencies are used to buy and sell goods domestically. But what if an executive who had Swiss francs really needed to trade them for U.S. dollars? The foreign exchange market makes it possible to conduct these international transactions. She or he may be traveling from Switzerland to the United States on a big business trip and wants dollars to spend. Or maybe the executive has a big bank account full of Swiss francs but needs to import some fantastic American-made computer parts from a company that wants to be paid in U.S. dollars. The foreign exchange market is where national currencies are traded for one another, and in this case, Swiss francs traded for U.S. dollars.

The exchange rate is the price at which one currency can be expressed in terms of another currency. Trading is conducted by major banks and dealers. Currency conversion occurs at the current exchange rate. While most nations' exchange rates are allowed to float, some nations have a fixed exchange rate. Often, due to its strength, the U.S. dollar is used as a standard way to express all rates. Check out some of the country currencies and their values in relationship to the dollar.

Major Currency Exchange Rates as of January 2, 2008 (Noon Buying Rate New York City).

Foreign Currency	Symbol	Per U.S. $	In U.S. $
Australian dollar	$	1.1348	0.8812
British pound	£	0.5044	1.9824
Canadian dollar	$	0.9922	1.0079
Euro	€	0.6785	1.4738
Hong Kong dollar	$	7.8107	0.1280
Japanese yen	¥	109.70	0.0091
Swiss franc	₣	1.1174	0.8949

The first column is the foreign currency with the second column displaying the currency symbol. The third column is the number of units of another nation's currency that equals one U.S. dollar. For example, 1.1174 Swiss francs are worth the same as one U.S. dollar. The fourth column is the U.S. dollar value of each unit of foreign currency. In this case, the Swiss franc is worth $0.8949. Note that these values have nothing to do with price parity—in other words, 1.1174 Swiss francs won't buy, in Switzerland, what one U.S. dollar would buy in the United States.

Here's an example. Susie Switzerland sold Andy American a handcarved desk at a price of 10,000 Swiss francs. How many dollars would Andy need to buy the desk? The Swiss franc exchange rate in U.S. dollars is 0.8949.

10, 000 Swiss Francs × 0.8949 = $8, 949

Andy would need $8,949 to buy the handmade desk.
Source: Federal Reserve Bank of New York.

Monetary Triva!

Coin Life
According to the U.S. Mint, the average life of a circulating coin is 30 years. Contrast this long life to the life of an average $1 bill—just 21 months. Coins sure know how to live!

CYCLICAL UNEMPLOYMENT
A temporary form of unemployment that occurs from a downturn in the business cycle. It arises when the economy is in a depressed state—recession or depression—and is operating at less than full capacity and thus has less need for workers.

DEBIT CARD
A small card that looks similar to a credit card, but is different because there is no credit extended—you are paying *now*. A debit card thus functions more like cash or a personal check than a credit card. When you make a purchase at a store, the card reader will automatically debit, or subtract the amount from your bank account.

DEBT
An amount of money owed by one person or group to another. This form of credit is similar to an IOU and must be repaid according to the terms of the agreement. Common types of debt include government bonds, corporate bonds, and commercial paper. Most types of debt call for interest payments at specified periods and repayment on the maturity date. Debt is a common means of existence in developed economies, and is an obligation to repay.

DEBT CEILING
The total limit a governmental entity can borrow. The national debt ceiling is raised periodically by Congress. Effective September 29, 2007, the national debt limit was raised to $9.815 trillion. This is the maximum amount of money the U.S. government can borrow without receiving further authority from Congress.

DEBT INSTRUMENT
A written promise to repay money. A debt instrument could take many forms, including bonds, bank certificates, promissory notes, and mortgages.

DEFLATION
An overall decline in prices in an economy; the reverse of inflation. While inflation may be accompanied by increased output and favorable employment levels, deflation is almost always a negative economic trend, accompanied by unemployment and falling output.

DEMAND
The quantity of a good or service that purchasers are willing and able to buy at different prices.

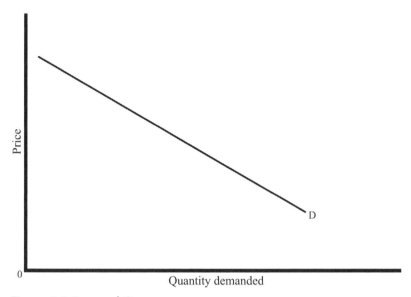

Figure 1.1 Demand Curve.

DEMAND CURVE

A graphical representation of the relationship between the price of a good or service and the quantity demanded. Price and quantity demanded are inversely related. Because a lower price increases the quantity demanded, the demand curve slopes downward from left to right (see Figure 1.1).

DEMAND-PULL INFLATION

A rise in the level of prices caused by excess demand at full employment. The total demand for goods and services exceeds the supply. Competition for the available supply of goods and services forces prices upward. A recent example is the run up in real estate prices.

DEPRESSION

A lengthy recession or severe downturn in the business cycle. Any or all of these may accompany a depression: consumer panic, a sustained level of high unemployment, falling prices, and a prolonged decline in business activity. A depression generally refers to the most extreme slump in business activity in history, the Great Depression. This depression centered in the United States and Europe from 1929 through the early 1930s, having devastating effects on the world economy. Earlier depressions also occurred in the United States in the 1870s and 1890s.

With unemployment rampant, bread lines were common during the Great Depression. A long line of people waiting to be fed in New York City in 1932. *Source:* The National Archives.

Women and children pick green beans at the Dodicha Vegetable Cooperative in the developing nation, Ethiopia. The beans will be sold to a local exporter, who will sell them to supermarkets in Europe. This USAID project has helped link the small farmers to overseas exporters. *Source:* USAID/Kristina Stefanova.

DEREGULATION

The removal or relaxation of government controls. The goal of deregulation is to increase competition and promote efficiency in the marketplace. A recent target of deregulation has been the telecommunications industry, which has resulted in more competition, innovative technology, and falling prices in the industry.

DEVELOPING ECONOMY

An economy with a low level of per-capita GDP and an underdeveloped market structure.

News Flash!

Low Standard of Living in Developing Nations

The United States is projected to have a per capita (per person) Gross Domestic Product (GDP) of $47,159.66 for 2008 (in nominal, or noninflation-adjusted, dollars). GDP is the output of a country, the market value of all final goods and services produced within a nation's borders for the year. Viewing this production number on a per-person basis is often seen as a rough indicator of a nation's economic well-being. The per-capita measure gives a ballpark idea of how well off the average person would be if everyone received an equal portion of the country's production. Contrast the strong U.S. standard of living with those of a group of less-industrialized economies. Although an international player, emerging market China may have the world's largest population at just over 1.3 billion people; 130 million Chinese still fall below the international poverty level. Its per capita GDP is projected to be just $2,574. Developing economy Ethiopia is poverty stricken; agriculture makes up almost half of its GDP ($219). Frequent droughts and poor cultivation have contributed to making it one of the poorest countries in the world.

The United States, however, is one of just seven major advanced economies identified by the IMF, and is the largest and most technologically powerful economy on the globe. Living in the United States provides a high standard of living, low inflation, and strong employment—opportunities abound for a great education, nutrition, health care, and abundant material possessions.

Per Capita GDP, current prices (U.S. $)
(2008 estimated)

Bangladesh	$520.28
China	$2,574.13
Ethiopia	$218.63
India	$941.55
Nicaragua	$979.63
Peru	$3,777.08
Philippines	$1,590.68
Russia	$9,508.27
Venezuela	$8,269.47
Vietnam	$880.80

Source: The International Monetary Fund, Staff Estimates for 2008 (decimals have been rounded).

DIMINISHING RETURNS, LAW OF

The tendency for smaller and smaller increases of output during the production process. Technically, the marginal physical product of a variable input declines as more of it is utilized with a fixed input. For example, as more workers are hired, each worker has less capital to work with and will yield smaller increases in output. So in a factory setting, the first worker makes fifteen chairs a day, the second worker twenty, the third worker fourteen, the fourth worker twelve, the fifth worker ten, etc. Diminishing returns set in after the second worker is hired because after the second worker is hired, per unit output begins to fall. As a rule, diminishing returns tend to set in fairly quickly during the production process.

DISCOUNT RATE

The rate of interest at which banking institutions borrow money from the Federal Reserve District Banks.

DISECONOMIES OF SCALE

The extent an operation or business is beyond the optimum scale; also referred to as decreasing returns to scale. Long run average total costs rise as more of a quantity is produced. As plant size grows, for example, production becomes less efficient. Diseconomies could result from internal problems with managing workers in such a large environment. Workers may feel alienated in such a large plant and not perform productively. Bureaucracy, internal conflict, and excess management pay can also cause diseconomies of scale to exist.

DISPOSABLE PERSONAL INCOME (DPI)

Personal income minus personal taxes. Individuals can spend or save this portion of their money.

News Flash!

Teens Spending Billions

The day of your birth marked a mini-spending boom for the economy. Your arrival brought the purchase of baby clothes, food, furniture, diapers, and no doubt a multitude of announcement cards from your proud parents, and baby presents from friends and family. As you grew up, your parents spent money providing for you, further propelling the economy. But at some point, likely when you were around 5 or 6 years old, you began making minor spending decisions on your own. Your first purchase may have been a toy or book with the $5 Grandma gave you for Christmas. Or perhaps it was bubble gum you bought with the 50 cents you earned for taking out the trash. Guess what? You have come a long way baby!

Teenagers today spend billions annually in the United States and influence everything from clothing styles to music and movies to food and cell phones. Teenage Research Unlimited in Northbrook, Illinois, projects America's 12-to-19-year-old group spending at $176 billion annually for 2007.

Just to give you an idea of how powerful that number really is, teen-buying-power could total the entire gross domestic product (current dollar, advance estimates 2006) of Vermont, North Dakota, Wyoming, Montana, and Delaware. And we would even have about $3 billion in spending change left over.

Vermont	$24.2 billion
North Dakota	$26.4 billion
Wyoming	$29.6 billion
Montana	$32.3 billion
Delaware	$60.4 billion

Teen Population Rising

Don't expect the spending of this influential group to die down. The Census Bureau estimated the U.S. teen population (ages 15–19) numbered 21.3 million in 2006, and is projected to total 36.7 million in 2100. Their younger counterparts (ages 10–14), total 20.6 million in 2006 with growth projected at 36.2 million for 2100. Teenagers are a powerful and growing segment of the U.S. economy.

DIVERSIFICATION

The spreading of an investment portfolio over a number of different investments to reduce risk. A portfolio should be diversified between assets categories and within asset categories. Combine asset categories to reduce risk exposure, such as stocks, bonds, cash, mutual funds, and real estate. For example, to diversify stocks, pick stocks in different industries and of different company sizes.

DIVIDEND

The portion of a corporation's net earnings that are distributed to stockholders. This amount is decided upon by the firm's board of directors. Typically, dividends are paid quarterly.

DIVISION OF LABOR

The breakdown of jobs so each worker specializes in an activity that best utilizes his or her skills in the production process. When jobs are simplified and narrowed, productivity increases because skills are refined and workers don't waste time moving from task to task.

DOUBLE COINCIDENCE OF WANTS

For a trade to take place in a barter economy, it is necessary that a double coincidence of wants occur between the two traders. What each individual is willing to exchange must be exactly what another individual wants for a trade to occur.

DUMPING

Selling goods in a foreign market at a low price, a price that domestic producers regard as unfair. The price is either below the cost of production or a price below the domestic producers' price. Dumping may simply be used intermittently to remove unwanted inventory on the part of a foreign producer, or could be part of a long-term plan to force a domestic producer out of business.

DUOPOLY

A market structure in which there are only two firms producing a good or service; an oligopoly in which there are only two members.

EARNINGS

The profit a business produces within a given time frame. Earnings typically refer to after-tax profits, before dividends have been paid to stockholders. Earnings per share refer to these profits divided by the number of shares a corporation has outstanding.

E-COMMERCE

Electronic commerce; conducting business over the Internet.

ECONOMIC GROWTH

An increase in output, or real gross domestic product (GDP). This number is measured every quarter by the Bureau of Economic Analysis (BEA) on an annualized basis. U.S. economists generally agree that growth in the range from 3 to 5 % is acceptable. Anything lower tends to signal a sluggish economy, while higher numbers suggest the economy may be booming, accompanied by too much inflation.

News Flash!

Special Events Pump Millions into Local Economies

Along with increasing a city's profile and cultural activities, special events bring big business to a region. Visitors and attendees pump money into local restaurants, shopping centers, neighborhood stores, hotels, and transportation. The government gets a boost too, as federal, state, and local revenues go up from all the business activity. Jobs—both full and part-time—are created and incomes burgeon. Check out some of the phenomenal numbers.

The average economic impact of the Super Bowl on a host city is between $300 and $400 million, according to the nonprofit Arizona Super Bowl Host Committee. The Arizona Super Bowl XLII, February 3, 2008, was held at the University of Phoenix Stadium in Glendale. The typical person attending the Super Bowl stayed four nights in a hotel and spent between $1,500 and $2,000 while at the event. See www.azsuperbowl.com.

The Ohio Quarter Horse Association (OQHA) hosts the All-American Quarter Horse Congress each October at the Ohio Expo Center in Columbus. The show is the world's largest single-breed horse show, receiving more than 16,000 horse show entries and bringing more than 650,000 people to the Columbus area over the 3-week period. The event brings over $110 million to the central Ohio region. See www.oqha.com.

The Tampa Bay Business Committee for the Arts (BCA) is a not-for-profit organization that promotes business support for the arts. The organization's recently commissioned impact study showed the arts bring over $402.2 million annually to Hillsborough and Pinellas counties. The study found that local arts organizations hosted 5.5 million visitors annually; provide 7,000 jobs, and salaries of $147 million. See www.tbbca.org.

ECONOMIC IMPACT

Economic impact is the change in wealth that results from an event, project, institution, or business. Economic impacts are typically estimated in increased jobs, sales, household income, and revenue generated within a region.

ECONOMIC INDICATOR

A statistic that provides antidotal information about economic activity. Economic statistics, interpreted wisely, will allow one to note important trends in the economy and further make better-educated financial and business decisions.

The Fabulous Five Economic Indicators

Each day you are bombarded by a multitude of economic indicators, hundreds in fact—everything from unemployment and production numbers, to price data. Most are useful in some realm, and some are just silly, like the old "briefcase indicator"—former Fed chief Alan Greenspan's full briefcase would indicate an interest rate change is on the way, while a slim briefcase would suggest no rate change.

You will find a host of economic indicators reported by the news media. That's great news if you are an economist or financial analyst; you have plenty of data to sort through, analyze, and evaluate. The more data, the better, for a professional forecaster. Let's face it; the real world—that's the rest of us—needs to follow only a few measurements to get a feel for the health of the U.S. economy. It is good to track a handful—five will provide a picture of the economy. Viewing only one at a time can be problematic because of mixed readings and revisions of the data. The economy can be tough to read, but here is a great start. Follow the "Fabulous Five" indicators, which will give you a pulse on the general direction of the U.S. economy.

Indicator	Definition	Released by	How Often	Why Important	Hint
S&P 500	An index of 500 large cap stocks that are widely held, representing 75% of the market and $1.53 trillion in assets.	Standard & Poor's www.marketwatch.com/quotes/$spx	Daily	Stock market leads economic activity.	A rising market suggests investors are positive, buying big, and the economy will boom; a negative trend signals tough times ahead.
CP1-U	Measures price changes for a market basket of goods and services typically purchased by urban consumers (87 % of the population).	Bureau of Labor Statistics www.bls.gov	Monthly	Most widely used measure of inflation in the economy. Used as an economic barometer of price changes in the economy, to adjust consumers' income payments (such as Social Security), and to adjust economic series for price changes.	Fed seeks to maintain low inflation, but watch out because rising inflation tells you costs are going up!

(*Continued*)

(*Continued*)

Indicator	Definition	Released by	How Often	Why Important	Hint
Housing Starts	Measures initial construction of residential units (single-family and multi-family).	U.S. Census Bureau and the Department of Housing and Urban Development www.census.gov	Monthly	Provide clues on the trend of the construction industry and a multitude of spin-off businesses such as furniture, carpeting, wallpaper, appliances, and home decorations.	When the number is rising people are investing in the American dream, and home building and decorating are stimulating the economy.
Initial Claims for Unemployment Insurance	New unemployment claims show the number of people who filed for unemployment insurance for the first time	U.S. Department of Labor www.dol.gov	Weekly	Good leading indicator of economic activity and job market.	The more people filing for state unemployment claims suggests a weakening job market and tough times ahead for the economy; a falling trend in claims suggests people are called back to work, companies are hiring, and production is booming.
Real GDP (Growth Rate)	Annual growth rate of GDP (total value of goods and services produced within the borders of the United States) at constant prices.	Bureau of Economic Analysis www.bea.gov	Quarterly	Best benchmark indicator to measure a country's economic growth.	Strong real GDP growth suggests a bustling economy; weak or negative GDP growth suggests a depressed economy.

ECONOMIC POLICY

Governmental action designed to influence economic outcomes. An example of an economic policy would be a reduction in the federal personal tax rate in order to increase consumer spending, thus stimulating the economy. Conversely, an increase in personal taxes could be used to dampen consumer spending and economic growth in order to bring down inflation.

ECONOMIC PROFIT

Any profit greater than that which will ensure a businessperson will remain in business. Economic profit, sometimes also referred to as above-normal profit or excess profit, is any profit greater than normal profit. Typically, economic profit will be earned only in the short run due to an imbalance of market supply and demand, which will be eroded by new businesses entering the market. The exception, prevalent in oligopoly and monopoly firms, is when above normal profits exist over the long run. Monopoly powers exist from barriers to entry, allowing high pricing of the good.

ECONOMIC REGULATION

Government-enforced rules in the interests of promoting competition and guarding against unfair business practices. Although the rules take a multitude of different forms, economic regulation is focused on prices, advertising, and the guidelines for industry entry or exit.

ECONOMICS

The study of how to best allocate scarce resources among competing options. Our resources (land, labor, capital, and entrepreneurship) cannot provide all the goods and services people wish to have, and economics explores how to best allocate these scarce resources among competing ends.

ECONOMIC THEORY

Rules and principles that act as a guide to explain the functioning of an economy. Monetarist theory, for example, maintains that money supply and output should be kept at the same level of growth to keep inflation from occurring.

ECONOMIES OF SCALE

Reductions in minimum average costs that come about through increases in output. Also referred to as increasing returns to scale, it is any scale of operations up to the optimum scale. Economies often make it possible for larger firms to produce goods more cheaply than smaller firms. Economies may arise because increased output permits specialization among workers; each worker will perform one job in which he or she has become highly skilled. A large company may purchase specialized machinery that produces high volumes or a low per-unit cost. Economies could also arise when the entire industry grows and services become available such as specialized training, which reduces the costs to all firms. Low financing costs may also translate into economies of scale.

ECONOMIST

An expert in the field of economics. Economists often teach at the college level or work in the economics department of a major bank, business, or government agency.

News Flash!

Famous Economics Majors

Studying economics is definitely cool and can lead to powerful career positions. It might surprise you that even Mick Jagger of the Rolling Stones was enrolled for the B.Sc. Economics (1961–1963) at the prestigious London School of Economics before dropping out for rock and roll fame. Check out some of the well-known successful people who were economics majors in college:

• Tiger Woods, professional golfer

• John Elway, former NFL Denver Broncos quarterback

• Edwin J. Feulner, president of the Heritage Foundation, a public policy research organization, or think tank

• Sandra Day O'Connor, former Associate Justice of the United States Supreme Court and current Chancellor of the College of William and Mary

• Ted Turner, media entrepreneur

• President Gerald Ford, Jr., the thirty-eighth President of the United States

• President Ronald Reagan, the fortieth President of the United States

• President George H.W. Bush, the forty-first President of the United States

• Alan Greenspan, former Federal Reserve Chairman

Think Like An Economist

Emily Economist is working on an economic problem for Carrie Custom Cowboy Hats, Inc. In a free market, the forces of supply and demand move the price toward the level where the quantity demanded will equal the quantity supplied. At a price higher than equilibrium, Carrie will have a surplus of cowboy hats. But at a price lower than equilibrium, there will be a shortage of hats. By solving this problem Emily knows she will discover the equilibrium price and quantity. Emily has worked hard to estimate the following supply and demand function (don't worry about how) for the cowboy hats:

$$Q_D = 50 - 2P$$

$$Q_S = -10 + P$$

P = Price, Q_S = Quantity supplied, Q_D = Quantity demanded.

Here are the steps Emily took to find the equilibrium price and quantity for the cowboy hats.

At the competitive market equilibrium, quantity demanded equals quantity supplied.

$$Q_D = Q_S$$

$$50 - 2P = -10 + P$$

$$60 = 3P$$

$$20 = P$$

Substituting the equilibrium price of \$20 into either the supply or demand function,

$$Q_D = 50 - 2(20)$$

$$Q_D = 10$$

Emily discovered the free market equilibrium price for Carrie's custom cowboy hats to be \$20 and the quantity 10.

ECONOMIST, HETERODOX

A heterodox economist is an unconventional or unorthodox economist. He or she does not accept the underlying teachings of mainstream economists. This would include any area of study that moves away from the mainstream like social economics, feminist economics, behavioral economics, Marxist economics, or Post-Keynesian economics. While the mainstream focuses on free-market theories, social economics, for example, is centered on integrating social, political, and cultural influences into economic analysis.

ECONOMIST, MAINSTREAM

A mainstream economist accepts the prevailing thoughts and influences in economics. He or she analyzes the economy with a similar approach and uses the same basic underlying economic models.

EFFICIENCY

Obtaining the maximum output from given resources.

ELASTICITY

The response of consumers to a change in price is measured by the price elasticity of demand.

Price elasticity = % change in quantity demanded ÷ % change in price.

Since quantity demanded decreases when prices increase, the price elasticity of demand is always negative. If the absolute value of price elasticity is larger than 1, demand is called elastic. This type of demand exists when a percentage change in price causes a greater percentage change in quantity demanded. Big purchases like computers, cars, and homes tend to be sensitive to price changes.

For example, assume that a 15% price increase in the price of a computer causes the amount of computers purchased to fall by 25%. The price elasticity of demand would be 0.25/0.15 = 1.67. (Price elasticities are displayed in absolute value terms, so the negative is dropped from the numerator.) This means that a 1% change in the price of computers triggers a 1.67% change in quantity demanded. The computer purchase is price elastic and consumers responded strongly to the price increase.

If the price elasticity value has an absolute value from 0 to 0.99, demand is inelastic. A change in price has relatively little effect on quantity demanded; the percentage change in price exceeds the percentage change in quantity demanded. Medicine, coffee, tobacco, and gasoline (over the short term) all tend to be relatively insensitive to a price change.

There are other measures of elasticity: income elasticity of demand (how changes in your income make it more or less likely you will purchase an item); cross elasticity of demand (how the changing price of one commodity affects demand for another); and the elasticity of supply (measures the extent which quantity supplied of a commodity responds to a change in price of that item).

EMBARGO

A government prohibition on trade with a certain country. An embargo is often employed as a political punishment because the effects of an embargo often depress an economy. An example of a well-known embargo is the Cuban Economic Embargo.

News Flash!

Cuban Economic Embargo

The longest-standing economic embargo dates back to 1962, when the United States instituted a full economic embargo with Cuba. Americans may not trade with Cuba. The embargo was instituted to destabilize the regime of dictator Fidel Castro. Americans also are prohibited from traveling to (except under special circumstances), or investing in, Cuba.

Cuba has not transitioned into a democracy and lifting sanctions against Cuba is routinely debated. Many feel it is time for a new Cuban policy. Critics argue that there are many Americans who would like to travel to Cuba, and their dollars would enrich the Cuban economy. Opening the trade and travel doors would benefit the Cuban people with lower-cost U.S. goods, along with tourist dollars and jobs. American businesses and consumers would also benefit economically from trading with Cuba. Others are dead set against opening the door to Cuba, feeling that the embargo will eventually influence the country to become a democracy.

EMERGING ECONOMIES

The classification of emerging economies varies. Universally, these economies have low and mid per-capita incomes and are striving for economic development.

News Flash!

China's Emerging Market

China was on the fast track in 2006. With 10.7% real growth, it is an emerging economy on the way to superstardom. GDP hovers at $2.6 trillion, while per capita, or per person level of GNI (gross national income) was just $2,010. Exports were at a level of $969 billion. The annual growth in China's exports that year was a staggering 27% and shows no signs of slowdown.

EMISSION CHARGE

A fee imposed on polluters, based on the measurements or estimates of the quantity or quality of pollution. It is also referred to as an emission tax.

ENTREPRENEUR

A person who starts his or her own business based upon a perceived opportunity. Entrepreneurs see opportunities for new or better products or services and bring their new ideas to market. Or they see a better way to produce or deliver existing products. Entrepreneurs generally have a business vision and the determination to bring it to reality. With these new ideas come opportunities for profit, but also the risk that the businesses will fail.

Entrepreneur Extraordinaire, Steve Jobs

Steve Jobs, at age 52, is an entrepreneur extraordinaire, not just in one business sector, but in both the computer industry and the entertainment industry. He is the cofounder and current CEO of Apple, a multimedia technology firm with $19 billion in annual sales. His personal fortune is estimated at near $5 billion, yet he is known for his simple uniform of jeans and a black turtleneck. Jobs founded Apple in 1976, along with Steve Wozniak, shifting the use of computers from the business arena to include personal use by everyday people as well.

Jobs dropped out of Reed College in Portland, Oregon, after only a semester, when he could not afford to pay the tuition. He then teamed up with his friend Steve Wozniak to sell personal computers, which they assembled in Jobs's parents' garage. With these humble beginnings, the Apple Corporation was founded, the name based on Jobs's favorite fruit. In December 1980, when Jobs was a mere 25 years old, Apple became a publicly traded firm, making Jobs a multimillionaire. Jobs was forced out of the company in 1985, after a power struggle, and then cofounded NeXT Software Inc.; but he returned to Apple in 1996, when Apple bought NeXT.

Today Apple develops, sells, and supports a series of personal computers, computer software, computer hardware, and the popular music-related products—the digital music player (IPOD), online music store (itunes), and the iPhone. Jobs also cofounded Pixar Animation Studios in late 1985, which has created the computer-animated featured films *Toy Story, A Bug's Life, Toy Story 2, Monsters, Inc., Finding Nemo, The Incredibles, Cars,* and

Ratatouille. In 2006, Pixar merged with The Walt Disney Company, where Jobs sits on the board of directors. Prior to Pixar's merger with Disney, Jobs was Chairman and CEO. Jobs grew up in California's apricot orchards, now known as Silicon Valley, where he resides with his wife and three children.

News Flash!

What Is a Google?

You may "google" on a daily basis, but what does the word actually mean? Google is a play on the term "googol." A googol is a large number: 1 followed by 100 zeros. Google's name reflects the company's mission to organize the limitless amount of information available on the Web.

Google Guys: Sergey Brin and Larry Page

Google, today the world's largest search engine, gets 200 million queries a day and typically returns relevant results in a fraction of a second. Co-founders Larry Page and Sergey Brin launched Google in September 1998. Page and Brin had just one employee, an office in a garage, and started with just 10,000 search queries a day. But out of humble beginnings began great things.

Brin, with a $14.1 billion net worth, and Page, with a $14 billion net worth, were the youngest people on the "400 Richest Americans" list for 2006. Both just 33 at the time, they ranked as the twelfth and thirteenth richest people in America. Not bad for a company that had its origins in a Stanford University dorm room.

The two met at Stanford while pursuing doctoral degrees in computer science. Although they initially did not click, arguing about every topic they discussed, they ultimately found common ground developing a new online search system. Initially they called their search engine BackRub, coined after its ability to analyze back links pointing to a particular Web site, and ranking results according to popularity. The name changed to Google, and with $1 million from family, friends, and acquaintances, the company was launched in Menlo Park, California, in September 1998. The office space was attached to the garage of a friend who sublet the space to the Google's staff of three. Meager beginnings for a *Fortune* 500 company that now generates substantial revenue—$10.6 billion in 2006—through online advertising targeted by keywords. The company has also grown to a team of 13,786 full-time employees (as of June 30, 2007).

Page now runs the product division at Google. He comes by his interest in computers naturally; his father is Dr. Carl Victor Page, Michigan State University computer science professor. He became an honors graduate from the University of Michigan, where he earned a Bachelor of Science degree in engineering, with a concentration in computer engineering. Page now resides in San Francisco.

Brin, a native of Moscow, received a Bachelor of Science degree with honors in mathematics and computer science from the University of

Maryland at College Park. He received his master's degree from Stanford, where he is currently on leave from the Ph.D. program in computer science. Brin holds the title president of technology at Google, and resides in Palo Alto, California.

Google went public with its initial public offering on August 18, 2004, at a price of $85 per share. Shares of their Class A common stock are traded on the NASDAQ under the symbol GOOG. In the third quarter of 2007, the stock's price had broken the $500 mark. It appears the sky is the limit for Brin, Page, and this forward-thinking technology firm.

Snowboarding Entrepreneur, Jake Burton Carpenter

Jake Burton Carpenter, age 53, is the founder of the world's leading snowboard firm. His middle name represents the world-famous Burton Snowboards Inc., selling snowboarding equipment and apparel across the globe. Headquartered in Burlington, Vermont, the company also has locations in New York; Wrentham, Massachusetts; Irvine and Santa Barbara, California; and international offices in Innsbruck, Austria, and Tokyo, Japan.

He works hard and plays hard, with a goal of traveling the globe snowboarding at least 100 days a season, testing new Burton products and taking runs with fellow riders. The Burton Company encourages riding, offering a free season pass to employees for Stowe, a mountain resort in Vermont. This privately held company had humble origins dating back to 1977, when Jake founded Burton Snowboards, working out of a barn on his Vermont farm. Today, Jake and his company have played a key role in bringing this sport from a fun wintertime activity to a worldwide mainstream sport. Snowboarding is so recognized today that in 1998 it made it into the Winter Olympic games in Nagano, Japan.

Snowboarding combines the elements of surfing, skateboarding, and skiing. In his home state of Vermont, Jake began modifying the Snurfer (snowsurfer) in the late 1960s until 1977, when he started Burton with the first production prototype. He shaped snowboards out of wood, fixing rubber straps on them for binding. Jake combined some skateboarding and surfing experience with the Snurfer.

Jake, who graduated from New York University with a degree in economics, spent 113 days riding last season. His company manufactures two-thirds more snowboards than any other company in the world and has distribution centers worldwide. Burton has some of the best snowboarders in the world on its team. Jake Burton Carpenter's passion for snowboarding has defined him not only as a snowboarder, but also a legendary entrepreneur.

Author Entrepreneur, J. K. Rowling

The Sunday Times Rich List 2007 is a guide to the richest 1,000 people in Britain and Ireland. Ranked at 136 is self-made billionaire and English author Joanne (J. K.) Rowling—the big time for anyone, much less a single mother who lived on welfare at one time. Today, at age 42, her net worth is listed at £545 million, which translates into just over $1 billion U.S. dollars. Rowling is wealthier than her own Queen Elizabeth, the head of state, who ranked just 229 with £320 million, or in U.S. dollars—$635,799,000. And at 619 on the list, with a net worth of £112 million—$222,527,000 in U.S. dollars—was soccer star David Beckham and his wife, former Spice Girl Victoria Beckham. Even rocker Ozzy and wife Sharon Osborne ranked below at number 700 with £100 million, or $198,610,000 in U.S. dollars. But J. K. is not just a big player in Britain. *Forbes* lists her as 891 on the World's Billionaires list.

How did J. K. amass such a fortune? It is the old saying, "Do what you love and success will follow." J. K. has been writing almost continuously since she was just 6 years old. Today she is the author of the Harry Potter fantasy series. The seventh and last installment of the series, *Harry Potter and the Deathly Hallows*, was published in July 2007. World sales of the books have reached a staggering 325 million copies.

J. K. graduated from the University of Exeter, complying with her parents' urging and choosing French as her area of study. It was in 1990 (while on a flat-hunting trip to Manchester with her boyfriend) that she found herself traveling back to London on her own aboard a crowded train. Here the idea for Harry Potter simply fell into her head. The train was delayed for four hours, and even though she didn't have a pen, she spent the time wisely dreaming up the characters for the series. After arriving in Manchester, she wrote feverishly.

After her mother's untimely death from multiple sclerosis, J. K. chose to spend some time in Portugal as an English teacher. She married a journalist in Portugal, and her daughter Jessica was born in 1993. The couple quickly divorced and J. K. moved back to Edinburgh, Scotland, with her baby daughter. Living on welfare benefits, she completed her first book. It took a year for her agent to find a publisher. She was rejected by many. Then, in August 1996, she finally got the call she had been waiting for. A small London publisher, Bloomsbury, had made an offer. J. K. currently lives in Scotland with her second husband, Neil Murray, and three children.

ENTREPRENEURSHIP

Organizing a business entity, based upon a perceived opportunity, and assuming both the risk and reward. The risk of an entrepreneurial endeavor is high; many fail. True entrepreneurship—doing something that hasn't yet been done—often involves a higher level of innovation and determination than opening a typical small business like a franchise.

ENVIRONMENTAL ECONOMICS

An area of economics concerned with the effects of economic activity on the whole environment. The objective of environmental economics is to help people make better decisions about the use of natural resources—namely air, water, and land.

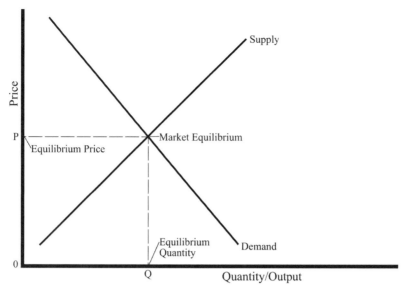

Figure 1.2 Equilibrium Price.

ENVIRONMENTAL PROTECTION AGENCY (EPA)

A U.S. federal agency, established in July 1970, is working to develop and enforce regulations and implement environmental laws enacted by Congress. The agency's annual budget is roughly $17 billion. The EPA's 18,000 employees work toward cleaner air, purer water, and better-protected land. In recent years, between 40 and 50 % of EPA's enacted budgets have provided direct support through grants to state environmental programs.

EQUILIBRIUM PRICE

The price at which the quantity demanded of a good is equal to the quantity supplied for that good. On a graph it is the price at which the supply and demand curves for the good intersect. At the equilibrium price the quantity of a good that consumers are willing and able to buy is exactly equal to the quantity of a good sellers are willing and able to sell. But no equilibrium price is permanent; when demand or supply changes, market equilibrium will change as well (see Figure 1.2).

EURO

Since January 2002, the euro has been Europe's single currency. The euro and its symbol, €, is the currency of fifteen European Union countries: Belgium, Germany, Greece, Spain, France, Ireland, Italy, Luxembourg, The Netherlands, Austria, Portugal, Finland, Slovenia, Cyprus, and Malta. The seven paper note denominations, ranging from the €5 to the €500 note, have a common design in all these fifteen countries. The eight denominations of coins include different national designs on one side and a single European design on the other. The European Central Bank (ECB) is responsible for the overall authorization of euro banknote issues, but the practical details of placing the banknotes into circulation are carried out by the central banks of the member countries. The member countries are responsible for issuing euro coins.

EUROPEAN CENTRAL BANK (ECB)

The central bank of those members of the European Union that share a common currency, the euro. Since January 1999, the European Central Bank has been responsible for setting the official short-term interest rate in countries using the euro as their currency. The ECB, headquartered in Frankfurt, Germany, and the national central banks, constitute the Euro system—the central banking system of the euro area.

EUROPEAN UNION (EU)

An international organization of European countries formed in 1950 in order to reduce trade barriers and increase cooperation of its (then) six member countries: France, West Germany, Netherlands, Italy, Belgium, and Luxembourg. Today, the European Union consists of twenty-seven countries: Austria, Belgium, Cyprus, Czech Republic, Denmark, Estonia, Finland, France, Germany, Greece, Hungary, Ireland, Italy, Latvia, Lithuania, Luxembourg, Malta, Netherlands, Poland, Portugal, Slovakia, Slovenia, Spain, Sweden, United Kingdom, Bulgaria, and Romania. The EU has evolved from a trade organization into the most powerful economic and political group in the world.

EURO SYSTEM

The Euro system consists of the European Central Bank (ECB) and the national central banks of the member states, which have adopted the euro as their currency. There are currently fifteen national central banks in the Euro system. The Euro system has been charged with maintaining price stability and conducting monetary policy for the euro area since January 1999. It is overseen by the governing council and the executive board of the ECB.

EXCHANGE

Trading goods or services with another person or business for other goods or services of equal value. This trade may be direct, as in "to barter," or it may involve money as a medium of exchange.

EXCHANGE RATE

The price of one country's currency in terms of another country's currency. Often, the U.S. dollar is used as the standard in which to express another country's rate. For example, imagine a British pound is

Harvesting yellow onions near Toppenish, Washington, for export to Pacific rim countries. *Source:* Doug Wilson/USDA.

Agricultural Research Service scientists helped preserve the U.S. cotton export market to China by helping its industry understand internationally recognized quality standards. *Source:* National Cotton Council/USDA.

worth $2. A dollar would buy £½. A U.S. traveler who had $100 of fun money to spend on his trip in England could buy things that would total £50.

EXCISE TAX

A federal or state tax on the sale of select luxury goods. Excise taxes fall on items such as alcohol, cigarettes, and tobacco, and for that reason are occasionally referred to as "sin taxes."

EXPLICIT COSTS

Costs that require an outlay of money. Explicit costs involve actual payments a firm makes such as supplier payments, employee salaries, and rent.

EXPORT

A good or service that is produced in one country and sold to another. For example, televisions produced in Japan and sold in Mexico are part of Japan's exports. One country's exports are another country's imports.

News Flash!

U.S. Imports More Than It Exports

The United States has a sizable trade deficit, which means it imports more goods and services than it exports. Take a look at the international trade in goods. You can see what types of goods are sent (exported) to other countries and the kinds of goods brought in (imported) to the United States. Below each subheading are the top four goods, listed in descending order of dollar amount.

U.S. Trade in Goods
2006
(Presented on a Balance of Payment basis; percentages may not total due to rounding)

U.S. Exports $1.023 trillion
Foods, Feeds, Beverages 6.4%

1. Corn
2. Meat, Poultry, etc.
3. Soybeans
4. Other Foods

Industrial Supplies and Materials 26.6%

1. Chemicals-Organic
2. Plastics Materials
3. Petroleum Products, other
4. Fuel Oil

Capital Goods (except automotive) 39.9%

1. Semiconductors
2. Civilian Aircraft
3. Computer Accessories
4. Industrial Machines, Other

Automotive Vehicles, Parts, and Engines 10.4%
Consumer Goods 12.5%

1. Pharmaceutical Preparations
2. Other Household Goods
3. Gem Diamonds
4. Toys, Games, and Sporting Goods

Other Goods 4.2%
U.S. Imports $1.861 trillion
Foods, Feeds, Beverages 4.0%

1. Fish and Shellfish
2. Wine, Beer, and Related Products
3. Fruits, Frozen Juices
4. Meat Products

Industrial Supplies and Materials 32.5%

1. Crude Oil
2. Petroleum Products
3. Gas—natural
4. Fuel Oil

Capital Goods (except automotive) 22.5%

1. Computer Accessories
2. Telecommunications Equipment
3. Computers
4. Electric Apparatus

Automotive Vehicles, Parts, and Engines 13.8%
Consumer Goods 23.8%

1. Pharmaceutical Preparations
2. Other Household Goods
3. Apparel, Household Goods, Cotton
4. TVs, VCRs, etc.

Other Goods 3.2%.

Source: U.S. Census Bureau, U.S. Bureau of Economic Analysis, Department of Commerce.

EXPORT SUBSIDY

A government payment to a business firm to encourage the exportation of a good. The subsidy is intended to keep the price of the good below production costs; often used to protect an essential or new industry where not bound by international agreement. The U.S. government often pays a subsidy to farmers and buys surplus crops at prices above the domestic market price. The government then sells the crop at low prices in foreign markets. The intent of the U.S. farm subsidy program is to protect farmers' income.

EXTERNALITY

The impact of one person's actions on a third party. Many activities provide a benefit or a cost to people not directly involved in the activity. Externalities are commonly referred to as external effects, or spillovers. A positive externality is referred to as an external benefit. For example, if your neighbor is meticulous about caring for her yard and it increases the value of your property, it is beneficial to you. A neighbor's beekeeping business could also benefit the next-door farmer by providing pollination services. A negative externality is referred to as an external cost. If the factory up the street from your home emits strong smoke, the pollution will affect your health negatively. A very loud car radio is a negative externality by not only disturbing your sense of tranquility, but harming your eardrums as well.

FACTORS OF PRODUCTION

Any resource used in the production process of a good or service. These are typically divided into the broad categories of land, labor, capital, and entrepreneurship.

FEDERAL DEPOSIT INSURANCE CORPORATION (FDIC)

Created by the Glass-Steagall Act of 1933, to insure bank or savings association deposits. The FDIC currently insures deposits up to $100,000 per depositor, per insured bank. Certain retirement accounts, like an Individual Retirement Account, are insured up to $250,000 per depositor, per insured bank. FDIC insurance is backed by the full faith and credit of the U.S. government.

News Flash!

See the FDIC Insurance Grow

The FDIC was established in 1933, in response to the economic devastation of the Great Depression, when bankrupt banking institutions were unable to refund depositors' money. During the depression years of 1929 to 1933, a total of 9,755 banks closed their doors. Depositors lost a whopping $1.4 billion. So when on January 1, 1934, the FDIC began insuring accounts at $2,500 per depositor, it was a major step toward restoring the public's confidence in the banking system. Today, FDIC insurance—at the basic $100,000 level—is still being used to protect bank deposits.

Chronology Time Line

• In response to widespread banking failures, on *June 16, 1933*, President Franklin D. Roosevelt signs the Banking Act of 1933, part of which organized the FDIC and made possible the institution of nationwide deposit insurance.

• *January 1, 1934*: Temporary funding for FDIC insurance, at $2,500 per account.

• *July 1, 1934*: Permanent funding for FDIC insurance, with the insurance increased to $5,000.

• *1950*: Deposit insurance increased to $10,000.

• *1966*: Deposit insurance increased to $15,000.

• *1969*: Deposit insurance increased to $20,000.

• *1974*: Deposit insurance increased to $40,000.

• *1980*: Deposit insurance increased to $100,000.

• *2006*: Congress raised the limit on deposit insurance coverage to $250,000 for select retirement accounts only.

Source: FDIC.

FEDERAL FUNDS RATE

Highly sensitive interest rate on overnight loans between member banks of the Federal Reserve System. This rate changes daily and is the key indicator of money market trends.

FEDERAL OPEN MARKET COMMITTEE (FOMC)

The most important monetary policymaking body of the Federal Reserve System. The Federal Open Market Committee (FOMC) conducts monetary policy through open market operations, which include the buying and selling of government bonds and thus influences the availability and cost of money and credit in the economy. The FOMC holds eight regularly scheduled meetings during the year where they set the target for the federal funds rate. The FOMC consists of twelve voting members: the seven members of the Board of Governors, plus five of the twelve Federal Reserve Bank presidents. The president of the Federal Reserve Bank of New York always serves as a voting member, and the other presidents serve rotating 1-year terms.

FEDERAL RESERVE NOTE

Paper money issued by the U.S. Federal Reserve. It is legal tender in the United States. A Federal Reserve Note, printed in denominations of $1, $2, $5, $10, $20, $50, and $100, has no other backing but the full faith and credit of the U.S. government. Because of the strength of the government and its ability to tax, the notes circulate freely.

Monetary Trivia!

The Lifespan of a Bill

Check out the average lifespan of a Federal Reserve Note by denomination:

Denomination	Life Span
$ 1	21 months
$ 5	16 months
$ 10	18 months
$ 20	24 months
$ 50	55 months
$100	89 months

Source: The Bureau of Engraving and Printing.

FEDERAL RESERVE SYSTEM (FED)

Established in 1913 as the central bank of the United States to regulate the banking system and monetary policy. The Fed consists of twelve regional Federal Reserve Banks (Boston, New York, Philadelphia, Cleveland, Richmond, Atlanta, Chicago, St. Louis, Minneapolis, Kansas City, Dallas, and San Francisco), and twenty-five branches. National banks must join the Fed system and state banks have the option of joining. The seven-member board of governors, located in Washington, DC, has the main charge of approving the discount rate (the interest rate at which member banks can borrow from the Fed), setting reserve requirements (the percentage of bank deposits banks must keep on hand or with the Fed as vault cash), and supervising the printing of currency at the mint. The twelve-member Federal Open Market Committee (FOMC) consists of the seven members of the board of governors plus five of the twelve regional Federal Reserve district bank presidents who serve on a rotating basis. This group is responsible for approving the purchase and sales of government securities by the Fed, which controls monetary policy and thus interest rates. The Board of Governors members are appointed by the President of the United States and confirmed by the Senate for a 14-year term, yet the group still maintains a great deal of autonomy when it comes to setting policies. The Chairman of the Board of Governors, who historically exercises considerable influence over the board members, is also appointed by the President and confirmed by the Senate for a 4-year term, which allows each U.S. President to appoint a Fed Chairman.

The Eccles Building, headquarters of the Federal Reserve System, is located in Washington, DC. The Federal Reserve, created in 1913, is the central bank of the United States. The Federal Reserve is able to affect the level of interest rates through its control of the nation's monetary policy. *Source:* © Pixtal, SuperStock, Inc.

News Flash!

Fed Leaders
Chairmen of the Federal Reserve Board, 1914–present.

Charles S. Hamlin	August 10, 1914–August 9, 1916
W.P.G. Harding	August 10, 1916–August 9, 1922
Daniel R. Crissinger	May 1, 1923–September 15, 1927
Roy A. Young	October 4, 1927–August 31, 1930
Eugene Meyer	September 16, 1930–May 10, 1933
Eugene R. Black	May 19, 1933–August 15, 1934
Marriner S. Eccles	November 15, 1934–January 31, 1948
Thomas B. McCabe	April 15, 1948–March 31, 1951
Wm. McC. Martin, Jr.	April 2, 1951–January 31, 1970
Arthur F. Burns	February 1, 1970–January 31, 1978
G. William Miller	March 8, 1978–August 6, 1979
Paul A. Volcker	August 6, 1979–August 11, 1987
Alan Greenspan	August 11, 1987–January 31, 2006
Ben. S. Bernanke	January 31, 2006–present

Source: The Federal Reserve Board.

FEDERAL TAX LIEN

In the United States, a lien (a legal claim against property) is placed on all the property of an individual who fails to pay his or her federal taxes. The lien attaches to all property, such as a person's home, boat, or motorcycle. Liens are public record until fully paid.

FEDERAL TRADE COMMISSION ACT

A federal law passed in the United States in 1914, to create the Federal Trade Commission (FTC) to oversee antitrust policies. Designed to prevent monopolies and unfair methods of competition, the act also monitors unjust and deceptive business practices.

FIAT MONEY

Money that is declared by the government to be legal tender, having no intrinsic value. Fiat money is distinguished from earlier forms of money, which consisted of materials that were themselves of value, such as gold or silver coin, or paper notes convertible into such coin. Most of the world's money today is considered to be fiat money and its cost of production is minuscule.

FIDUCIARY

A person, company, or association that holds assets in trust for a beneficiary. A fiduciary has a legal responsibility to act in the best interest of the beneficiary and invest the money wisely.

FINAL GOODS

Goods that are consumed directly, and not used in the consumption or production of another good. Examples of final goods include books, cell phones, cars, and calculators.

FINANCIAL INTERMEDIARY

Any organization, such as a bank or financial institution, that serves to bridge the gap between saving surplus units and borrowing deficit units. An intermediary, as it is often called, collects deposits from savers and makes loans to borrowers.

FISCAL POLICY

A government's use of spending and taxation to affect the level of the overall economy. For example, a government that wanted an increase in overall spending in the economy may decide to lower personal tax rates, in the hope that people may spend more of their retained income. Conversely, a government that wanted to bring in overall spending in the economy might reign in government spending.

FISHER, IRVING (1867–1947)

An American economist and professor of political economy at Yale University from 1898 to 1935. He did his greatest work in mathematical economics. Fisher received his undergraduate degree from Yale, in mathematics, and graduated first in his class. He used his mathematical knowledge to further the field of numerical economics, studying monetary applications, and did graduate work in both mathematics and economics. In *The Purchasing Power of Money* (1911) he developed the widely recognized quantity theory of money, often referred to as the Fisher equation: $MV = PT$ (M is the stock of money, V is the velocity or turnover of money in circulation, P is the price level, and T is volume of transactions in goods and services), and used it to explain the causes of inflation. In *The Making of Index Numbers* (1922) Fisher developed an ideal inflation measure. In *The Theory of Interest* (1930) he explains the determination of the interest rate as being governed by individual's time preference (having money now versus having money at a later date) and the balance of available funds. In 1930, Fisher was a joint founder of the Econometrics Society and was named its first president.

FIXED COSTS

The portion of the costs that do not change with the level of output. For example, the costs of the factory and equipment used to produce goods.

FLAT TAX

A proportional, fixed rate, assessed on all levels of income. This taxation system is simple and often advocated on the premise of fairness. For example, if a flat tax rate were established at 12%, a low-income earner would pay the 12% rate on his or her modest income as well as the multimillionaire paying the 12% on his or her earnings. The rate would be 12% of each dollar earned, regardless of the income status of the earner. The U.S. federal tax system is currently a progressive system, whereby higher-income earners pay a greater percentage of their income in taxes. The flat tax system has been adopted by several states.

FREE RIDER

An individual who is not willing to pay for a good or service and relies on others to pay. Because of the free-rider problem, certain goods and services, especially public goods such as national defense, are produced by the government. The government then finances the public goods by imposing a tax on the entire population.

FREE TRADE

A policy of open, unhindered trade between countries. Goods and services flowing between countries are not subject to tariffs, quotas, or export subsidies. In reality, most governments are involved in regulating trade in some form.

FRICTIONAL UNEMPLOYMENT

The unemployment that results from the process of job seeking: when people are between jobs, just entering the working world, or coming back to work. Economists estimate that at any given time, 2 to 3 % of the labor force is frictionally unemployed. Examples of the frictionally unemployed: students who have just graduated from high school or college and are looking for work; a mom who has decided to reenter the workforce; and the thirty-something relocating to the West Coast to search for better job opportunities.

Free trade boosts okra exports in Nicaragua. The members of the Araya family planted a range of different crops—corn, sorghum, and sesame—on their 50-hectare farm before USAID suggested they try growing okra for export to the United States. USAID is supporting a program to build Nicaraguan trade by helping thousands of producers like the Arayas diversify crops, improve quality, and gain new markets. *Source:* USAID.

Icon Economist, Milton Friedman (1912–2006)

Milton Friedman was a leading proponent of monetarism, or the Monetarist School of Economic Thought. Monetarists believe money controls the economy. Friedman was the leader of this school, which originated and remains at the University of Chicago, where he served as an economics professor for 30 years (1946–1976). The Monetarist's major tenet is that too much money causes inflation, or rising prices. In order to keep inflation at bay, the Fed should keep the rate of money-supply growth at the same rate as output, or GDP. The monetarist philosophy was strictly adopted by the Fed on one occasion, to bring down the double-digit inflation of the late 1970s and early 1980s. Central bankers today monitor the level of money flowing into the economy; they and economists learned from Friedman that inflation is a monetary phenomenon.

Friedman was the recipient of the 1976 Nobel Prize in Economic Sciences "for his achievements in the fields of consumption analysis, monetary history and theory, and for his demonstration of the complexity of stabilization policy." He authored a multitude of major works in economics including *Taxing to Prevent Inflation* (1943), *A Theory of the Consumption Function*

(1957), *Inflation: Causes and Consequences* (1963), *A Theoretical Framework for Monetary Analysis* (1971), and *Monetary Trends in the United States and the United Kingdom* (1982). Friedman's permanent income hypothesis that individuals consume not on current income but their permanent income (the average of their lifetime wealth and earnings), is standard fare in economics texts today and an important contribution to economic theory. After Friedman's retirement from the University of Chicago, he joined the Hoover Institution at Stanford—a think tank dedicated to the study of politics, economics, and international affairs—where he remained doing economic research until his death. He passed away on November 16, 2006, at age 94.

Milton Friedman (1912–2006), famous monetarist and Nobel Prize winner in Economic Sciences. *Source:* The University of Chicago.

G7, G8, AND G77

The group of seven, commonly abbreviated as G7, stands for the seven most industrialized nations in the world—the United States, Britain, France, Italy, Canada, Germany, and Japan—that meet regularly to coordinate fiscal and monetary policies. The international organization, designed to promote a more stable world economic system, was officially established in 1985. In 1998, Russia was added to the group, changing it to the G8.

In 1964, a group of seventy-seven countries—predominately developing countries—formed a coalition known as the G77. The group's aim is to articulate and promote their collective economic interests, as well as enhance negotiating capacity on major economic issues in the United Nations system. Today the group consists of 132 countries but has retained its title due to its historical significance. The group has acted in a number of important roles under the umbrella of the United Nations in international economic cooperation and development—making statements, and sponsoring or negotiating resolutions at global conferences and meetings. The group advocates initiatives that favor redistributing wealth to developing countries.

GALBRAITH, JOHN KENNETH (1908–2006)

A Canadian-born economist, author, teacher, ambassador, and presidential adviser, John Kenneth Galbraith did it all. Galbraith was born in 1908, in Iona Station, Ontario, becoming an American citizen in 1937. He received his Ph.D. in agricultural economics in 1934, from the University of California, Berkeley. The same year he accepted a teaching position at Harvard, where he spent his academic career, although he took time off for political pursuits. He was active in politics, notably in the 1950s and 1960s; he campaigned with Adlai Stevenson in 1952 and 1956, and was presidential adviser to Senator John F. Kennedy during the 1960 presidential race. Galbraith was Kennedy's ambassador to India from 1961 to 1963.

A liberal thinker, he was known for his development of Keynesian economics—advocating government spending to solve the nation's social dilemmas—and for his work on the economic power of the large corporation. He was a prolific writer. His most influential book, *The Affluent Society* (1958), critiqued the rising affluence of the American economy and the good it would bring for society.

GAME THEORY

Game theory is a mathematical method used to analyze how two or more people behave in strategic situations, where actions and counteractions occur. In game theory, each person must make decisions on what the other person is likely to do. This method is often used to help understand the optimal course of action in mind games like chess, but it is also used in economic and political negotiations.

GENERAL AGREEMENT ON TARIFFS AND TRADE (GATT)

An international organization dating from January 1948, and affiliated with the United Nations. Over 100 nations were members of GATT, which supported liberalization of world trade. It supported free trade among member nations by encouraging elimination of tariffs and other barriers to trade. In January 1995, GATT was replaced by the World Trade Organization (WTO).

GIFFEN GOOD

A good or service in which a price increase raises the quantity demanded, and price decreases reduce quantity demanded. Giffen goods are named after English economist Sir Robert Giffen (1837–1910), who first discovered this theoretical possibility, when he observed poor people buying more bread as the price rose.

Giffen goods violate the law of demand, which states that price and quantity demanded are inversely related (when one goes up, the other goes down). There is debate in the economics profession if any such goods in real life exist. To meet the qualifications, a good would need to be an extreme example of an inferior good and have poor substitutes. Scenarios examined have involved basic foods, such as in bread and potato famines in which the poor needed the basic food items and were unable to afford the more luxurious food items. As the price of the basic food item rose, the poor ended up buying more of the essential commodity.

GLOBALIZATION

The word *globalization* describes the increased connectivity of the world's economies. As people, finances, capital, and trade move more rapidly between countries, there is growing economic interdependence across borders.

Global Economic Data

Economists use economic data and statistics to compare and contrast the economic health of nations. Following is a list of selected data for a handful of countries for 2008. All of the nations listed are advanced economies, but nevertheless, you will still notice fluctuations in economic well-being. GDP per capita, a ballpark measure of a nation's prosperity, displays wide swings. Luxemburg is estimated to have a per-person output of over $100,000 for 2008, while Taiwan checks in at $16,672. It may be tough to find a job in Greece with an unemployment rate of 8.5. And while Japan may have virtually nonexistent inflation, Greece, the United States, Portugal, and Slovenia all are predicted to have a modest flirtation with rising prices.

Measurements	Means
Per Capita GDP, Current Prices (U.S. dollars)	Per Person Standard of Living
Inflation, Consumer Prices (Annual Percentage Change)	Rising Prices
Unemployment Rate (% of total labor force)	State of the Job Market

Country	Per Capita GDP	Inflation	Unemployment Rate
Canada	$39,934	2.0	6.2
France	$39,449	1.8	7.8
Germany	$38,774	1.6	7.6
Greece	$32,788	3.2	8.5
Italy	$35,455	2.0	6.8
Japan	$34,864	0.8	4.0
Luxemburg	$104,309	2.1	4.8
Portugal	$21,018	2.4	7.3
Slovenia	$21,840	2.4	6.4
Taiwan	$16,672	1.5	3.7
United Kingdom	$46,259	2.0	5.1
United States	$47,159	2.5	5.0

Source: International Monetary Fund (IMF Staff Estimates for 2008).

Monetary Trivia!

Gold Bricks

Approximately sixty foreign governments, central banks, and international organizations store gold at the Federal Reserve Bank of New York. The Fed does not charge for storing the gold, but does charge a handling fee when gold comes in, moves within the vault, or is shipped out. Good thing!

Moving gold is a strenuous task. Gold is stored in big blocks that look like construction bricks. Gold stackers work in shifts to permit rest breaks, and they wear strong, magnesium shoe covers. The weight of a gold brick? A hefty 27 lbs!

GOLD STANDARD

A monetary system in which a country's currency is convertible to a fixed amount of gold. The United States abandoned the gold standard in 1933.

Monetary Trivia!

Gobs of Gold

In 1933, the U.S. government abandoned the gold standard and people could no longer redeem currency for gold. Gold nonetheless remained on hand from this early practice, and the gold reserves of the United States total about 262 million troy ounces (in 2003). It is officially valued at just over $11 billion. But valued at the approximate market price of gold, about $800 an ounce in 2007, the government's gold reserves are worth over $200 billion.

GOODS

Goods are items of value that are real or tangible, such as cars, computers, homes, and books. U.S. economic output is roughly 28% goods based, and 72% service based.

News Flash!

Federal Spending Gone Wild

The federal government spends public money to provide many essential goods and services like national defense, Social Security, Medicare, Medicaid, education, food, and housing assistance. But with a national debt totaling near $9 trillion, and spending to exceed revenues by $239.4 billion for fiscal 2008, some economists argue that lawmakers could do a better job of monitoring government purchases to bring them back in line with revenues. Check out some of the crazy federal government outlays.

• Over half of all farm subsidies go to corporate farms with average household incomes of $200,000.

• Washington recently spent $1.8 million to help build a private golf course in Atlanta, Georgia.

• The Conservation Reserve program pays farmers $2 billion annually to not farm their land.

• The federal government made at least $37 billion in overpayments in 2005. Current estimates range between $40 billion and $100 billion in annual overpayments.

• Congress recently gave Alaska Airlines $500,000 to paint a Chinook salmon on a Boeing 737.

• Washington spends $60 billion annually on corporate welfare, versus $43 billion on homeland security.

• The Advanced Technology Program spends $150 million annually subsidizing private businesses, and 40% of this goes to Fortune 500 companies.

Source: The Heritage Foundation.

GOVERNMENT FRANCHISE

When a local, state, or federal government grants an exclusive right to one organization to be the sole provider of a good or service. A government franchise provides the basis for a monopoly and is a barrier to entry for other firms wanting to enter the market. The United States Postal Service, as the sole provider of daily mail, is an example of a federal government franchise or monopoly.

GREAT DEPRESSION

On October 29, 1929, known as "Black Tuesday," the stock market crashed, marking the beginning of the Great Depression in the United States. The downturn extended worldwide, resulting in high unemployment, depressed production, low profits, depressed personal income, severe poverty, and stagnant trade. The Great Depression lasted until the economic recovery of the early 1940s.

GREAT SOCIETY

President Lyndon Johnson's Great Society (1964–1968) domestic spending programs were federal programs designed to improve the life of all Americans. The Great Society programs of Medicare, Medicaid, food stamps, and the establishment of the Department of Housing and Urban Development are all still in effect today and consequently have had a long-term economic impact on the U.S. economy.

Federal Reserve Board Chairman Alan Greenspan, and Treasury Secretary John Snow, participate in a meeting of the G7 finance ministers and Central Bank governors (April 16, 2005). *Source:* The Department of the Treasury.

Icon Economist

Alan Greenspan (1926–)
American economist and thirteenth chairman of the U.S. Federal Reserve System (1987–2006). A Republican, Greenspan's monetary policy while at the Fed largely consisted of interest-rate targeting. During his early years at the Fed (namely from 1988 to 1989 and from 1994 to 1995), Greenspan was concerned that too much production would bring on a spiral of inflation, and raised interest rates in order to dampen spending. This tactic earned him the name of "Inflation Hawk." His later years at the Fed consisted of an opposite tactic—lowering interest

rates. As the economy entered a recession in the early 2000s, Greenspan's tactic to stimulate the economy was to constantly lower interest rates in an effort to encourage consumers to borrow and spend, thus stimulating the economy.

Greenspan's education consists of a bachelor's degree, a master's degree, and a doctorate in economics from New York University. Prior to joining the Fed, he ran Townsend-Greenspan, a New York economic consulting firm that compiled economic data and ran industry forecasts for large banks and companies. A political person, he headed the Social Security Commission for former President Ronald Regan and was the Chairman of the President's Council for Economic Advisors for former President Gerald Ford. He is also known as being a great saxophone player, touring with the Henry Jerome Swing band for 1 year shortly after high school graduation.

Greenspan's term as Fed chair expired on January 31, 2006. He skillfully guided the U.S. economic structure for more than 18 years. Upon retirement, Greenspan sold his memoir—*The Age of Turbulence: Adventures in a New World*—for a reported upfront advance of more than $8.5 million.

News Flash!

The Briefcase Indicator

Economic indicators are statistics that track the economy's performance and permit analysis of future performance. Weekly initial claims for unemployment insurance gives an early peek at the employment picture, monthly building permit data foretells a construction boom or bust, and the S&P 500, representing all key business sectors, provides a wide view of the stock market. But what does a briefcase tell you? If it is the CNBC's "Briefcase Indicator," it can suggest a great deal, albeit in a fun approach. When Alan Greenspan was at the Fed, the briefcase indicator, reported by CNBC, tried to predict Fed action by looking at the thickness of Alan Greenspan's briefcase as he walked into the Federal Open Market Committee meetings. The theory goes that if the briefcase was thick, the attache was filled with documentation to discuss with other members at the meeting, so a change in the federal funds rate would occur. But if his briefcase was thin, the rate would remain unchanged. There were some investors that thought this unusual indicator had credence, but due to a minimal level of accuracy, it largely showed that economists do have a humorous side.

GROSS DOMESTIC PRODUCT (GDP)

Gross Domestic Product (GDP) is the broadest measure of economic activity for a country and consequently one of the most important economic terms business people must understand. It is the total amount of all new goods and services produced within the domestic borders of a country during a specified time period, normally for a given year. It is calculated by adding all consumer, investment, and government spending for the year, plus net exports (the value of what a country imports less the value of what foreigners spend on a country's exports—a negative number in the case of the United States). GDP provides a strong benchmark of a country's size and relative strength or weakness. Every new purchase in an economy falls into one of the categories. Previously owned items, like a used car or a formerly owned home, do not fall into this benchmark number. Financial transactions, like stock or bond trades, will not register here either. But the new computer you just purchased, as well as your recent dental bill will all show up as consumer purchases. The building of a new corporate office suite or a new dream home will count in the investment category. And government purchases, which happen to be roughly one-third of all the spending in the U.S. economy, show up in a number of ways. The payment of your local police department as well as the federal government defense spending all fall into the government category of GDP spending. For countries that export more of their goods than they import, GDP will register a positive total in the net exports category. But for countries like the United States that are historically big importers, this category will register a negative number and pull down the GDP total a bit. The GDP number for the United States stands at around $13 trillion a year, the largest output number for any country. To stay in tune with the economy, one must keep tabs on the growth rate of GDP, a number published quarterly (along with updates) by the Bureau of Economic Analysis (www.bea.gov).

GROSS NATIONAL PRODUCT (GNP)

A former, widely used measure of economic performance of citizens of an economy. Gross National Product (GNP) equals GDP plus the income earned by residents from investments abroad, minus the income sent home by foreigners who are living domestically.

GROWTH RATE

The percentage rate increase (or decrease) of an economic variable. It often refers to the economy's rate of GDP growth. The growth rate of GDP is released on a quarterly basis by the Bureau of Economic Analysis, and measured in annualized terms. Although there is no set definition on the proper rate of growth for the economy, most economists maintain that a growth rate from 3 to 5% is generally healthy and means the economy, employment, and production is flourishing. Numbers in the 1 to 2% range, along with negative growth rates, suggest the economy is stagnating. Businesses may not be producing as much and it is more difficult to find a job. Excessive GDP growth rates (6% and higher) may signal that the economy is expanding too strongly and inflation may rear its ugly head. The growth rate could also refer to a financial growth rate like an increase (or decrease) in earnings, sales, dividends, or assets.

News Flash!

Delaware Has the Highest Per Capita GDP

Gross Domestic Product (GDP) by state is the counterpart to the national GDP figure. The state of Delaware had the highest per capita real GDP at $59,288 (2006, advance estimate). Delaware's high ranking is influenced by its large concentration of businesses in the finance and insurance area. The state with the lowest per capita real GDP was Mississippi at $24,062, 36% below the national average.

Source: Bureau of Economic Analysis.

HARD MONEY

Currency of a nation that is economically and politically stable. Hard money, also referred to as hard currency, is widely accepted around the world. An example: U.S. currency. Hard money sometimes refers to precious metals in the form of coins.

HEDGE

An action taken to offset investment risk. Hedging involves deliberately taking on a new risk to offset an existing one. For example, people often hedge against inflation. An investor would purchase an asset, such as gold, real estate, or fine art, expecting that its price will rise faster than the rate of inflation.

HIGH-POWERED MONEY

Money in the form of commercial bank reserves, plus currency. The term originated from the monetarists school. Such money is considered high-powered because the reserve requirement, via lending, will produce a multiplied change in the bank deposits. Banks required to maintain a reserve ratio of 10%, for example, can allow total deposits to expand by 1/0.10 or 10 times for every dollar of new money in the banking system.

HUMAN CAPITAL

The knowledge and skills acquired by the workforce that improve productivity. Education is a major investment in human capital because it increases output; examples include going to college, attending a computer seminar, and on-the-job training courses. Life experiences and knowledge can also improve a worker's job productivity.

HYPERINFLATION

Unusually high inflation, or a persistent increase in prices of 100% or more a year. Hyperinflation leads to a breakdown in the monetary system, rendering money nearly useless as a medium of exchange, and seriously disrupting economic activity. During hyperinflation people try to spend their money very quickly before prices rise again. Money is a poor store of value during hyperinflation, causing many people to shift funds to hard assets like gold, which retains its value during inflationary times. Hyperinflation is a fairly rare occurrence in the developed world, the most notorious case being the Germany hyperinflation of the early 1920s. The United States has not experienced hyperinflation since the Civil War (1861–1865).

HYPOTHESIS TESTING

Testing an unproved theory. In economics, testing is generally concerned with a casual relationship between two variables. An assumption that might be tested is whether reduced personal tax rates cause increased economic growth. After gathering historical data on personal tax rates and real GDP growth rates, statistical tests would be conducted to examine the casual relationship. Because economic data can be inaccurate, statistical tests can never prove a statement true, only that the relationship appears to be valid. At best, there appears to be a direct relationship between reductions in personal income taxes and increases in economic growth.

IMPERFECT COMPETITION

This refers to all forms of market structure in which some degree of competition exists, but not to the extreme of perfect competition in which all firms sell an identical product at the going price. Imperfect competition includes monopolistic competition, oligopoly, and duopoly. In this structure, a firm has at least some control over the market price of its good or service.

IMPLICIT COSTS

The opportunity cost of production for which no direct dollar payment is made. Implicit costs commonly include the lost interest on owner funds withdrawn from investments and placed in the business. Owner salaries that are not withdrawn from the business are another implicit cost. Economists include both explicit, direct dollar payments, and implicit costs, when calculating true profit.

IMPORT

A good or service consumed in one country, which has been bought and shipped in from another country. For example, cars sold in the United States but produced in Germany are part of U.S. import totals. One country's imports are another country's exports.

INCOME EFFECT

A change in the price of a good or service will impact the spending power, or real income of individuals. A price decrease will increase the real income of the consumer. With a change in real income, the income effect can shift either way. If, for example, a good or service is demanded more as income falls—for example, used cars, budget noodles, or cheap cuts of meat—it is called an inferior good. But more typically, goods that are demanded more as income rises, like books, clothes, and steak, are called normal goods.

INCOME ELASTICITY OF DEMAND

The ratio of a proportional increase in the quantity demanded of a good to the proportional increase in income, while price is held constant. The measure shows how responsive the quantity demanded is to a change in income. A good that has an income elasticity of demand less than one, which means that as income rises, the good accounts for a smaller and smaller portion of the consumer's income. This is called a necessity. A good that has an income elasticity of demand greater than one means that as income rises, the good accounts for an increasing portion of the consumer's income. This is called a luxury. When the income elasticity of demand is one, it means that at any given price, the portion increase in the quantity of a good demanded is directly proportional to the increase in income.

INCOME STATEMENT

An accounting report, often referred to as a profit-and-loss statement. An income statement summarizes an organization's profit or loss over a given time period, usually over a quarter or year. Revenues less expenses will result in the net income, or loss, for the period.

INCOME TAX

A method of taxation based upon earnings, levied by the federal government and by certain state and local governments. The origin of the U.S. income tax system dates back to 1913, with the passage of the Sixteenth Amendment to the Constitution, granting Congress the power to impose tax on personal income. Taxes on excess business profits and estates followed with the 1916 Revenue Act. In most countries, including the United States, the system is progressive, meaning wealthier people pay a higher percentage of tax than poorer individuals. The two forms of income tax are personal income tax, levied on households and unincorporated businesses, and corporate income tax, levied on net income of corporations.

INFERIOR GOOD

Items for which demand falls when the incomes of the buyers rise. For example, the demand for packaged noodles falls as the income of recent college graduates rise. Goods that are not classified as inferior are normal goods.

INFLATION

An overall increase in prices in an economy; the result is a fall in the purchasing power of money. It occurs when there is too much money trying to buy too few goods. As a rule, everything costs more. It becomes more expensive to buy a car, eat out, go to the doctor, or go to the movies. The two main measurements of inflation in the United States are the consumer price index (CPI), measuring price changes of items bought by a typical consumer, and the producer price index (PPI), measuring price changes of raw materials used in the production of goods.

In the early 2000s, U.S. prices increased at a low rate, in the 1 to 2 % range. Moderate inflation can be expected with economic growth. But for much of the decade in the 1970s, for example, the inflation rate was in the low teens, and was declared enemy number one. Severe inflation causes social dilemmas, so keeping inflation at a low level is a main concern of economic policymakers and central bankers all over the world.

Monetary Trivia!

The U.S. "$" Sign

How did the U.S. dollar sign originate? A widely accepted theory is the result of the evolution of the Mexican or Spanish "Ps" for pesos, or piastres, or pieces of eight. This theory maintains that the "S" gradually came to be written over the "P," resembling the "$" sign. The United States adopted the dollar sign for its currency.

Source: The Bureau of Engraving and Printing.

Monetary Trivia!

Which Bank Account Should I Pick?

Eddie Entrepreneur is deciding which of two banks he should choose to invest his hard-earned dollars in a 1-year CD. Eddie has collected $1,000 from his tutoring business, Eddie's Easy As. Both town banks offer identical time deposits, except Community Bank offers 5% compounded semiannually, and City Bank offers 5% simple interest paid annually. Where should Eddie deposit his hard-earned tutorial earnings?

You are correct. Community Bank's compound interest will provide a greater return, $.63 more to be exact, for financially savvy Eddie. Compound interest is calculated when interest actually earns interest. And the more frequently compounded, like daily or quarterly, it would be an even better deal. At Community Bank, Eddie is paid a 5% annual rate, twice a year. For half of the year, the interest computation totals $25(0.05 × $1,000) ÷ 2. New interest will now be calculated on a figure of $1,025. At year end, the interest actually earns interest $25.63(0.05 × $1,025) ÷ 2. Total interest earned for the year totals $50.63, and Eddie has $1,050.63. The annual percentage yield is 0.05063 or 5.063%.

Simple interest is calculated on the amount of the investment alone. At City Bank, Eddie would be paid back the 5% interest at year end, as well as his initial investment. At 5% simple interest paid annually the calculation is simple: $50(0.05 × $1, 000). With simple interest, at the end of the year Eddie would receive $1,050, his $50 interest plus the initial investment of $1,000.

Want to calculate compound interest with your money? Use the compound interest formula.

$$A = P \times (1 + r/n)^{nt}$$

$A =$ amount of money accumulated

$P =$ principal amount deposited

$r =$ annual rate of interest

$t =$ number of years the amount is deposited

$n =$ number of times per year that interest is compounded

Complete the formula to see where we got the $1,050.63.
Answer: $1,000 \times (1 + 0.05/2)^{(2)(1)} = \$1.050.63$
Try another example. Let us assume you earn 5% compounded quarterly, on that $1,000.

$P = \$1,000$

$r = 0.5\%$

$t = 1$ year

$n = 4$ times per year

$A = 1,000 \times (1 + 0.05/4)^{(4)(1)}$

$A = \$1,050.95$

You can see that Eddie does a little better if he invests in a time deposit that earns 5% interest quarterly. He would earn $50.95 in interest rather than the semiannual $50.63 interest.

INITIAL PUBLIC OFFERING (IPO)
An initial public offering is the first time a company offers ownership shares (stock) to the public. IPOs must be registered with the U.S. Securities and Exchange Commission.

INSTITUTIONAL ECONOMICS
The study of how the role of man-made institutions affects economic behavior. It combines institutions (social, law, and political aspects) to formulate economic analysis. This approach was founded by American economist and sociologist, Thorstein Veblen (1857–1929), in the early twentieth century.

INTEREST RATE
The cost of using, or the reward for lending, money. It is expressed as a rate per period of time. The interest rate is usually shown on an annual basis.

Monetary Trivia!

The Rule of 72
Here is a simple way to estimate how long it will take you to double your money. Divide 72 by the interest rate you are currently earning. Let's say you are earning 6% on a $1,000 money market deposit account.

$72 \div 6\% = 12$ years

In 12 years you will have $2,000, assuming you do not withdraw any money from the account. Use the rule of 72 to visualize your money growing!

INTERMEDIATE GOODS
Goods used in the consumption or production of another good. Intermediate goods are not counted in the Gross Domestic Product totals. An example of an intermediate good is the wheat used to make bread.

INTERNAL REVENUE SERVICE (IRS)
The IRS is a bureau of the Department of the Treasury. The organization is the tax collection agency for the United States, administering the Internal Revenue Code enacted by Congress. In 2006, the IRS collected more than $2.5 trillion in gross collections and processed more than 228 million tax returns.

INTERNATIONAL MONETARY FUND (IMF)
The International Monetary Fund (IMF) was established in 1945, along with the World Bank, after the Bretton Woods Conference. The organization's purpose is to promote international monetary cooperation, currency exchange stability, and orderly exchange arrangements; to foster economic growth and high

Headquarters building of the International Monetary Fund, Washington, DC. *Source:* International Monetary Fund.

levels of employment; and to provide temporary financial assistance to countries to help ease balance of payments adjustment. The IMF provides temporary loans to less-developed countries to restore conditions for sustainable economic growth. Funding for the IMF comes from the treasuries of its 185 member countries.

The Executive Board of the International Monetary Fund, Washington, DC (April 19, 1999). *Source:* International Monetary Fund.

INVESTMENT

Economists refer to investment as using money to add to capital, meaning adding to goods, which are not used in consumption. This could be acquiring buildings, land, or equipment. A secondary use of the term, generally reserved for finance, refers to ownership of financial assets such as stocks or bonds.

INVISIBLE HAND, THE

The idea that society as a whole is better off if individuals pursue their own interests. Famous economist Adam Smith coined the phrase in *Wealth of Nations* (1776), stressing the role the so-called "invisible hand" played in coordinating society's interests. If people are guided by selfish motives, they will work hard to earn a dollar. This drive to do well will result in more goods being produced. It also fosters competition, which drives down prices. Result in both cases: Society is better off.

JOINT VENTURE

A temporary partnership formed by individuals or corporations set up for the purpose of pursuing a specific business goal. Parties agree to share in profits (or losses) and management. Joint ventures are often undertaken to spread risk, and by people or companies that want to partner but do not want to merge. After the specific project is completed the joint venture ends.

JUNK BONDS

Bonds issued by firms whose credit ratings are below investment grade. In order to compensate holders for risk, junk bonds pay higher interest rates. These bonds are typically purchased for speculative purposes. Also referred to as high-yield, or speculative bonds.

John Maynard Keynes (1883–1946) penned *The General Theory of Employment, Interest, and Money. Source:* Library of Congress.

Icon Economist

John Maynard Keynes (1883–1946)
Keynes was a British economist who introduced his theory for pulling the economy out of the depression in his major published work, *The General Theory of Employment, Interest, and Money* (1936). Keynes noted that the economy does not automatically maintain a level of full employment as the Classical Economists believed. According to him, the economy could get stuck in a glut, with significant unemployment and curtailed production. The economy could not rely on businesses to borrow funds and stimulate production, so instead, it was the responsibility of the government to stimulate the economy. He called for the government to spend, and spend

big! Keynes suggested the government develop government works programs to create jobs and get money in people's hands, which would be spent to further stimulate the economy. His work would develop into the Keynesian School of Economic Thought; economists of this school believe the economy should be controlled through fiscal policy—adjusting government spending and/or taxes—to deliberately slow or stimulate the economy.

Keynes was educated at King's College at Cambridge University, where he studied mathematics and philosophy. Upon graduation, he was a civil servant in the India Office for just a year—he found the work boring—and returned to Cambridge to lecture. During World War I, he worked for the British Treasury and was responsible for Britain's war financing. He also represented Britain at the Paris Peace Conference, but resigned because he felt the German war reparations (financial compensation for damages during war) imposed by the Allies would keep Germany impoverished. In *Economic Consequences of Peace* (1919), he predicted such payments were much too high and would exhaust Germany's capacity to pay. Keynes resigned from the Treasury, went back to teaching, and pursued a financial career in London.

Assistant Secretary of the U.S. Treasury, Harry Dexter White (left) and John Maynard Keynes, honorary advisor to the U.K. Treasury, at the inaugural meeting of the International Monetary Fund's Board of Governors in Savannah, Georgia, United States, March 8, 1946. *Source:* International Monetary Fund.

Keynes was influential in post-World War II reforms. In 1944, he led the British delegation at the United Nations Monetary and Financial Conference. The conference is commonly referred to as Bretton Woods because it was held at the Mount Washington Resort in Bretton Woods, NH. The conference set up the International Monetary Fund (IMF), and the International Bank for Reconstruction and Development (IBRD). A year before his death, in 1945, Keynes assisted in negotiating a major loan from America to Britain to help rebuild after the war. On April 22, 1946, Keynes passed away at age 63 after suffering a heart attack just days earlier. While Keynes was gone, his ideas and theories ruled academic institutions and political settings through the 1970s. Keynes is regarded by many as the most influential economist of the twentieth century.

KEYNESIANS

A school of economics, named after John Maynard Keynes, dominating economics roughly from Keynes' publication of *The General Theory of*

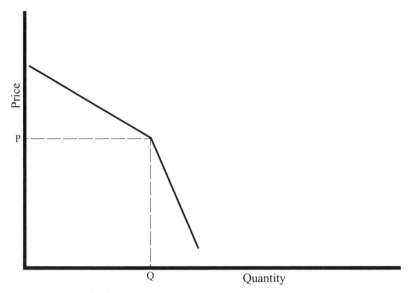

Figure 1.3 Kinked Demand Curve.

Employment, Interest, and Money in 1936 to the late 1970s. Keynesians generally favor government intervention to stabilize the economy. Keynesians promote using fiscal policy—deliberate changes in government spending and/or taxes—to stimulate or slow down the economy.

KINKED DEMAND CURVE

The demand curve resulting from an oligopoly. If an oligopolist raised its price above the kink, competitors would not match price hikes and sales for the firm would fall sharply. But if the oligopolist cuts its price below the kink, others would reduce their prices so sales for the firm would rise very slowly. Neither price increases nor decreases are productive for the oligopolist. This type of situation creates a tendency for prices to be sticky at their existing levels (see Figure 1.3).

LABOR

The physical and mental efforts of human beings in the production process.

LAGGING INDEX

A monthly index release by The Conference Board, a private research group. The index is actually a compilation of seven lagging indicators all rolled into one easy number to provide verification of past economic activity. The lagging index lags behind the highs and lows in the economy. The lagging index turns up months after the whole economy hits an expansion period, and turns down months after the whole economy hits a recession. The indicators in the lagging index are: average duration of employment (inverted—meaning a negative change is positive); change in inflation for services; ratio of consumer credit to personal income; change in labor cost per unit of output; ratio of manufacturing and trade inventories to sales; and commercial and industrial loans outstanding.

LAGGING INDICATORS

Indicators that have a historical tendency to lag, or turn after the whole economy moves. Lagging indicators are high after economic activity has reached its high point and low after the economy has hit its low point. The most well-known U.S. lagging indicator is actually a composite of seven lagging indicators; the Lagging Index is produced monthly by The Conference Board, a private research group.

LAISSEZ-FAIRE

The principle that there should be no government interference in guiding the economy. The term is French for "allow to do." Most economists who adopt a laissez-faire philosophy still believe in a minimal role for government in legal structure, national defense, and law enforcement.

LAW OF DEMAND

According to law of demand, the quantity of a good or service demanded in a given time period increases as its price falls, all else being equal. For the rare occasions when a good or service does not conform to the law of demand, see Giffen Good.

LAW OF SUPPLY

According to the law of supply, the quantity of a good supplied in a given time period increases as its price increases, all else being equal.

LEADING INDEX

A monthly index released by The Conference Board, a private research group. The index is actually a compilation of ten leading indicators all rolled into one easy number to give a prediction of upcoming economic activity. The leading index, on average, turns up 4 months before the whole economy hits an expansion period, and turns down 9 months before the economy hits a recession. The individual indicators are: state unemployment insurance claims (inverted, because a rise in claims means more people are out of a job and bad news for the economy); building permits; vendor performance (companies that are receiving slower deliveries); manufacturers' new orders for consumer goods and materials; manufacturers' new orders for nondefense capital goods; average weekly manufacturing hours; stock prices; index of consumer expectations; interest rate spread; and real money supply.

LEADING INDICATORS

Indicators that have a historical tendency to take turns before the whole economy moves. Leading indicators hit lows before the economy hits a low, and rise before the economy expands; therefore, leading indicators forecast the highs and lows in the business cycle. The most well-known U.S. leading indicator is actually a composite of ten leading indicators: the Leading Index, produced monthly by The Conference Board, a private research group.

LENDER OF LAST RESORT

Central banks typically lend money to banking institutions that are experiencing liquidity struggles. The Federal Reserve is the lender of last resort for the U.S. banking system. Banks may borrow from the "discount window" so that a shortage of funds at one bank will not upset the flow of money and credit in the economy.

LOAN

A sum of money lent with conditions. The borrower agrees to repay the lender the funds in installments or all at once, typically with interest.

LONG RUN

A period of time long enough for all inputs to be varied (no fixed costs). In other words, all things can be changed—new capital equipment can be a purchased, office space can be leased, employees can be added or released, etc.

LUCAS, ROBERT E., JR. (1937–)

American economist, economic theorist, leader of the New Classical School, and the principal formulator of rational expectations theory. This theory holds individuals may anticipate and affect government policies. His work, which gained prominence beginning in the 1970s, questioned government policy to influence the economy. This challenged the Keynesian macroeconomic tradition. He is also known for the classic "Lucas Critique" (1976, *Econometric Policy Evaluation: A Critique*), which is a criticism of the use of econometric models for evaluating alternative economic policies because built-in parameters of the model were actually influenced by past policies. Lucas won the Nobel Prize in Economic Sciences in 1995 "for having developed and applied the hypothesis of rational expectations, and thereby having transformed macroeconomic analysis and deepened our understanding of economic policy."

Lucas attended the University of Chicago, earning a B.A. in history in 1959, and a Ph.D. in economics in 1964. He taught at Carnegie Mellon University before returning to teach at the University of Chicago in 1974, where he has spent his entire academic career. In 1980 he became the John Dewey Distinguished Service Professor of Economics, a title he still holds at the university.

LUXURY

A good that has an income elasticity of demand greater than one, such that, as income rises, the good accounts for an increasing portion of the consumer's income. Wealthy people thus spend a higher portion of their income on luxury goods than do poorer individuals.

M1

The narrowest definition of the money supply. Everything in M1 is liquid and easy to spend. M1 consists of currency held by the public, traveler's checks, demand deposits (funds in a bank account that you can access "on demand" by writing a check), and other checkable deposits (NOW accounts, automatic transfer service accounts, credit union share drafts, and demand deposits at thrift institutions).

M2

A broader measure of money supply, is M2. It consists of everything in M1 plus balances in savings accounts, time deposits less than $100,000, and money market mutual funds.

MACROECONOMICS

This area of concentration in economics is concerned with the aggregate segments of the economy—the determination and analyses of gross domestic product (output), inflation, and employment, among other things.

Icon Economist, Thomas Robert Malthus (1766–1834)

Malthus was an English economist who caused controversy with his theory that the world's population, unless controlled, would outgrow the ability to support itself. He held that the population would tend to overshadow the available food supply. In *An Essay on the Principle of Population* (1798, revised edition 1803), Malthus claimed the population grew at a geometrical ratio and the ability of the earth to support itself via the food supply grew at an arithmetical ratio. In the first edition, Malthus wrote that only war, famine, and disease could stunt the burgeoning population. In his revised work he admitted that "moral restraint" (if people might wait to marry later and avoid reproducing outside of marriage) might be a preventive check to the inevitable doom. Although Malthus's mathematical calculations were inaccurate, his population theory is still influential today where it concerns wages and poverty; thus he anticipated a fundamental concern in modern macroeconomic theory.

Thomas Robert Malthus (1766–1834), population advocate, clergyman, and author of *An Essay on the Principle of Population as It Affects the Future Improvement of Society. Source:* © Pixtal, SuperStock, Inc.

MARGINAL BENEFIT

The additional benefit from an increase in an activity. If the marginal benefit of an activity exceeds the marginal cost, economists maintain the activity should be pursued. As an example, assume you are at an outdoor concert and deciding if you should stay for the second show. The first group was rock, but the upcoming group is classical, and you think staying may educate you on songs and bring up your grade in music to an A. Mom and Dad pay $10 for each A, so you estimate the marginal benefit of staying at $10. You already paid the $7 fee to get in the outdoor arena and would only need a $2 cola to keep you going through the second concert. Because the marginal benefit ($10) exceeds the marginal cost ($2) of attending, you listen to the second group.

MARGINAL COST

The additional cost from an increase in an activity. For a firm, it is the increase in total costs caused by increasing output by one additional unit.

MARGINAL PHYSICAL PRODUCT

The change in total output divided by the change in input quantity, or the increase to output from a per-unit increase in input. For example, the marginal physical product might increase due to the change in production output that occurs when adding an additional worker. It is assumed that marginal physical product initially increases, but then declines as the quantity of labor employed increases, or when diminishing returns set in.

MARGINAL PROPENSITY TO CONSUME

The change in consumption resulting from an additional unit of income. Or in other words, it is the proportion of additional income a person desires to consume. The sum of the marginal propensity to consume, plus the marginal propensity to save, is always one.

MARGINAL PROPENSITY TO SAVE

The change in savings resulting from the additional unit of income. Or in other words, it is the proportion of additional income a person desires to save. The sum of the marginal propensity to save, plus the marginal propensity to consume, is always one.

MARGINAL REVENUE PRODUCT

The revenue gained by a firm when an additional worker is hired. It is the marginal revenue product that determines how much labor will be hired.

MARGINAL UTILITY

The additional, or incremental, satisfaction obtained from utilizing a good or service. Additional quantities of a good will eventually yield increasingly smaller increments of satisfaction. Thus, the marginal utility of a good or service declines as more of it is consumed in a given time period, something referred to as the law of diminishing marginal utility. A simple example would be eating hamburgers when you are very hungry. The first hamburger is extremely satisfying, the second hamburger may be OK but not nearly as pleasing (diminishing marginal utility has occurred), while the third hamburger gives you a stomachache (referred to as negative utility).

MARKET FAILURE

When an unregulated market fails to provide an ideal situation. Pollution is an example of market failure in which the government had to step in and regulate to correct the problem.

MARKET POWER

The power to alter the market price of a good or service.

MARKET STRUCTURE

The characteristics of a market, namely the number and relative size of firms in an industry. The structure of the market affects pricing and competition. A perfectly competitive industry has many firms selling an identical product, none of which has a significant impact on pricing. A monopolistically competitive industry has many firms selling similar, but not identical products; the firms exhibit a limited amount of control over price. In an oligopoly industry, four or fewer firms produce 50% or more of the market, selling an identical or more commonly differentiated products (like the wide variety of gum products available). In a duopoly, two producers supply the market and have great control over pricing. The ultimate price maker is a monopoly firm. The single supplier derives excess profits and produces at a lower rate than other markets.

MARSHALL, ALFRED (1842–1924)

An English economist who spent most of his academic life as a professor of economics at Cambridge University (from 1885 to 1908). Much of microeconomics originates from Marshall's work, yet he is also well known for mentoring his student, John Maynard Keynes. Marshall's work was concerned with the theories of costs, value, and elasticity. The core of Marshall's work is the power of demand and supply to generate equilibrium prices. His best-known book, *Principles of Economics* (1890), was a standard reference and economic text until the 1930s.

MARX, KARL (1818–1883)

German philosopher espousing the belief that capitalism would be replaced by communism. Marx was convinced capitalism was destined for failure and highlighted his beliefs by documenting the historical progression of capitalism and pinpointing its flaws. In 1848, Marx coauthored with German businessman Friedrich Engels (1820–1895) the now-famous *Communist Manifesto*, the first comprehensive statement of modern communism. The book predicted that the proletariat would overthrow the bourgeoisie ruling class in a Communist revolution. The collapse of capitalism did not come true as predicted by Marx. Some countries did establish communist governments in the twentieth century, but most have failed.

MARXIST ECONOMICS

A school of economics inspired by nineteenth century economist and philosopher Karl Marx, designed to analyze the social and economic development of capitalism. While the Marxist economic ideology that the communist style of rule will prevail has been discredited, since Soviet-style governments have either collapsed or moved toward a more capitalist economic system, the Marxist historical evolutionary analysis of capitalism is strong.

MEDIUM OF EXCHANGE

An article or instrument that is generally accepted in exchange for goods and services Money acts as a medium of exchange in today's economy.

MEMBER BANKS

A bank that is a member of the Federal Reserve System. National banks are required to join, while state banks have the option of joining.

MICROECONOMICS

This area of concentration in economics is concerned with the specific segments of the economy—how individuals, businesses, and governments make decisions and interact in the marketplace. Examples might include how a consumer makes a decision between substitute goods at the grocery store, how a business firm makes production decisions to maximize its bottom line, and how a local government's decision to raise property taxes affects the area housing market.

MILL, JOHN STUART (1806–1873)

An English philosopher and classical economist, Mill was an intellectually gifted child, beginning the study of Greek at age 3. He was strictly educated by his father, James Mill, also an economist. The rigorous academic stress left the younger Mill emotionally depressed, with few social skills. After suffering a nervous breakdown, he became a prolific writer in the field of philosophy and economics. His major work, *Principles of Political Economy* (1848), which essentially summarized the prevailing theories of classical economic thought, became a standard textbook in economics for over 40 years. Mill accepted the major theories of the classical economists, but brought the classical theories to further completion by having a more positive outlook than Malthus and Ricardo, believing the working class could look forward to the day when they would be educated, stifle their numbers, enjoy economic growth (however stationary), and the fruits of their labor. Among his accomplishments, Mill was the first to note the concept of opportunity cost—you must give up something to get something else.

MINIMUM WAGE

A level of pay for workers set by the government. Proponents argue that a government must set a base level of pay to protect less-skilled workers, so they are able to maintain a basic standard of living. Opponents, including economists, maintain that minimum wage rises above the market's equilibrium wage, increasing job loss. Opponents also charge that minimum wages cause inflation, directly by raising worker pay, and indirectly when businesses pass on labor costs to customers. Currently, the Fair Minimum Wage Act of 2007 raises the minimum wage from $5.15 an hour, where it had been for 10 years, to $5.85, effective July 24, 2007; $6.55 effective July 24, 2008; and $7.25 effective July 24, 2009.

News Flash!

First Minimum Wage Set at a Quarter

In 1938, President Franklin Roosevelt signed into law the Fair Labor Standards Act, which among other things established the first minimum wage at $0.25 an hour. A quarter may not sound like a great deal of money today, but look at the bag of food items you could get for your quarter in 1938:

Hershey's Milk Chocolate Bar	$0.05
Loaf of Bread	$0.09
Canned Tomatoes	$0.08
Three Penny Tootsie Rolls	$0.03
Total:	$0.25

According to Bureau of Labor Statistics records, that quarter in 1938 could have gotten you a half gallon of delivered milk (25 cents); a chuck roast (22.8 cents); a dozen oranges (26.7 cents); or 10 lbs of potatoes (21.3 cents).

Monetary Trivia

World's First Million-Dollar-Monster Coin
On May 3, 2007, the Royal Canadian Mint introduced a pure bullion gold coin with a face value of $1 million in Canadian dollars. This coin is not only the world's highest face-value coin, but it is the biggest, too—its 21″ diameter and 1″ + thickness is roughly equivalent to the size of an extra-large pizza. Originally designed as a unique showpiece to introduce the new Gold Maple Leaf 1-ounce bullion coins, the RCM decided to mint limited quantities of the supercoins after several buyers expressed interest. To read more about the supercoins and to learn about the Royal Canadian Mint's coin manufacturing, consult the RCM Web site at www.mint.ca.

Monetary Trivia!

The 5-Cent Fact
Yes, there really is nickel in your nickel. The nickel is the only U.S. coin to be called by its metal content name. It does contain 25% nickel, but the remaining 75% is copper.

MINT, UNITED STATES
The United States Mint was created on April 2, 1792, by an act of Congress. Its mission is to produce an adequate volume of circulating coinage for the nation to conduct business. The Mint produces between 11 billion and 20 billion coins each year. It is a self-funded agency that makes upwards of $1 billion a year, which it turns over to the general fund of the U.S. Treasury. The Denver and Philadelphia Mints produce the coins we use in daily transactions, while the San Francisco Mint produces commemorative proof sets. The nation's $100 billion commodity assets are stored as gold bullion at Fort Knox, Kentucky, and the West Point Mint stores silver, gold, and platinum.

Monetary Trivia!

States Celebrated on the Quarter
States are honored in the U.S. Mint's 50 State Quarters Program, so be sure to check out your state quarter. A 10-year program, spanning from 1999 to 2008, releases five new state quarters each year. So every 10 weeks you will see a new quarter, released in the order in which the states were admitted to the Union. Every state coin design is stunning and unique. State designs

are displayed on the tail side of the quarters, while the head side continues to display George Washington's image.

New Quarter Releases to the Federal Reserve Bank

Release Date	*State*	*Statehood Date*
1999		
January 4, 1999	Delaware	December 7, 1787
March 8, 1999	Pennsylvania	December 12, 1787
May 17, 1999	New Jersey	December 18, 1787
July 19, 1999	Georgia	January 2, 1788
October 12, 1999	Connecticut	January 9, 1788
2000		
January 3, 2000	Massachusetts	February 6, 1788
March 13, 2000	Maryland	April 28, 1788
May 22, 2000	South Carolina	May 23, 1788
August 7, 2000	New Hampshire	June 21, 1788
October 16, 2000	Virginia	June 25, 1788
2001		
January 2, 2001	New York	July 26, 1788
March 12, 2001	North Carolina	November 21, 1789
May 21, 2001	Rhode Island	May 29, 1790
August 6, 2001	Vermont	March 4, 1791
October 15, 2001	Kentucky	June 1, 1792
2002		
January 2, 2002	Tennessee	June 1, 1796
March 11, 2002	Ohio	March 1, 1803
May 20, 2002	Louisiana	April 30, 1812
August 2, 2002	Indiana	December 11, 1816
October 165 2002	Mississippi	December 10, 1817
2003		
January 3, 2003	Illinois	December 3, 1818
March 13, 2003	Alabama	December 14, 1819
May 22, 2003	Maine	March 15, 1820
August 7, 2003	Missouri	August 10, 1821
October 16, 2003	Arkansas	June 15, 1836
2004		
January 26, 2004	Michigan	January 26, 1837
March 29, 2004	Florida	March 3, 1845
June 1, 2004	Texas	December 29, 1845
August 7, 2004	Iowa	December 28, 1846
October 16, 2004	Wisconsin	May 29, 1848
2005		
January 3, 2005	California	September 9, 1850
March 13, 2005	Minnesota	May 11, 1858
May 22, 2005	Oregon	February 14, 1859
August 7, 2005	Kansas	January 29, 1861
October 15, 2005	West Virginia	June 20, 1863
2006		
January 3, 2006	Nevada	October 31, 1864
March 13, 2006	Nebraska	March 1, 1867
May 22, 2006	Colorado	August 1, 1876
August 7, 2006	North Dakota	November 2, 1889
October 16, 2006	South Dakota	November 2, 1889

Release Date	State	Statehood Date
2007		
January 29, 2007	Montana	November 8, 1889
April 2, 2007	Washington	November 11, 1889
August 3, 2007	Idaho	July 3, 1890
September 3, 2007	Wyoming	July 10, 1890
November 5, 2007	Utah	January 4, 1896
2008		
Date to be determined	Oklahoma	November 16, 1907
Date to be determined	New Mexico	January 6, 1912
Date to be determined	Arizona	February 14, 1912
Date to be determined	Alaska	January 3, 1959
Date to be determined	Hawaii	August 21, 1959

Source: The U.S. Mint.

MIXED ECONOMY

An economic system that blends competitive private enterprise with some degree of governmental control. Most of the industrialized capitalistic nations are mixed economies. The United States is an example of a mixed economy.

MONETARISTS

A school of economics, inspired by Milton Friedman, which won many followers in the late 1970s and early 1980s. The monetarists' main belief is that the rapid growth of money causes inflation, a premise understood by all economists today. The monetarists believe the economy can be stabilized by keeping the growth rate of money proportional to the growth rate of output.

MONETARY POLICY

Government or central bank guidelines concerning money supply, interest rate targets, and credit conditions that in turn influence broad economic goals such as growth, inflation, and employment. In the United States, the Federal Reserve Board that controls monetary policy. The Fed has three options to control monetary policy: open market operations, the most influential and frequently used monetary policy tool, which consists of buying and selling government bonds in the open market; changing the bank reserve requirement on checkable type deposits; and lastly, changing the discount rate (the interest rate charged by the Fed to other financial institutions). If the Fed wants to stimulate the economy, it can buy bonds, lower the reserve ratio, and/or lower the discount rate. Conversely, if the Fed believes the economy is expanding too fast and inflation might rear its ugly head, it can sell bonds, raise the reserve ratio, and/or increase the discount rate. By affecting the level of money in the economy, interest rates, and credit terms, the Fed can strongly influence the amount of money spent in the United States.

MONEY

Something generally accepted in payment for goods and services or in the payment of debts. Money is a medium of exchange. Today this may be a physical substance in the form of coins and paper money, or bank deposits in the form of book entries. Primitive economies existed on barter as a means of exchange. The use of money depends on others believing it can be exchanged for things of value. Money is also a store of value, although during periods of high inflation it may not be the best store of value.

> **Monetary Trivia!**
>
> **You Thought Silverware Was Just for Eating?**
> Legend has it that George and Martha Washington gave some of their silverware to the United States Mint so it could make the first U.S. silver coins.

MONEY LAUNDERING

Acts designed to conceal the location, source, or ownership of money. Those involved in drug trafficking, tax evasion, or other illegal activities want to disguise the ownership of funds in order to avoid government reporting and tax requirements. Money laundering is a problem of global concern because it disrupts the financial security and thus the economic development and prosperity of a country.

MONEY MULTIPLIER

A number that shows how an original deposit can expand the money supply. The multiplier is $1/R$, where R stands for the reserve requirement. For example, if a bank receives a deposit of \$50,000 and the reserve requirement is 10 %, \$500,000 could be created from the original deposit ($1/0.10 \times \$50,000 = \$500,000$).

MONOPOLISTIC COMPETITION

A market structure in which many firms produce a similar, but not identical, product. Each firm produces a good or service somewhat different from its competitors. The differences may be real (for example, a white cotton shirt may have a different shaped collar, a unique fabric weave, or a slim cut), or they may be imaginary or perceived differences through powerful advertising. So each firm has a market that is slightly distinct from its competitors, giving monopolistically competitive firms a degree of market power. Monopolistic competition, in which there is limited market power (the ability to alter price), is different from a pure monopoly, in which a single producer can be a price maker. This form of market structure is also distinct from the theoretical perfectly competitive market structure, in which everyone makes the same product and no one has the power to price, because each product is slightly different. Monopolistically competitive firms, as the name suggests, combine some aspects of both monopoly and competitive firms. Excess profit encourages firms to enter the industry, but the market adjusts and firms ultimately earn a normal profit in the long run. The bulk of businesses in the United States are monopolistically competitive firms. Examples include veterinary offices, law practices, gas stations, fast food restaurants, and hair salons. While there are numerous competitors for each business, each offers the same basic good or service—animal health care, legal advice, a fill-up, a quick meal, or a haircut—with a slightly different twist and delivery.

MONOPOLY

A situation that exists in the market in which there is only one producer or seller for a product. To be a true monopoly, there must be no close substitutes for the product or service. The monopoly will make profits in excess of a competitive business, and is often referred to as a price maker. Under monopoly, prices are higher and output lower than in perfect competition.

Competition is the backbone of the American economic system, resulting in choice and lower prices, and consequently monopolies are illegal in the United States. The exception is those firms that have been granted the right to be exclusive by the government. In certain instances, the government deems it most beneficial for citizens to limit the number of firms to only one or two. An example is the U.S. Post Office, which has a government monopoly on the delivery of mail. Another is a government-regulated public utility like your local electric company or water provider. In these situations, the government not only ensures delivery of the services, but also ensures that prices are in the best interest of the consumer.

If a true monopoly does exist, the barriers to entry are so high it is virtually impossible for any new firms to exist. Few companies have a true monopoly, but many exhibit degrees of monopoly power, particularly with a specific product in their line. For example, McDonald's Big Mac, Coca Cola's Diet Coke, or Campbell's Chicken Noodle Soup, all have strong market recognition and market clout.

MONOPOLY FRANCHISES

Government granting to a firm (or firms) the exclusive right to supply a particular good or service. This right automatically creates a barrier to entry for potential competing firms. The U.S. Postal Service is an example of such a franchise and has exclusive rights for use of the postal mailbox and daily mail delivery. Public utilities have exclusive rights to provide gas, electricity, and water to select areas. There may be a sole producer, or two or more, which have been given franchises for select areas.

MONOPSONY

A market situation where there is only one buyer of a good or service. As the sole buyer, a monopsonist will have an impact on the market price. A reduction in units purchased will reduce price, while buying more units will increase price. An example might be the U.S. Government buying armaments from a defense contractor.

MORTGAGE

Instalment debt on real property, such as houses, condos, buildings, or land. The borrower gives the lender a lien on the property as security for the loan.

MUNICIPAL BOND

A bond issued by a city, county, or state government to finance projects such as highways, hospitals, sewage treatment, or university buildings. Munis, as they are commonly called, are exempt from federal tax. They are usually exempt from state and local tax, notably if you live in the state in which the bond was issued.

Because of the tax savings, munis will typically pay a lower rate than similar term and quality corporate bonds.

MUTUAL FUNDS

A professionally managed investment that pools capital from many investors to invest in stocks, bonds, options, futures, money market instruments, or other securities. Investors purchase mutual funds shares directly from the fund, or through a broker or an investment advisor. Shares are redeemable; the fund (or broker or investment advisor) will buy back any shares the investor wishes to sell. Mutual funds offer diversification benefits due to large numbers of securities held, professional portfolio management, and liquidity.

NASH, JOHN (1928–)

An American mathematician and Nobel Laureate who was the feature of the 2001 film, *A Beautiful Mind*. He established the mathematical foundations for game theory. The film details his mathematical genius, as well as his long struggles with paranoid schizophrenia. Nash's Princeton University dissertation (1950) would revolutionize economics and later be known as Nash Equilibrium, an equilibrium concept for noncooperative games. Nash jointly won the Nobel Prize in Economic Sciences in 1994 with German mathematician Reinhard Selten, and UC Berkeley economist John C. Harsanyi, "for their pioneering analysis of equilibrium analysis in the theory of noncooperative games." Nash currently is a Senior Research Mathematician at Princeton University.

NASH EQUILIBRIUM

Game theory originates from studies of strategy games like chess or poker. Such strategic tactics arise in business situations, so game theory is useful in economic analysis. A Nash equilibrium, named after John F. Nash's work in game theory, exists if there is a set of strategies with the essential factor that no player can gain by a change in strategy as long as all other players keep their strategies unchanged.

NATIONAL ASSOCIATION OF SECURITIES DEALERS AUTOMATED QUOTATION SYSTEM (NASDAQ)

Founded in 1971, the NASDAQ is the largest U.S. electronic stock market. Trading does not take place on the floor as with traditional exchanges, but via a sophisticated computerized network. Corporate headquarters are at One Liberty Plaza in New York City. NASDAQ has more listed stocks (near 3,200) and trades more volume (at roughly 2 billion daily) than any other U.S. stock exchange. Companies traded cover all areas of business, including biotechnology, communications, financial services, media, retail, technology, and transportation.

NATIONAL BUREAU OF ECONOMIC RESEARCH (NBER)

The NBER was founded in 1920, as a private, nonprofit, nonpartisan economic research organization. The NBER is widely regarded as the world's leading nonprofit economic research organization. The Bureau's main office is in Cambridge (Massachusetts), with branch offices in Palo Alto (California), and New York City. At any one time, the NBER has over 600 top-tier economics and business professors as research associates, performing research on a variety of economic issues confronting society. The research institution makes its findings known through a variety of publications and economic working papers, but in an effort to assure the public of its impartiality, the NBER and its researchers abstain from making recommendations on policy.

NATIONAL DEBT

The total outstanding borrowings by the federal government. It consists of such obligations as treasury bills, treasury notes, treasury bonds, and savings bonds. National debt is the debt that has been accumulated over the years. It is calculated by adding up yearly deficits, less surpluses. Some of the gross debt is held by government agencies, so the net national debt, which excludes debt held by government agencies, is lower than the gross debt. As of the end of fiscal 2007, U.S. gross national debt stood at $9 trillion, with net debt at $5 trillion.

NATURAL MONOPOLY

Occurs when a market is most efficiently supported by only one firm, based upon the cost advantages a single firm has. One firm, for example, can sometimes provide a good or service at a lower per-unit cost than two or more other firms. An example would be a small island that has limited population and can only support one grocery store. The local grocery on the island is a natural monopoly. Public utilities, like gas and electric companies that require a network of cables, often involve natural monopolies. It is more cost effective for the government to grant one company the right to provide utilities due to the high investment cost.

NATURAL RATE OF UNEMPLOYMENT

The rate of unemployment that would prevail if the economy were producing at its full potential. The natural rate of unemployment contains both a structural unemployment (between 2 and 3%) and a frictional unemployment (between 2 and 3 %) component. Any attempt to force unemployment below its natural rate will result in accelerating inflation. Economists suggest somewhere between 94 and 96% is the natural rate of employment.

NECESSITY

A good having an income elasticity of demand less than one, such that as income rises, the good accounts for a smaller and smaller portion of the consumer's income. Poorer individuals thus spend a higher portion of their income on necessities than do the wealthy.

NEW CLASSICAL ECONOMISTS

A group of economists, also called rational expectationists, who believe government economic policy will only have an effect if people do not anticipate government actions. New classical economics is the most influential school of economic thought of the 1980s, 1990s, and 2000s. This school maintains government policies are largely ineffective, and not necessary or helpful. According to new classicals, people anticipate the consequences of government fiscal and monetary actions and change their actions to counteract the government economic policy. As an example, a tax cut may be designed to increase spending in the economy. People rationally expect the tax cut to lead to larger government debt,

The New York Stock Exchange building is both a city and a national landmark. A design of master architect George P. Post, its six massive Corinthian columns give a feeling of strength and stability to the financial institution. The building opened its doors for business on April 22, 1903, and continues to be the center of the financial district. *Source:* © Brand X, SuperStock, Inc.

which will ultimately need to be paid off. People save money because they know the government will eventually raise taxes to pay off the debt. Consequently, because people hold onto their tax money, it cancels out the intended stimulating effect of the tax cut. University of Chicago economist Robert E. Lucas (1937–) is the strongest proponent of rational expectations. Lucas received the 1995 Nobel Prize in Economic Sciences "for having developed and applied the hypothesis of rational expectations, and thereby having transformed macroeconomic analysis and deepened our understanding of economic policy."

NEW YORK STOCK EXCHANGE (NYSE)

The oldest U.S. stock exchange, dating back to 1792 when a group of twenty-four brokers met under a buttonwood tree at what is today 68 Wall Street and signed the original brokers' agreement agreeing to trade securities. The New York Stock Exchange (NYSE), nicknamed the "Big Board," is located at 11 Wall Street in New York City where investors buy and sell listed companies' common stock and a host of other securities. The companies listed on the NYSE represent a total global value of approximately $25 trillion.

NOMINAL GROSS DOMESTIC PRODUCT (GDP)

Nominal GDP measures production in current prices and is also referred to as current-dollar GDP.

NONPROFIT

An organization that does not seek to make a profit; a nonprofit enterprise. Nonprofits can and do make profits, but financial gain is not the focus of the organization. Profits are not distributed to owners, directors, or stockholders, but are used to fund the operation of the organization. Governments generally do not tax nonprofits because they better society. Examples of nonprofits include some hospitals, churches, foundations, museums, and arts councils. The bulk of nonprofits fall under 501(c)(3) of the IRS Code and are organizations which are "charitable, religious, educational, scientific, literary, testing for public safety, fostering national or international amateur sports competition, and preventing cruelty to children or animals."

NORMAL GOOD

Items for which demand increases when the incomes of the buyers rise. Most goods people buy are normal goods. For example, the demand for new cars, furniture, and clothing rises as the income of young professionals rise. Goods not classified as normal are inferior goods.

NORMAL PROFIT

This is the minimum amount of profit a firm must earn to stay in business. Normal profit is the opportunity cost to the businessperson. Levels of profit higher than this tend to cause new firms to enter the industry. Conversely, profits lower than normal profit tend to cause firms to leave the industry. The exact percentage will vary, depending on market conditions.

NORMATIVE ECONOMICS

An area of economics concerning what ought to be, based on opinion or beliefs of how the economy should be run or organized. An example of a normative statement: "Internet transactions should be taxed in order to treat all business entities equitably."

NORTH AMERICAN FREE TRADE AGREEMENT (NAFTA)

The North American Free Trade Agreement (NAFTA) began on January 1, 1994, creating the world's largest free trade area. This agreement removes most tariff and trade barriers among three countries: the United States, Canada, and Mexico. On January 1, 2008, the last scheduled tariffs and quotas were eliminated, joining North America in free trade.

News Flash!

Gobs of Gum

Gum is big business in the United States. Domestic retail gum sales approach $3 billion a year. According to Wrigley, guess how many servings of gum per year the average American consumes?

a. 5

b. 35

c. 180

If you guessed high—180 servings of gum—you are correct.

OLIGOPOLY

A market structure in which four or fewer firms produce 50% or more of the goods or services for the market. The products supplied by this market may be identical or, more commonly, differentiated. Oligopolists earn above-normal profits that are protected by barriers to entry from other firms. The gum business in the United States, dominated by Wrigley's and Cadbury Schweppes, is an example of an oligopolist industry. The product "gum" is differentiated, among other ways, by making teeth whiter, being sugar free, giving us fresh breath, and taste. Other U.S. oligopolist industries include cigarettes, breweries, and motor vehicle manufacturing. Each firm has a fairly large share of the market, so much so that each must consider the reactions of the rival firms when making a change in output or price. This market may not engage in much price competition, relying instead on heavy advertising and marketing efforts to establish strong brand loyalty. Typically there is price leadership; the big firm in the industry sets the price and others tend to hover around that price because price competition would eat into the profit of all firms.

News Flash!

Check Out Concentration Ratios

If you want to get a ballpark idea of the level of market power—the ability to control prices—check out the four-firm concentration ratio tabulated by the U.S. Bureau of Census. Economists generally maintain that four or fewer firms that control 50% or more of the market define an oligopoly, where above normal profits characteristically exists.

Below are a few examples of the oligopolist industries in the United States. The top four firms in each of these industries control over half the industry market sales.

Four Firm Concentration Ratios

Cigarette Manufacturing	95.3
Breweries	90.5
Motor Vehicle Manufacturing	85.0
Breakfast Cereal Manufacturing	82.1
Underwear and Nightwear Knitting Mills	79.6
Cookie and Cracker Manufacturing	70.9
Creamy Buttery Manufacturing	66.9
Women's Footwear (except athletic manufacturing)	61.2
Paper Mills	56.1
Doll and Stuffed Toy Manufacturing	50.8

Source: U.S. Bureau of Census, Concentration Ratios: 2002.

OLIGOPSONY

A small number of buyers control the market. These buyers have a large amount of influence over purchases and thus, market price in a given market. The big four television networks ABC, CBS, NBC, and Fox, compose an oligopsony with a great deal of control over programming.

OPEN MARKET OPERATIONS

The Federal Reserve's primary tool of monetary policy. This tool consists of the Fed's buying and selling of treasury securities in the secondary market to affect bank reserves and bond prices and hence interest rates.

OPPORTUNITY COST

Giving up the next best opportunity in order to obtain the most desired goods or services. As an example, if you spend $10 on pizza, you give up spending the money on your second favorite food, barbecued chicken wings. A production factory may find it most profitable to produce lead pencils, while producing pens is the second most profitable venture. The opportunity cost of producing lead pencils is the value of the factory space, equipment, and labor if the company had produced pens instead, because if lead pencils had not been produced, all the resources used in making lead pencils could have been used to produce pens.

ORGANIZATION FOR ECONOMIC CO-OPERATION
AND DEVELOPMENT (OECD)

The Organization for Economic Co-operation and Development (OECD) is a Paris-based group consisting of thirty member countries committed to democracy and a market economy. The OECD, dominated by the United States and the European Union, was formed in 1961. It is globally respected for its economic publications and statistics in the fields of macroeconomics, trade, development, education, science, and innovation. The OECD is well-known for its individual country surveys and reviews. Learn more at www.oecd.org.

OUTPUT

The result of economic activity. Output is whatever is produced by using the factors of production. Output and Gross Domestic Product (GDP) are often used interchangeably in economic circles.

OVER-THE-COUNTER (OTC)

Trading in securities is carried out via computers and phone, rather than on the floor of a traditional exchange.

PARTNERSHIP

In the United States One of the three major types of business organizations (the other two being proprietorship and corporation). A partnership is an unincorporated business owned by two or more people, which may or may not have employees.

Partnerships have a few advantages over corporations and proprietorships. A major plus over corporations is ease of entry. Any group of individuals can start up a partnership business because no incorporation paperwork or fees are necessary. The owners can do what they choose and make all the business decisions without having to consult a board of directors as corporations do. Partnerships also pay income taxes based on the personal tax rates of the owners, which are often lower than corporate rates. A partnership can raise more funds than a proprietorship because they can obtain the funds, or borrow, based on the wealth of two or more owners.

Partnerships also have major disadvantages to the corporation or proprietorship. Unlike corporate entities, partnerships are not shielded by limited liability. In other words, if the business fails, the owners are personally responsible for all debts of the business. This means creditors could potentially take some of your prized possessions to pay a debt. Furthermore, each partner is responsible for all debt of the firm, even if she or he had nothing to do with incurring them. In other words, if your partner makes bad decisions, you too are responsible. This is a drawback versus the proprietorship, where the only person you are responsible for is yourself. With a partnership, there is no continuity of operation because the death of one of the owners technically terminates the business. However, the remaining owners may reorganize.

PATENTS

A legal protection that provides exclusive rights for production of a particular product to the inventor. The patent process is country-specific and gives the patent holder rights for a certain number of years. Generally, U.S. patents provide the inventor 20 years of exclusive rights to produce the particular product. The positive side of patents is that the process encourages research and development by people or companies who are then rewarded with the possibility of monopoly profits for a set number of years. The negative side of patents—accruing to society—is that patent protection can limit further improvement and technological innovation.

PEAK

The point in the business cycle between a recovery and a recession. The point in the business cycle between a recession and a recovery is referred to as a trough. Both peaks and troughs are known as turning points.

PER CAPITA

The per-member, or per-person, contribution of some economic variable, such as the per-person income, debt, or real GDP contribution of a country.

PER-CAPITA GDP

A country's per-person output contribution. To calculate per capita GDP, divide GDP by the population. Current dollar per-capita GDP in the United States is $45,958 (2007, Q3). Economists also view per capita real GDP (inflation-adjusted GDP), which measures $38,382 for a similar period. Per capita real GDP, because it has been adjusted to a base year to keep purchasing power constant, is thus useful for comparing year-to-year changes in actual output per person.

PERFECT COMPETITION

A theoretical set of market conditions in which there are so many buyers and sellers that no individual buyer or seller can influence the price. All firms are selling an identical product and no seller or buyer can influence price. Therefore, perfectly competitive firms are defined as price takers. They must accept the going price for the good or service to make the normal rate of return. There is free entry into this market. Firms will come into the market if they see above-normal profits are being earned, eventually forcing profits down until just a normal return exists.

Few markets come close to replicating perfect competition. The closest examples to this structure are agricultural products, like eggs, milk, corn, and wheat. Each agricultural commodity is essentially the same regardless of which farm was responsible for the production. Economists use perfect competition to explain the profit conditions of real world market structures of monopolistic competition, oligopoly, duopoly, and monopoly.

PERFECT INFORMATION

Buyers and sellers have complete information on the location and prices of goods and services. The possession of such knowledge is characteristic of a perfectly competitive market. Any divergence from such knowledge depicts the market structure of monopolistic competition, oligopoly, duopoly, or monopoly.

PERMANENT INCOME

The theory that people consume not on current income, but permanent income. The permanent income theory of consumption was discovered by Milton Friedman and first coined in his famous text *The Theory of the Consumption Function* (1957). People tend to smooth out the pattern of their consumption over their lifetime by averaging their income streams. Thus, consumers transfer spending from comfortable periods in their life to times when they are less well off. People accomplish this smoothing out of spending by saving in some periods and dissaving in others.

PHILLIPS CURVE

A curve illustrating the historical short run tradeoff between inflation and unemployment. The relationship is inverse, meaning there is a tradeoff between the two. For example, when inflation rises, there is less unemployment, and vice versa (see Figure 1.4).

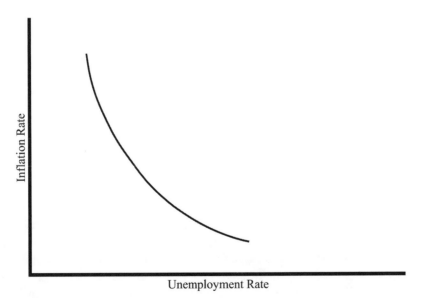

Figure 1.4 Phillips Curve.

PORTFOLIO

A collection of holdings of investments, often referred to as an investment portfolio. Holdings may consist of one or more stocks, bonds, mutual funds, CDs, real estate, or other assets.

POSITIVE ECONOMICS

An area of economics concerning what is, based on how the economy is run or organized. An example of a positive statement: "When the minimum wage rate is increased above the equilibrium wage rate, unemployment will increase."

PREFERRED STOCK

Shares of ownership in a company with several unique aspects that differentiate it from common stock. Unlike common stockholders, preferred stockholders do not enjoy voting rights in the company. Preferred stockholders receive dividend payments before common stockholders may get paid. They are generally entitled to dividends at a specified payment every quarter. For example, if you buy a 4% preferred stock share, you may receive $40 a year, or $10 a quarter on an investment of $1000. Preferred shares are traded on an exchange and over-the-counter, just like common stock. Because the payment stays steady, the market price of preferred shares tend to fluctuate in part based on interest rates. If the company goes bankrupt, preferred shareholders will be paid a settlement before common shareholders.

PRICE CEILING

A government imposed limit on how high a commodity is allowed to sell for, or how high a price is allowed to be charged. It is a maximum allowable price by law. During World War II, the U.S. government set price ceilings on rent to keep wartime workers in affordable housing. Although the federal government lifted this practice after the war, many local governments have continued the practice of rent control on the premise that it creates affordable housing. Price ceilings are effective if they are below the equilibrium price and create a situation of shortages. In other words, the quantity demanded at the price ceiling exceeds the quantity supplied.

PRICE FLOOR

A government imposed limit on how low a commodity is allowed to sell, or a wage is to be paid. It is a dictate that you must pay at least this much for a good or labor service. The U.S. government routinely sets price floors on certain agricultural products, and since 1938 has maintained a price floor on wages, referred to as the minimum wage. Price floors are effective if they are set above the equilibrium price and create a situation of excess supply. In other words, the quantity supplied at the price floor exceeds the quantity demanded.

PRICE LEADERSHIP

One firm in an industry leads in changing prices, and other sellers follow. In an effort to maximize profits and not undercut one another, many oligopolists use price leadership rather than explicit agreements to coordinate their prices.

PRICE MAKER

A business that has some latitude over the price it can charge. Businesses that are price makers face downward-sloping demand curves. (That is, the higher the price they charge, the lower the quantity demanded for the product, and vice versa.)

PRICE SUPPORTS

Government intervention in the selling of agricultural commodities. With price supports, commodity prices are set at a rate higher than market equilibrium. The government may purchase any unsold surplus or pay the farmer a subsidy to cover the difference between market price and support price. The premise of such supports is to increase farmers' incomes. Price support schemes in the United States began in 1926.

PRICE TAKER

A business whose production size is so small in relation to the entire market supply that its activities have no significant effect on the total quantity or prevailing market price. Price takers face a horizontal demand curve with all products selling at the same price, regardless of the quantity sold.

PRIMARY MARKET

The market in which investors purchase newly issued securities, with the money going to the issuing company. Subsequent trading takes place on the secondary market.

PRIME RATE

The interest rate banks charge their most credit worthy business and personal customers. The prime rate (the "prime") tends to be uniform throughout the banking industry and changes when the top-tier banks change their prime rate. Banks often use prime as a base rate and will charge their less creditworthy companies prime plus a point or two.

PRIVATE COSTS

The costs of providing a good or service as it appears to the individual or business supplying it.

PRIVATE GOOD

A good or service that is both rival and excludable. Rival means that when consumed or used by one person it diminishes use by another person. Excludable means that you can exclude others from consumption. Examples of private goods are doughnuts, clothing, and cars. When you eat a doughnut it is no longer available for others to consume. Also, you can exclude someone from consuming if they do not pay for the doughnut. Most ordinary goods are private goods and are provided by the market for profit.

News Flash!

It Costs Big Bucks to Raise a Family

No doubt, you have heard from your parents how expensive it is to raise a family. Food, clothing, cell phones, education, vacations—expenses can add up quickly. For kids between the ages of 9 and 17, families spend from

$10,250 to $11,290 annually on each child. Here's just how much it costs middle-class America to raise a family each year.

Estimated Annual Expenditures on a Child by Husband-Wife Families (Overall United States, 2005)

AGE OF CHILD

	9–11 Years	12–14 Years	15–17 Years
Housing	$3,360	$3,640	$3,120
Food	$2,080	$2,090	$2,330
Transportation	$1,500	$1,640	$2,080
Clothing	$490	$820	$730
Health Care	$850	$860	$910
Child Care & Education	$830	$610	$1,040
Miscellaneous (Includes personal care items, entertainment, and reading materials.)	$1,140	$1,330	$1,080
Total	$10,250	$10,990	$11,290

Figures are based on middle-income families with before-tax income from $43,200 to $72,600, average of $57,400. For each age category, expense estimates represent average child rearing expenditures for each age. The figures represent estimated expenses on the younger child in a two-child family.

Source: U.S. Department of Agriculture, Center for Nutrition Policy and Promotion, Expenditures on Children by Families, 2005.

PRIVATIZATION

In the strictest form, the act of privatization involves transferring ownership from the government to the business or private sector. This often occurs by selling government-owned assets. An example: State-owned university housing being sold to a private business firm to operate and manage. In a broader sense, privatization relates to merely the transfer of responsibility for services or goods from the government to private business firms. Contracting out the operation of a city convention center to a private business firm meets the broad definition of privatization.

Privatization is often done to discard goods and services operations that operate at a loss for the government. Another reason is that an outside business firm can infuse money, technology, and skill that is often unavailable to government-run entities, and thus bring enhanced service.

PRODUCER SURPLUS

The measure of the benefit to a producer from participating in a market. Simply stated, it is the difference between what a producer is willing to accept in payment for a good or service and the price the producer actually receives. Consumer surplus plus producer surplus measures the total economic surplus, or economic benefit, generated for both consumers and producers.

Producer Surplus in Action

Freddie Financier is explaining producer surplus to his little sister, Frannie, who is an up-and-coming artist. Frannie just sold her first painting for a cool grand! Of course, her big brother was the first to get the big news, telling Freddie she would have taken $125 for the picture but got $1,000 instead. Help Freddie calculate the producer surplus for his little sis.

$1,000 - $125 = 875

That is correct. Frannie Financier, living up to her name, received a big $875 producer surplus. This huge economic benefit will certainly encourage Frannie to keep painting.

PRODUCT DIFFERENTIATION

The range of products serving a similar function but with minor differences. These differences may be either real or perceived. Items could differ by the quality of component parts, material, and workmanship. Or advertising could create an illusionary allure of uniqueness. Goods often tend to have both real and perceived differences. By differentiating their products, companies establish brand loyalty and thus have more control over market price.

PRODUCTION POSSIBILITIES

Alternative combinations of final goods and services that could be produced in a given time period with all available resources and technology.

PRODUCTIVE EFFICIENCY

Goods and services, the output of the economy, are produced at the least possible cost. This occurs when competitive pressure on prices is pushed to the maximum limit.

PROFIT

The difference between total revenue and total cost. The basic incentive for operating a business is the expectation of profit.

PROFIT MAXIMIZATION

Profits are maximized for all types of market structures at the rate of output where MR (marginal revenue) = MC (marginal cost). To illustrate whether the MR = MC rule holds, see what happens when MR and MC are not equal. When MC is greater than MR, the true costs of producing one more unit of output would exceed the additional revenue brought in by one more unit, and profits are lower than necessary. When MR is greater than MC, the additional revenue for producing one more unit of output is greater than the costs for producing one more unit; so increased production will result in greater profits.

PROGRESSIVE TAX RATE

An income tax system whereby those who have higher incomes pay a higher percentage of their income in taxes than those with lower incomes. The U.S. income tax system is based on a progressive system.

PROLETARIAT

The exploited working class, according to Marxist theory. At the time, many workers owned no property and struggled to sell their labor, often ending up working 18-hour days in unsafe, unclean factory conditions. In 1848, in the *Communist Manifesto*, Karl Marx and Friedrich Engels predicted the proletariat would overthrow the bourgeoisie ruling class in a communist revolution.

PROPRIETORSHIP

In the United States, one of the three major types of business organizations (the other two being partnership and corporation). A proprietorship is an unincorporated business owned by one person, which may or may not have employees.

Proprietorships have a few advantages over corporations. A major plus is ease of entry. Anyone can start up a proprietorship business because there are no fees or incorporation paperwork required. The owner can do what he or she chooses and makes all business decisions. Proprietorship owners pay income taxes based on personal tax rates, which are often lower than corporate rates.

Proprietorships also have major disadvantages. Unlike corporate entities, proprietorships are not shielded by limited liability; in other words, if the business fails, the owner is personally responsible for all debts of the business. This means creditors could potentially take some of your prized possessions to pay a debt. It is often very difficult for a proprietorship to borrow funds for operation because any loans are based on the single owner's assets and credit worthiness. There is no continuity of operation because the death of the owner terminates the business.

PUBLIC CHOICE THEORY

A branch of economics that deals with the economic analysis of politics. As man is self-interested, so too are politicians, according to this theory. Government officials pursue their own agendas over public good. This theory was developed by Nobel Prize winner James McGill Buchanan (1919–).

PUBLIC GOOD

A good or service that is both nonrival and nonexcludable. Nonrival means that when consumed or used by one person, it does not deprive others from using it. Nonexcludable means it is impossible to exclude people from the good's consumption. Examples of public goods are national defense, the legal system, and air quality. Because people cannot be excluded from using public goods, they are difficult to provide by the private market. Public goods are generally provided by the government and financed by taxation.

PURCHASING POWER PARITY (PPP)

In comparing Gross Domestic Product of countries, data must be converted to a common currency in order to eliminate price differences among countries. These are rates of conversion that equalize the purchasing power of different currencies. Once converted to a common currency, comparison of GDP and its major aggregates allows international comparisons of economic size and well-being.

PUT OPTION

A contract that gives the holder the right to sell a stock at a particular price, or strike price, within a fixed period of time.

QUANTITY DEMANDED

The amount of a good or service that buyers are willing and able to buy at a specific price.

QUANTITY SUPPLIED

The amount of a good or service that sellers are willing and able to sell at a specific price.

QUANTITY THEORY OF MONEY

A classical view that uses the equation of exchange, or the Fisher equation, to explain the causes of inflation. (The Fisher equation states that $MV = PT$, where M is the stock of money, V is the velocity or turnover of money in circulation, P is the price level, and T is volume of transactions in goods and services.) The quantity theory of money holds that any change in the supply of money should lead to a direct proportional change in the price level. Classical economists assumed that the velocity of money and transactions are constant, at least in the short run. Although there have been revisions and debate to the strict classical view, economists still maintain that the growth rate of money influences the inflation rate.

QUOTAS

In international trade, a quantity limit placed on the import of a specific good. Quotas, like tariffs, are used to give an advantage to domestic producers of a specific commodity or product. Since there are quantity restrictions on the incoming good, there will likely be less of the select good on the domestic market, thus keeping the price of the good higher than the free flow of goods would dictate.

RATIONAL EXPECTATIONS

An economic theory that suggests players in the economy form their expectations based on a rational outlook, using available information and incorporating past experience.

RATIONALITY

People making decisions based upon cost and benefits alone. A rational person accepts a proposal or takes action if the benefits outweigh the costs. Altruism and kindness do not enter into the decision.

REAL ESTATE

Land and all physical property attached to it. Real estate is also referred to as real property. Examples of real estate include houses, secured mobile homes, office buildings, apartment buildings, undeveloped land, and agricultural use.

So You Want to Invest in Real Estate?

If you thought buying a house, apartment building, or office was the only way to invest and make a buck in the real estate market, think again. Check out some of the different avenues to try your hand in the real estate market. But it's no sure thing and real estate can be very risky, so be sure to study your investments carefully and comprehend risk issues.

Real Estate Investment Trusts (REITs)—These companies invest funds in real estate. To qualify, companies must pay 90% or more of their income to shareholders. So REITs may present a high dividend yield. REITs trade on major exchanges so you can purchase and sell shares. Equity REITs invest in or own real estate; mortgage REITs lend money to developers or invest in mortgages on real estate; hybrid REITs are a combination of the two.

Real Estate Mutual Funds—A mutual fund, which pools money to invest in equity securities of real estate-related companies, including REITs. An advantage to a real estate mutual fund is that it generally requires a minimal investment and provides diversification. Sector funds, such as real estate, are common with the major mutual fund families. Check out your favorite mutual fund for offerings.

Real Estate-Related Stock—According to the Bureau of Labor Statistics, the construction industry is the only major goods-producing sector expected to show positive employment growth. The industry is projected to rise by roughly 1 million employees to reach 7.8 million in 2012. The industry includes companies providing maintenance, repair, and improvement services. When looking for investment opportunities, don't forget opportunities in the renovation and upkeep area. Home improvement stocks, like flooring retailers, plumbing manufacturers, and hardware suppliers, can sometimes flourish even when the economy is tough, since people like to invest in their houses.

REAL GDP

The inflation-corrected measure of GDP; all new goods and services produced within the domestic borders of a country during a specified time period, normally for a given year. Real GDP, expressed in base-year prices, is also called constant dollar GDP. For 2007 (Qtr.3-final), current-level GDP stood at $13,970.5 trillion, while real GDP, adjusted for pricing effects, stood at $11,658.9 trillion for the same year.

REAL RATE OF INTEREST

The interest rate less the inflation rate.

RECESSION

Generally, an economic phase in which general economic activity slows down and the economy starts to contract. The average recession is 10 months long, while the typical expansion period is 5 years long. During a recession, production slows and unemployment rises. An old economic rule of thumb is that two consecutive quarters of declining output indicate a recession.

RECIPROCITY

A principle of international economic relations where country X grants country Y certain rights, on the condition that Y grants the same rights to X. International trade agreements often contain reciprocity requirements.

REGULATION

Government-enforced rules to alter the behavior of individuals or firms. In modern economies, regulation is plentiful. Although these rules take a multitude of different forms, they are in the interest of health and safety (social regulation), or to promote competition and guard against unfair business practices (economic regulation).

RENT CONTROL

A price ceiling that sets limits on the rent allowed to be charged for housing. Rent control was initially a federal program used during the World War II era to keep rents low for the workers coming into big cities to do factory work for the war effort. Since the federal program was disbanded, over 200 American cities have instituted rent control, largely as an effort to help the poor. In order for rent control to be effective, the rent control price must be below the prevailing equilibrium price. While rent control does have the immediate effect of making housing more affordable, a market shortage of housing results because quantity demanded exceeds the quantity supplied at the below equilibrium price. Because landlords must charge below-equilibrium rates in rent-controlled areas, one result of rent control is poor maintenance of existing units and less new construction of rental units.

REQUIRED RESERVES

The minimum amount of reserves that banks must legally hold against their checkable deposits. Banks may hold more than the legal requirement for demand and liquidity expectations. For example, if an annual street festival is held in a community, the local bank may keep a larger amount of cash on hand because customers have a high demand for cash during festival week.

RESERVE RATIO

The amount of cash and other liquid assets member banks in the Federal Reserve System are required to maintain with the Fed. The reserve balances are usually a specified percentage of their checkable deposits. By raising or lowering the reserve ratio requirement, the Fed can tighten or loosen money in the economy.

RETURN ON INVESTMENT

A ratio that measures the efficiency of a business. As a guideline, a company that is earning a return on investment lower than its cost of capital is inefficient.

Called ROI for short, it is calculated by dividing the ratio of earnings to capital employed. Usually this is earnings before interest, taxes, and dividends, divided by total capital of the business (stock plus long-term debt).

News Flash!

Kroc Opens McDonald's Restaurant in 1955

When Ray Kroc opened his first McDonald's restaurant, the revenues for the first day of business totaled just $366.12. But the restaurant took off, and Kroc was smart enough to see a goldmine. He bought the chain from the McDonald brothers in California, and the rest is history.

Whatever your favorite—the classic McDonald's hamburger, Big Mac, Quarter Pounder, Chicken McNuggets, a Premium Salad, an Egg Mc-Muffin, or one of the other menu items—McDonald's strives to be your restaurant of choice. Today, the company has 52 million customers every day. With 31,046 McDonald's restaurants in 118 countries, the corporation is "focused on increasing McDonald's relevance to consumers . . . " And successful it is, with revenues growing by 9% to a record $21.6 billion in 2006.

Source: McDonald's 2006 Annual Report.

RICARDO, DAVID (1772–1823)

British economist and businessman who, in his book *Principles of Political Economy and Taxation* (1817), developed most of his well-known theories—particularly those of value and wages. Ricardo went to work at the age of 14 and retired a wealthy individual at the age of 42, allowing him time to devote to his academic and literary pursuits. His interest in economics was aroused after reading Adam Smith's *The Wealth of Nations* (1776). His theory of value held the value of a good is determined by the amount of labor needed in its production. Ricardo's theory of wages, which eventually became known as the Iron Law of Wages, maintained the wages of laborers should be kept at the lowest possible level because the unlimited supply of labor would ensure a surplus supply at the subsistence wage level. Ricardo was a proponent of international trade. His doctrine of comparative costs showed that all countries benefit from free trade.

ROBINSON, JOAN VIOLET (1903–1983)

A British economist and prolific author who had such a myriad of economic contributions that she is widely regarded as the most celebrated female economist. Robinson, born Joan Maurice, studied economics at Girton College in Cambridge, England. Upon graduation, she married fellow economist, Austin Robinson. The couple spent the next few years in India, where Austin served as a tutor to the Maharajah of Gwalior.

Robinson returned to Cambridge to teach following her time in India. She taught at Cambridge until her retirement in 1971. She became a full professor and a fellow of Girton College in 1965. Robinson became the first female fellow of King's College in 1979.

Robinson's first significant book was *The Economics of Imperfect Competition* (1933), in which she developed a model of competition between perfect and monopoly. During the 1930s, Robinson participated in the Cambridge discussions, a small group of economists—including her husband Austin—who meet on a regular basis to discuss Keynes' works. In *Introduction to the Theory of Employment* (1937), Robinson simplified the main principles that Keynes put forth in *The General Theory* (1936). She later became interested in Marx as an economist and published *An Essay on Marxian Economics* (1942). Robinson eventually become a leader of the post-Keynesian movement, publishing *The Accumulation of Capital* (1956), which extended Keynes's short-run analysis to long-run analysis of accumulation of capital. Robinson never earned the Nobel Prize in Economics, considered an unfair oversight by many.

SAVINGS RATE

Personal savings as a fraction of disposable personal income. Personal savings is the amount of money remaining after personal expenditures and personal current taxes. Personal savings is available to invest in financial assets like bank accounts or stocks, buying a house, or paying down principal on consumer debt. The trend for Americans has been to spend more and save less of their disposable income. The personal savings rate of Americans has steadily declined over the last 25 years, today hovering at near 1%, while reaching a peak in 1982 at 11.2%.

Falling Savings Rate

8.6%
The Personal Savings Rate for 1986

4.0%
The Personal Savings Rate for 1996

0.4%
The Personal Savings Rate for 2006

SAY, JEAN BAPTISTE (1767–1832)

French classical economist, best known for his law of markets, which he developed in *A Treatise on Political Economy* (1803). Say's Law of Markets, as the theory is called, notes that supply creates its own demand. Say denied there could ever be a glut of goods, thus making overproduction of goods impossible. This idea was important to the classical school of economics because it led to the conclusion that the economy would automatically correct itself if left free from government intervention.

SCARCITY

The imbalance between our desires and available resources. All countries, regions, and individuals deal with the issue of scarcity. This is because the available resources are insufficient to satisfy all of our desires, and that is the core issue in economics. Every time we choose to use scarce resources in one way, we give up the opportunity to use them in other ways.

SECONDARY MARKET

The market in which securities are bought and sold after the original issuance. Proceeds go to the investor or dealer, not to the issuing company.

SECURITIES AND EXCHANGE COMMISSION (SEC)

Congress established the Securities and Exchange Commission (SEC) in 1934, to enforce securities laws, to promote stability in the markets, and to protect investors. The regulations invoked by the SEC carry forth two main premises: businesses offering securities (bonds and stocks, for example) must be truthful about their companies and the securities they are selling; also, those selling securities (brokers, dealers, and the exchanges) must treat investors fairly and honestly. Headquartered in Washington, DC, the SEC is small by federal standards with roughly 3,100 employees and eleven regional and district offices throughout the United States.

SELLER

A person or business entity that offers goods and services to a buyer in the marketplace for a price.

SEN, AMARTYA (1933–)

Indian citizen, an economist who is the leader in the field of welfare economics and the economics of poverty. In 1988, he was awarded the Nobel Prize in Economic Sciences "for his contributions to welfare economics." Sen has become a voice for poverty elimination, studying causes of famine and solutions for famine prevention. He earned a B.A. from Presidency College in Calcutta in 1953, a B.A. in 1955, and a Ph.D. in 1959 from Trinity College, Cambridge, England. Sen has held a host of prestigious teaching appointments, most recently at Harvard University from 1987 to 1998. In 1998, he became the Master of Trinity College, Cambridge, returning to Harvard in January 2004, as Lamont University Professor. Sen is a prolific writer, with over twenty books to his credit, including *Collective Choice and Social Welfare* (1970), *Poverty and Famines* (1981), and *Development as Freedom* (1999).

SERVICES

Services involve one party charging another for labor, skill, or advice. The U.S. output is overwhelmingly a service-producing economy, at 72% services and 28% goods. Services are work that has value, such as that provided by a dentist, accountant, lawyer, hair stylist, nurse, or plumber.

SET-ASIDE

Government removal of land from agricultural production. The intent of a set-aside is to keep the agricultural commodity market from becoming flooded with a particular crop, and therefore keep prices high. Farmers are usually paid for such reductions in crop acreage. The term also refers to a government program in which a certain percentage of contracts or funding is reserved for businesses owned by women or minorities.

SHOCK

An unexpected event that affects an economy. Examples of shocks to the economy include natural disasters like the 2004 hurricane season, which placed a drag on the tourist industry in the South; the oil shocks of the 1970s, where the sudden price increases imposed by OPEC caused real incomes to fall; and spending on World War II, which stimulated the country out of the depression.

SHORTAGE

A situation that exists when quantity demanded is greater than quantity supplied.

SHORT-RUN

The period in which the quantity and quality of some inputs cannot be changed. For example, the general assumption is that, in the short-run, labor can change while capital is held constant. As the amount of labor used increases, in general, the output will also increase. A short-run production function shows how much each additional worker contributes to output.

SIMPLE INTEREST

Interest is paid only on principal. If you deposited $1,000 in an account, which earned 3% simple interest, you are paid the same interest each year—$30. At the end of 3 years you would earn $1,090.

Icon Economist, Adam Smith (1723–1790)

Smith was a Scottish moral philosopher—a moral philosopher studies how morals affect behavior—educated at Glasgow University in Scotland and Oxford in England. He was a professor of moral philosophy at Glasgow University. Often referred to as the "father of economics" for his *Inquiry into the Nature and Causes of the Wealth of Nations* (1776), he formed the foundation of classical economics. In the text, Smith was concerned with what created wealth in a society. His new ideas that technical productivity and division of labor (specialized work tasks for employees) increased economic growth, or wealth, challenged the traditional view that wealth was created by collecting gold and silver.

Adam Smith (1723–1790), "father of economics" and author of *The Wealth of Nations. Source:* Library of Congress.

Smith said people are led by self-interests, and the invisible hand of the competitive marketplace will guide and promote overall economic well-being. He was a strong proponent of the laissez-faire principle, maintaining the marketplace was harmonious and should have a minimum of government interference. Smith also advocated free trade (no tariffs) because it promoted competition.

SOCIAL COSTS

The opportunity costs to all the individuals in a society. Social costs include the private costs that fall directly on the individual or business partaking in an activity, along with any additional costs imposed on society. For example, when an individual smokes cigarettes, he or she may incur private costs of increased doctor visits, but the social cost of smoking may also add to health issues and consequent doctor visits of those individuals around the smoker. Social costs differ from private costs primarily due to the existence of externalities—third party effects for which no compensation can be drawn. Many times taxation is used so social costs can be reflected in private costs, and market prices will better represent the actual costs for the entire society.

SOCIAL ENTREPRENEURSHIP

Business innovation with a social cause. These innovative efforts are designed to identify and solve social problems. A highly respected social entrepreneur is Professor Muhammad Yunus, the founder and managing director of Grameen Bank, which provides small loans to the poor in Bangladesh without requiring collateral. The bank extends credit to the disadvantaged—7.31 million borrowers, with 97% of loans are extended to women—to break the cycle of poverty while creating opportunities for self-employment.

SOCIALISM

An economic system in which there is public ownership of the important factors of production—capital and land—and some degree of centralized planning to determine how, when, and to whom the goods are distributed. In today's socialist economies, the degrees of public ownership and centralized planning vary widely. Modern socialism simply describes a government-planned economy. Karl Marx described socialism as an intermediate stage in the transformation of capitalism into full communism.

SOCIAL REGULATION

Government enforced rules in the interests of safety, health, environmental protection, and highway safety.

SOCIAL SECURITY

The Social Security Act was signed by President Franklin D. Roosevelt in August 1935, and continues today. It was designed as a protective measure to guard against the widespread unemployment and poverty

This 1936 poster exhorts workers to register (through the Post Office) for a Social Security number in order to participate in the new program. *Source:* SSA History Archives.

prevalent in the depression years—social insurance. Under the original 1935 act, Social Security paid retirement benefits to the primary worker. In 1939, a change in the law added survivor benefits and benefits for a retiree's spouse and children. In 1956, disability benefits were added. The original 1935 law contained the first national unemployment compensation program, and aid to states for various health and welfare programs.

News Flash!

Social Security Payout
Over $585 billion in Social Security benefits went to close to 50 million Americans in 2007.

STAGFLATION

An unusual combination of stagnation, or a depressed economy, combined with inflation. Prices rise during stagflation but there is high unemployment and low business production. Stagflation was prevalent in the United States in the early 1970s, when oil prices rose significantly, thus fueling prices worldwide and causing economies to suffer.

STOCK

The issued capital of a corporation commonly referred to as a share. Because stock represents ownership in a firm, stockholders have equity in the company. In the financial world, stocks are sometimes referred to as equities. Stockholders make money on stocks by two means: receiving dividend payments—profits distributed to shareholders—and an increased share price.

There are two main classes of stock, common and preferred. Common stock is the main form of ownership in a corporation, carries voting rights, and typically pays a dividend when the company makes a profit. Preferred stock pays a fixed dividend and does not carry voting rights. Common stockholders may only receive a dividend if preferred dividends have been paid.

STOCK EXCHANGE

A market through which stocks, bonds, and other securities are traded. There are stock exchanges located throughout the world. The three principal exchanges in the United States are the New York Stock Exchange (NYSE), the American Stock Exchange (AMEX), and the National Association of Securities Dealers Automated Quotation system (NASDAQ). Requirements vary by exchange, but each has rules and criteria in order to be traded on the exchange. Overall, firms tend to be among the largest and most profitable. NYSE is the largest in the world; other major exchanges include Tokyo, London, Hong Kong, and Toronto. Stock exchanges benefit the economy, providing a secondary market in which ownership of assets can be transferred.

STOCKHOLDER

A person or an organization that owns one or more shares of stock in a corporation. This ownership position is also referred to as a shareholder.

The famous Wall Street Sign. Wall Street is a city street located in downtown Manhattan in New York, the center of the financial district. Home to the New York Stock Exchange, banking institutions, and investment firms, "Wall Street" commonly refers to the entire investment community. *Source:* © Photographers Choice, SuperStock, Inc.

How to Read a Stock Quote

Local newspapers, popular reads like *U.S.A. Today* and *The New York Times*, and of course major financial newspapers like *Barron's* and *Wall Street Journal*, all list stock quotes. Details vary by newspaper, but all are displayed in a fairly common format. The stock table lists essential data about the company's stock price and performance. But it is important to know how to decode the tedious statistical data; knowing how to interpret a stock quote will aid you in buying, selling, and holding decisions, placing you at the top of the class in being an astute investor.

Let us examine a basic stock quote for a fictitious company, "Zip Zag Zone" that is representative of what could be found in a newspaper financial section. Some newspapers will print abbreviated versions. Newspapers should list a guide to the tables, which explains specific stock footnotes such as new 52-week high, new 52-week low, and first day of trading.

Stock Quotation

(1) (2)	(3)	(4)	(5)	(6)	(7)	(8)	(9)	(10)
52-WK High Low	NAME	SYM	DIV	YLD	VOL	P/E	CLOSE	NET CHG
77.00 56.70	ZZZone	ZZZ	.40	6.7	9797	16.3	59.72	−0.29

Stock Market Terminology

(1) and (2), 52-Week High and Low. The first column lists the highest and the second column lists the lowest prices at which one share of stock traded during the last year (52 weeks). The stock's high price for the year was $77.00 and its low was $56.70.

(3) Company Name. This column lists the name of the company. Names will be abbreviated. This fictitious company's full name is Zip Zap Zone.

(4) Company Ticker. This column lists the company's ticker symbol, which will uniquely identify the stock. If you don't know the ticker symbol for your favorite stocks, check out the online searches www.finance.yahoo.com/lookup or www.marketwatch.com/tools/quotes/lookup.asp for United States, and even international tickers. The ticker in this example is ZZZ.

(5) Dividend Per Share. Dividends are annual payouts per share, based on the latest declarations. A blank space indicates no dividends are currently paid out. The annual dividend for this company is $0.40 per share.

(6) Dividend Yield. This column notes the dividend yield, which is the current return on investment. The dividend yield is calculated by dividing the current dividend by the closing stock price. In this example, a dividend of $0.40, divided by the closing price of $59.72, equals 6.70%.

(7) Trading Volume. This column lists the total number of shares of the stock traded for the day. The number is always listed in hundreds of shares, so just add 00 to the listing to get the total number of traded shares. On this particular reporting date, 979,700 shares of Zip Zap Zone were traded.

(8) Price/Earnings Ratio. This column compares the price per share to the earnings per share. The ratio is calculated by dividing the closing stock price by earnings per share for the last four quarters, a trailing *P/E*. This number is often viewed as a measure of value, showing how much investors are willing to pay for $1 of earnings. In this example, a closing price of $59.72 divided by earnings per share of $3.66 (not stated in the stock quotation) equals 16.3. Interpreted, investors are willing to pay 16.3 for $1 of earnings.

(9) Close. This column lists the last price at which a trade was made during the day, the closing stock price. This stock closed at $59.72 for the day.

(10) Net Change. This column represents the change between the closing price for the previous day and the current day's closing price. A positive net change says that the stock price rose today, while a negative net change says the stock price fell today. In this example, the stock closed down today, so the previous day's close was $59.72 plus $.29 or $60.01.

STOCK INDEX

An index is a statistical measure of the performance of the stocks represented in it. Each stock index represents a unique sector of the stock market. Component stocks in an index may be roughly the same capitalization, in the same industry or subindustry, or in the same stock exchange.

Major stock index prices are reported daily by the news media. Although they do not report individual stock, performance indexes provide a benchmark of the general direction of the market. Indexes are a quick way to get a feel for stock market activity for the day. Besides the informational content, indexes also give portfolio managers a guideline for comparing performance. Common indexes quoted are the Dow Jones Industrial Average (DJIA), NASDAQ Composite Index, and the Standard and Poor's 500 Index.

News Flash!

"Watch the Dow"

Throughout the day you may hear people say, "The market is up!" or "The market is taking a beating." When someone is talking about the stock market, typically they are referencing the Dow Jones Industrial Average (DJIA). It is the most commonly quoted stock index in the world, the lead index reported on the nightly news, and monitored for its every shift throughout the trading day. Watching the Dow is helpful to investors because its reliability and long-term track record signal the market's basic trend. Here is a quick peek at the Dow calculation and historical origins.

Dow Calculation

Even though the DJIA is viewed by many as representative of the overall stock market, the DJIA is a calculation of only thirty stocks. But these are not just any stocks; these are the big boys, so to speak—stocks that are widely held by individuals and institutional investors, and represent roughly 25 to 30 % of the total market value of all U.S. stocks.

Thirty Index Component Stocks of the DJIA
(Closing Prices, August 21, 2007)

3M Co	88.46
Alcoa, Inc.	34.60
Altria Group, Inc.	67.22
American Express Company	59.14
American International Group, Inc.	65.81
AT& T, Inc.	38.75
Boeing Co.	96.95
Caterpillar, Inc.	74.28
Citigroup, Inc.	48.06
Du Pont	47.75
Exxon Mobil Corp	83.15
General Electric Company	38.35
General Motors	31.08
Hewlett-Packard Co.	46.01
Honeywell Intl, Inc.	55.02
Intel Corporation	23.89
International Business Machines	109.04

Johnson & Johnson	61.67
JP Morgan Chase & Co.	46.20
McDonald's Corporation	48.47
Merck & Co., Inc.	49.77
Microsoft Corporation	28.07
Pfizer, Inc.	24.24
The Coca-Cola Company	54.03
The Home Depot, Inc.	34.30
The Procter & Gamble Company	64.46
United Technologies Corporation	72.94
Verizon Communications	41.71
Wal-Mart Stores, Inc.	43.70
Walt Disney Company	33.29

As you can tell, the DJIA is an index of thirty of the best-known companies in the stock market. These companies are referred to as "blue chip" stocks, representing leading companies in the industries that move the stock market. Most of the stocks included in the index are listed on the Big Board—the New York Stock Exchange.

The Dow is an easy-to-calculate, price-weighted index, more affected by the movement of higher-priced shares than lower-priced shares, regardless of shares outstanding. Simply add the prices of the closing prices for all 30 stocks, divide by the current divisor (0.123017848) to find the Dow. Therefore, the Dow is not quoted in dollars, as is often misunderstood by the public, but rather reported in points.

In this case, the 30 stocks total to 1,610.41 divided by 0.123017848 equals 13,090.86. On August 21, 2007, the Dow closed at 13,090.86. The divisor is adjusted on occasion to keep the index consistent through structural changes such as stock splits, component substitutions, mergers and acquisitions, and large dividend distributions. The companies that make up the Dow are changed from time to time, at the discretion of the managing editor of *The Wall Street Journal*.

Dow History

The Dow is over 100 years old, created on May 26, 1896, by Charles Dow, cofounder of Dow Jones & Co. Although initially not highly regarded, it soon began daily publication in the company's financial newspaper, *The Wall Street Journal*. The Dow index grew from its original 12 stocks, to 20 stocks in 1916, and 30 stocks in 1928, where it remains today.

The Dow (May 26, 1896)

American Cotton Oil
American Sugar
American Tobacco
Chicago Gas
Distilling & Cattle Feeding

General Electric
Laclede Gas
National Lead
North American Utility
Tennessee Coal & Iron
U.S. Leather (preferred)
U.S. Rubber

General Electric is the only company in the current DJIA that was in the original Dow. GE was removed twice over the years, only to be returned in subsequent component changes. When the Dow was first published, the index was 40.94. Hard to believe when the Dow has already flirted above the 14,000 mark? Certainly it was a different economic climate in 1896. But the key point is simple and remains the same: If stocks are doing well, the index will rise. If stocks are doing poorly, the index will fall.

STORE OF VALUE

Money is a store of value, although during periods of high inflation may not be the best store of value.

STRUCTURAL UNEMPLOYMENT

The unemployment resulting from changes in demand or technology in our dynamic economy. Structural unemployment exists under the natural rate of un-employment, when the economy is working at full potential. Economists estimate that at any given time, between 2 and 3 % of the labor force is structurally unemployed. Examples of the structurally unemployed: a bank teller who has been replaced by an ATM; a typist replaced by an automated computer; or the coal miner who cannot secure a new job due to the closing of numerous coal mines.

SUBSIDY

Typically, a payment by a government to a producer. Subsidy payments are used to keep prices below what they would normally be in the free market, or to support businesses that would otherwise struggle—a form of protecting domestic industries.

SUBSTITUTE GOODS

Goods that may typically be substituted for one another in consumption. These are goods that can be used in place of one another. When the price of product "A" rises, demand for the product "B" rises, as well. As an example, if the price of butter rises, the demand for margarine will rise.

SUBSTITUTION EFFECT

The effect on the demand for a good or service due to a change in relative prices, assuming the consumer is compensated enough to remain equally satisfied. The substitution effect is always negative, as people always switch their spending away from items whose prices rise, wanting to preserve their living standards. That is, as

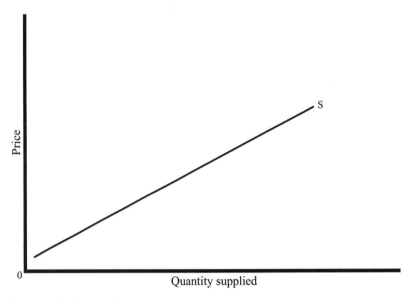

Figure 1.5 Supply Curve.

prices rise, the quantity demanded falls; and as prices fall, the quantity demanded rises.

SUNK COSTS

Costs that cannot be recovered even if a firm ceases operations. Sunk costs include such costs as advertising, marketing, and development.

SUPPLY

The quantity of a good or service sellers are willing and able to sell at different prices.

SUPPLY CURVE

A graphical representation of the relationship between the supply of a good or service and its price. Price and quantity supplied are directly related; a higher price increases the quantity supplied. The supply curve slopes upward from left to right (see Figure 1.5).

SUPPLY-SIDE ECONOMICS

An economic theory that holds real growth in the economy comes from factors affecting supply rather than demand. Supply-side policies were designed to increase aggregate supply in the economy. A main premise of supply-side economics, which gained prevalence in the early 1980s under the Reagan presidency, is that the high tax rates harm the incentive to work and save. Supply-side economics calls for a reduction in tax rates, especially harmful for businesses and wealthy individuals, in order to increase work and savings, and therefore investment and production. Overall, the supply-side policies of the Reagan years, while increasing output, did not lead to the rapid growth in the economy that was expected.

SURPLUS

This situation exists when quantity supplied is greater than quantity demanded.

TARIFF

A tax or duty levied on foreign imports. A tariff is a source of revenue for governments. There are two main types of tariffs: specific basis tariff, as an amount per unit—for example 30 cents per finished fabric garment; or an ad valorem tariff, expressed in percentage terms—for example 20% of the value of an imported car. Trade between countries generally has terms attached, and one of the most common restrictions is a tariff. A main argument for asserting tariffs is that if tariffs are issued, the level of foreign products will be limited in the domestic country. Consequently, consumers will buy more domestic made goods and services, which will benefit domestic producers of that particular good. These companies will have a greater likelihood of staying in business, and consequently, employees of these firms will have a greater likelihood of retaining their jobs.

Although the tariff is charged to the importer of a good, a problem with tariffs is consumers usually end up paying for tariffs. The importer passes along the cost of the tariff by charging a higher price for the product. The main argument for free trade is that tariffs disturb business productivity and the free flow of goods between countries, throwing it out of balance. This is a disadvantage to the consumer because not only will they be paying a higher price for certain goods, but their options may be limited as well.

The World Trade Organization (WTO) is the only international organization dealing with the rules of trade between nations. The goal of the WTO is to help producers of goods and services, and exporters and importers, conduct business. Country specific pacts, such as The North American Free Trade Agreement (NAFTA), between the United States, Canada, and Mexico, attempt to reduce trade barriers among a select group of countries.

TAXATION

A mandatory transfer of money from individuals, institutions, businesses, or groups to the government. The two basic forms of taxation are: direct tax—a tax on income, wealth, or capital; and indirect tax levied on sales of a good or service.

TAX AVOIDANCE

Reporting your income in such a way that tax is not legally due. This is a legal strategy and often involves hiring a professional accountant to seek out appropriate exemptions and deductions to reduce one's tax bill. Tax avoidance contrasts with tax evasion, which is an illegal activity.

TAX BASE

The total amount or coverage of what is to be taxed. For example, the income tax base for Small Town, United States, is the assessed value of incomes of the total population of that town.

TAX BURDEN

The total amount of money an individual, institution, business, or group must pay in tax. The tax burden includes not only the actual amount collected in taxes, but compliance costs too, such as hiring an accountant to organize and prepare tax forms.

TAX COMPETITION

A strategy whereby a country lowers its taxes, or even reduces its taxes to zero, in an effort to gain international funds and business.

TAX EVASION

A strategy that results in paying less tax than one's legal obligation. Tax evasion, which is illegal, may take several different forms. On the extreme, an individual with earnings may decide not to file a tax form. Other tax evaders may purposely claim deductions or exclusions that they are not entitled to, to reduce their tax bill. Illegal tax evasion contrasts with tax avoidance, which is a legal attempt to reduce one's tax bill.

TAX HAVEN

A country that allows foreigners an opportunity to reduce taxes (tax avoidance) or pay no taxes (tax evasion). Such tax havens may offer foreigners a legal option by banking with financial institutions in countries with reduced taxes, or an illegal option due to lack of record keeping on income that allows for tax evasion and money laundering.

THIRD WORLD

Roughly describes the economically underdeveloped countries of Asia, Africa, and Latin America. Countries classified as Third World commonly have conditions that may include one or more of the following: poverty, high birth rates, or economic dependence on more advanced countries.

TOKEN MONEY

Generally refers to coins and is sometimes called metallic money. The face value of token coins bears no relationship to the intrinsic value of the material (silver, gold, copper, zinc, etc.) of which it is composed. Years ago, for example, a $10 gold piece was actually worth $10 in gold if melted down, but today U.S. coins are token money.

TRADABLE POLLUTION PERMITS

A permit that firms can buy and sell, allowing them to continue to pollute at given levels. When permits are tradable, the level of pollution will be controlled to a certain quantity and the limited amount of pollution will be done by the firms that consider the cost of pollution control the highest. Rather than penalizing firms that pollute by a tax, tradable pollution permits let firms purchase the right to continue polluting.

TRADE-OFF

Choosing less of one option to get more of another. The trade-off for increased production is less clean air (more pollution).

TRANSFER PAYMENTS

Payments given by the government to an individual. The transfer does not involve any current exchange for work and is part of the process of redistribution of the economy's output. Income transfers include direct cash payments to individuals, such as Social Security, welfare, unemployment compensation, and FEMA disaster assistance. In-kind benefits involve a transfer of goods and services such as food stamps, housing assistance, Medicaid, and Medicare.

TRANSITIONAL ECONOMY

An economy that has had a developed socialist economic system, but has embraced the market system, and is in the process of shifting to capitalism.

TREASURY, U.S. DEPARTMENT OF

A U.S. government department, which has the basic functions of managing federal finances; collecting taxes; producing postage stamps, currency and coinage; managing government accounts and the public debt; supervising national banks and thrift institutions; advising on financial, monetary, economic, trade and tax policy; enforcing federal finance and tax laws; and investigating and prosecuting tax evaders, counterfeiters, and forgers. President George Washington appointed statesman Alexander Hamilton (pictured on the U.S. $10 bill) as the first Secretary of the Treasury in 1789. His financial program provided public credit where there was none before, and gave the infant nation circulating medium and financial machinery.

Treasury Secretary John W. Snow and U.S. Treasurer Rosario Marin provided their signatures to the Bureau of Engraving and Printing (BEP) for use on Series 2003 U.S. paper currency. "Having my signature on the currency of this nation is a great honor."—Secretary Snow. Snow was sworn in as head of the Treasury on February 3, 2003 and served until June 29, 2006. *Source:* The Department of the Treasury, March 5, 2003.

> **Monetary Trivia!**
>
> **Mint Matters**
> The United States Mint is a self-funded agency. The Mint turns in revenues beyond its expenses to the General Fund of the Treasury. The Mint receives more than $1 billion in annual revenues. During fiscal year 2006, the U.S. Mint transferred a total of $750 million to the Treasury General Fund.

TREASURY SECURITIES

Debt obligations of the U.S. government backed by its full faith and credit, exempt from state and local taxes. Treasury bills are short-term securities with maturities ranging from a few days to 1 year, and sold at a discount from their face value. Treasury notes have fixed maturities of 1 to 10 years, and Treasury bonds have maturities that range from 10 to 30 years. Both Treasury note and bonds pay a fixed rate of interest every 6 months. Treasury Inflation-Protected Securities (TIPS) are marketable securities with whose principal is adjusted to changes in the inflation rate.

TROUGH

The point in the business cycle between a recession and a recovery. The point in the business cycle between a recovery and a recession is referred to as a peak. Both troughs and peaks are known as turning points.

UNEMPLOYMENT

This situation exists when people want to work, but are unable to find jobs.

UNEMPLOYMENT RATE

The percentage of people in the civilian labor force who are unable to find a job. In the United States, the Bureau of Labor Statistics compiles the monthly unemployment rate from a random household survey on job and job search questions. The unemployment rate tends to rise and fall with the economy's business cycles. When an economy is in a downturn or recession period, unemployment is generally high, but when an economy is in an expansion phase or recovery, unemployment is very low.

UNIT ELASTICITY OF DEMAND

The condition whereby a percentage change in price causes an equal percentage change in quantity demanded, making total revenue constant. For example, a 30 % reduction in price of backpacks causes a 30 % increase in quantity demanded of backpacks. Unit elasticity of demand has a coefficient of one.

UNIT OF ACCOUNT

Money serves as a unit of account—a benchmark for comparing values of goods and services with one another. The monetary unit is set by a country's government. Goods and services in the United States are priced in dollars

U-SHAPED COST CURVES

Curves illustrating how the average costs of a firm vary with output increases. The steady decline of average fixed costs (AFC) combined with the later rising of

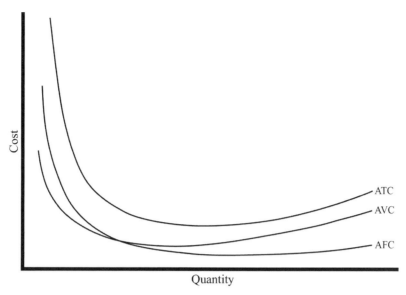

Figure 1.6 U-Shaped Cost Curves.

average variable costs (AVC) gives the average total cost curve (ATC) a U-shaped pattern (see Figure 1.6).

UTILITY

The amount of satisfaction or pleasure obtained from consumption of a good or service. In utility theory, economists maintain that the higher the satisfaction a good or service provides, the more a consumer will pay.

VARIABLE COSTS

The portion of the costs that change with the level of output. For example, labor and material costs.

VEBLEN, THORSTEIN (1857–1929)

American economist, sociologist, and founder of Institutional Economics. Veblen received a B.A. from Carleton College in 1880 and a Ph.D. in philosophy from Yale in 1884. He held a number of teaching positions, including University of Chicago, Stanford, and University of Missouri. In his most influential book, *The Theory of the Leisure Class* (1899), he coined the term "conspicuous consumption" whereby people consume to show pecuniary strength. In *The Theory of Business Enterprise* (1904), Veblen examined the conflict between the businessman, who is the controlling interest in business and profit motivated, and the efficiency interests of the engineer as to "avoid idleness, waste and hardship."

VENTURE CAPITAL

Money provided by individuals or business interests to fund entrepreneurial startups or expansion projects. Venture capitalists, in exchange for their investment, receive equity securities in the firm. The venture capitalist may look at several hundred investment opportunities before investing in only a few selected companies with favorable opportunities. Venture capital is important to the growth of the U.S. economy because it supports entrepreneurial action and innovation.

WALRUS, LÉON (1834–1910)

A French economist, best known for his application of mathematics to economics. Before teaching, Walrus dropped out of engineering school at Ecole des Mines, wrote novels, and was an administrator for a railway. He was appointed Chair of Political Economy at the University of Lausanne in 1870, and retained his position until retirement in 1902. His *Elements of Pure Economics* (1874 and 1877) provides a foundation for modern general equilibrium theory; often referred to as the father of general equilibrium theory.

WANTS

The desire for goods and services. In economics, society is assumed to have unlimited wants.

WEALTH

The total value of an individual's or a nation's financial assets, shares in companies, machinery, equipment, buildings, land, and other economic goods. It also includes personal skills that generate income and intellectual property such as copyrights, trademarks, and patents. Wealth consists of anything that can be traded for money.

News Flash!

World Wealth

According to estimates by the World Bank, the average world citizen has a total wealth of $90,210 (year 2000). Wealth consists of natural capital (such as nonrenewable resources, cropland, pastureland, forested areas, and protected areas), produced capital (such as buildings, machinery, equipment, and infrastructure), and intangible capital (such as raw labor, human capital, social capital, and the quality of institutions). Sound like a lot? Then contrast this with the U.S. per person wealth at $512,612, or the plummeting Ethiopia per-person wealth of just $1,965.

Source: *Where is the Wealth of Nations? Measuring Capital for the 21st Century*, The World Bank, 2006.

WEALTH EFFECT

The effect one's wealth has on his or her spending and savings. It is generally assumed that one with greater wealth will spend a larger portion of their current income.

WELFARE ECONOMICS

A term broadly associated with normative economics. The basic tenet of normative economics is concerned with value judgments on what ought to be in economics, whereas positive economics is concerned with facts or what is in

The Ghanaian authorities are signposting construction projects to high-light the tangible benefits of their participation in the IMF-World Bank Heavily Indebted Poor Countries Initiative. *Source:* International Monetary Fund.

economics. It is specifically concerned with the effects of economic activity on the welfare of society. Amartya Sen, academic scholar and advocate for elimination of poverty, won the Nobel Prize in Economic Sciences in 1988 "for his contributions to welfare economics."

WORLD BANK

The World Bank was established in 1945, along with the International Monetary Fund (IMF), after the Bretton Woods Conference was held. The main job of the organization is to provide low-interest loans, interest-free credit, and grants to developing countries for investment projects. The World Bank is made up of 185 member countries, jointly responsible for how the institution is financed and how its money is spent. The World Bank centers its efforts on sustainable poverty reduction through its two development institutions. The International Bank for Reconstruction and Development (IBRD) focuses on middle income and creditworthy poor countries, while the International Development Association (IDA) focuses on the poorest countries in the world.

WORLD TRADE ORGANIZATION (WTO)

An international agency that took the place of GATT in January 1995. WTO was designed to continue the work of GATT in supporting free trade among member countries, administering global trade agreements, and resolving trade disputes. There are 151 member countries.

X-EFFICIENCY

A firm, organization, or country that produces the maximum output technically possible from a given set of inputs. This may commonly be described as best practice technology.

X-INEFFICIENCY

A firm, organization, or country that fails to produce the maximum output technically possible from a given set of inputs.

YELLEN, JANET (1946–)

American economist, Janet L. Yellen serves as the President and Chief Executive Officer of the Federal Reserve Bank of San Francisco. Yellen has been affiliated with the Haas School of Business at UC Berkeley since 1980, where she now holds the title, Professor Emeritus.

Yellen, a Brown University economics undergraduate, received her Ph.D. in economics from Yale University. In addition to her academic experience at Berkeley, she was a Research Fellow at Massachusetts Institute of Technology, Assistant Professor at Harvard University, and a lecturer at the London School of Economics and Political Science.

She served as a member of the Board of Governors of the Federal Reserve System from 1994 through 1997, leaving to chair the President's Council of Economic Advisers through 1999. Yellen is the recipient of numerous honors and awards including the Maria and Sidney Rolfe Award for National Economic Service; Women's Economic Roundtable in 1997; an Honorary Doctor of Laws degree from Brown in 1998; and an Honorary Doctor of Humane Letters from Bard College in 2000.

Yellen is a prolific writer, focusing on a wide array of macroeconomic issues, including unemployment and labor market issues. Her research includes collaborations with her husband, Nobel Prize-winning economist and UC Berkeley professor, George Akerlof.

YIELD

The rate of return on a bond expressed in three major ways, always dividing the annual interest payment by the price of the bond. Most bonds sell for a par value of $1,000. For example, the nominal yield of a bond paying $50 a year, and a par value of $1,000, is 5%. Bond prices—the price at which one could sell the bond before its redemption date—move inversely to going interest rates in the economy. For example, as interest rates rise in the economy (let's say to 6% for this example), the price of this bond will fall. The reason is that other bonds of a similar quality and maturity will now be paying $60 a year but your bond is just paying $50. Obviously it is less valuable and the price on the bond will fall below par value. Current yield is calculated on the going market price of the bond. If this bond now sold for $900, the current yield would be $50/$900 = 5.6%. The redemption yield is the interest equivalent to the interest payment plus capital gains or losses, assuming the bond is held to its maturity.

ZONING LAW

A law governing what types of activities can be carried on in certain areas. These laws often attempt to minimize negative externalities, such as pollution, noise, or traffic. For example, many residential areas do not allow operation of a business from your home to cut down on all three externalities.

PART II

MONEY 101

Lesson 1

America's Central Bank

"Yogi Berra reminded us that prediction is very hard, especially about the future. In that spirit, the Federal Reserve continues to work actively to prepare for the possibility of financial stress."

—Federal Reserve Chairman, Ben Bernanke

You have probably been visiting the local bank with your parents since you were a small child. Perhaps you have fond memories of the great-tasting suckers handed out by friendly bank tellers. But did you know that banks are critical to our economy's health? A bank raises funds by collecting money from businesses and people. In turn, the bank provides them a checking account, savings account, money market deposit, or a certificate of deposit (CD). As payment for the use of their money, customers receive interest—a fee for use of their funds. Banks then loan this money out to businesses so they can expand production, and to people for making large purchases like houses and cars. Banks are described as financial intermediaries because they bring savers and borrowers together, keeping the economic wheels of our nation turning.

What is a central bank? No, it is not a bank located in the center of town. But good guess. A central bank is a financial institution that provides banking and financial services for the government and for the banking system. A central bank is usually the nation's ultimate monetary authority. It is a lender of last resort to banks, controls monetary policy, has regulatory power over the country's banking system, and issues currency. Other duties may include check-clearing services and acting as the government's bank. Most industrialized, and many developing, economies have central banks. The Bank of England, Bank of Japan, Reserve Bank of India, Bank of Canada, Swiss National Bank, German Bundesbank, and the United States Federal Reserve are all examples of central banks.

Where Do Central Banks Bank?

The Bank for International Settlements (BIS) is where central banks do their banking. Established in 1930, the BIS is the world's oldest international finance organization. The lead office is located in Basel, Switzerland, with regional offices in the Hong Kong Special Administrative Region of the People's Republic of China, and in Mexico City. The BIS offers short-term advances to central banks, along with numerous other financial services, which aid central banks and international monetary organizations in the management of their foreign exchange reserves. As a center for economic and monetary research, the BIS also provides a means for central bankers to share information.

AMERICA'S BANKING HISTORY

The Federal Reserve was not the first U.S. central bank. There were two prior attempts at central banking in the United States. The First Bank of the United States (1791–1811), headquartered in Philadelphia, was the largest corporation in the United States at the time. Its size and power frightened many citizens, and when its 20-year charter came up for renewal, the bank failed to receive a new charter from Congress by one vote. After a 5-year pause from central banking, the government tried again to establish a monetary authority. The Second Bank of the United States (1816–1836), also located in Philadelphia, was an even larger and more powerful financial institution than the First Bank. But the Second Bank met its early demise in 1832 when President Andrew Jackson, who was never fond of banking institutions, vetoed its recharter. The Second Bank continued operations, but on a downward spiral, until its charter officially expired in 1836.

The U.S. banking system was then left under the direction of the individual states for nearly three decades. At the time, state banks issued their own currency, to be redeemable in gold and silver. State bank examiners were expected to visit each bank and make sure there was enough specie backing the notes, but supervision was often faulty and many people were left holding worthless notes. Counterfeiting was also a serious problem. By 1860, more than 10,000 different types of bank notes had been distributed throughout the nation.

The next piece of major legislation, the National Banking Act of 1863, brought some relief to an unstable state banking system. It created a network of nationally chartered banks. It removed the ability of state banks to issue bank notes and gave the national banks sole responsibility for issuing currency. Without a bankers' bank, however, the U.S. financial system was subject to an inelastic money supply, bank panics, and severe cyclical fluctuations.

National banks were required to hold government securities against their bank notes. Therefore, money supply was inelastic and did not expand or contract according to the needs of business. Sometimes money was available for loans and business growth while at other times money was tight, causing periodic currency shortages and precipitating bank panics. Adding to the financial crisis was a system of immobile reserves. Bank reserves were held in specified reserve city banks and could not be shifted to areas where customer withdrawal demands had increased.

Monetary Trivia!

Do You Know Who Currently Produces U.S. Currency?

A. National banks

B. The Federal Reserve

C. The Bureau of Engraving and Printing

Banking panics, or runs, were common in the late 1800s and early 1900s. Featured here is a bank run on the Nineteenth Ward Bank. *Source:* Library of Congress.

Answer: The Treasury Department's Bureau of Engraving and Printing. While the Fed issues Federal Reserve Notes, the only U.S. currency now produced, the Bureau of Engraving and Printing has the manufacturing job. During the 2006 fiscal year, the Bureau of Engraving and Printing produced 33 million notes a day with a face value of approximately $529 million.

A flurry of bank "runs" erupted during the national banking period, namely 1873, 1884, 1890, 1893, and 1907. Runs, or banking panics, occurred when rumors circulated that a bank was in financial trouble or was about to have its charter pulled. Customers would line up at the bank and begin to withdraw their savings in cash. Panic would quickly spread to other banking institutions. There was no federal banking insurance until 1933, so when a bank could not cover such huge demands for cash, it was destined for failure. The most severe occurred in 1893, when the bank run was followed by a harsh depression.

The Panic of 1907 began at New York banks and trusts, and quickly spread across the country. Wealthy financier J.P. Morgan halted the crisis by influencing bankers to place funds in the troubled banking institutions. By this time government officials and politicians realized they needed a central monetary authority to maintain a healthy banking system.

President-elect Woodrow Wilson recognized the need for monetary reform. He summoned two top advisers to assist in the reform package: Representative Carter Glass from Virginia, soon to become Chairman of the House Committee

A crowd of depositors gathered in the rain outside the Bank of the United States after its failure. *Source:* Library of Congress.

on Banking and Finance, and the committee's top adviser, H. Parker Willis, a former economics professor at Washington and Lee University. Glass and Willis spent the better part of a year working on a central bank proposal, dubbed the Glass-Willis proposal. After much debate, on December 23, 1913, just 6 years after the last major panic and just months into his presidency, Woodrow Wilson signed a version of this proposal into law. The Federal Reserve Act called for "...the establishment of Federal Reserve Banks, to furnish an elastic currency, to afford means of rediscounting commercial paper, to establish a more effective supervision of banking in the United States, and for other purposes." The Federal Reserve, or Fed as it is commonly called, was open and ready for business on November 16, 1914.

THE FEDERAL RESERVE SYSTEM

The role of the Federal Reserve has evolved over the years. The Fed functions as the nation's money manager via a complicated quasi-governmental structure including (1) a Washington, DC-based Board of Governors; (2) a monetary policymaking body called the Federal Open Market Committee (FOMC); (3) twelve regional Federal Reserve Banks plus a total of twenty-five branches; (4) member banks who hold stock in their regional Federal Reserve Bank; and (5) various advisory councils. All work together to reach the nation's economic goals of stable prices, strong economic growth, and full employment.

Is the Fed a Government Institution?

The answer is yes and no. The Federal Reserve is often referred to as quasi-governmental because it is an independent arm of the U.S. government. The Fed is self-financed and does not request money from Congress for operations. In fact, after paying for operational expenses, each year the Fed turns over most of its revenue to the Treasury. The Chairman of the Federal Reserve Board of Governors testifies regularly before Congress on its activities and monetary policy, but daily decisions do not require Presidential or Congressional approval.

Mucho Money!

The Federal Reserve receives revenues—roughly $21 billion dollars a year—primarily from interest on its holdings of U.S. government securities acquired through open market operations. This self-financing institution, after paying its own expenses, then turns over the majority of its revenues to the U.S. Treasury to pay for the government's expenditures.

THE BOARD OF GOVERNORS

The Board of Governors, located in Washington, DC, oversees the operations of the Federal Reserve System—making supervisory and regulatory decisions, setting reserve requirements, and approving the discount rate. The Board is composed of seven members who serve staggered 14-year terms. Each member is appointed by the President and confirmed by the Senate. The Board Chairman and Vice Chairman positions are named by the President and confirmed by the Senate for 4-year terms and can be reappointed for additional 4-year terms as long as their Board terms have not expired.

The Board is in charge of two monetary policy tools: reserve requirements and the discount rate. Reserve requirements are the percentages of certain deposits banks are required to keep on hand. These reserves must remain in the bank's own vault or on deposit at the Fed. According to the Monetary Control Act (MCA) of 1980, the Board can set the reserve requirement on transaction accounts (checking accounts and other accounts that can be transferred to third parties) anywhere from 8% to 14%. The reserve requirement on transaction accounts is currently set at approximately 10%. When a customer brings in $100 to deposit in a checking deposit, the bank must keep $10 on hand or with the Fed, and is free to lend out $90. This is primarily how banks make money, by lending out depositors' money. If the reserve requirement were decreased, it would give the banking system the ability to create more money, and vice versa. Reserve requirements, however, are rarely changed and are not the main monetary policy tool.

The discount rate is the interest rate at which the Fed gives short-term loans to eligible banking institutions. This role is referred to as a "lender of last resort," because the Fed provides money to banking institutions when they have an emergency, as well as temporary or seasonal needs.

FEDERAL OPEN MARKET COMMITTEE

The Federal Open Market Committee (FOMC) conducts monetary policy through open market operations—the Fed's most flexible tool. The FOMC consists of twelve voting members: the seven members of the Board of Governors, plus five of the twelve Federal Reserve Bank presidents. The president of the Federal Reserve Bank of New York always serves as a voting member and the other presidents serve rotating 1-year terms. The President of the New York Fed holds this standing position because all open market operations, along with buying and selling dollars in international exchange, are carried out at the New York Fed. The nonvoting Reserve Bank presidents attend the FOMC meetings to participate in discussions and provide input on economic conditions in their districts. The Chairman of the Board of Governors also serves as Chairman of the FOMC (see Fast Fed Facts for current Chair).

FEDERAL FUNDS RATE

The FOMC holds eight regularly scheduled meetings each year in Washington, DC. At each of its meetings, the FOMC decides on its target for the federal funds rate, the rate at which banks borrow overnight reserves from one another. Immediately following each meeting, the FOMC announces its policy decision—to raise, lower, or keep unchanged the target for the federal funds rate—and by how much. The statement after each meeting also provides a brief explanation for the decision, based upon economic conditions. The decision to raise, lower, or maintain the federal funds target is always made with the goal of keeping inflation low and stable, while maintaining a strong economy.

Although it is a complicated process, the Fed can push the federal funds rate lower by purchasing government securities. Open market purchases by the Fed add to the reserves in the banking system, which puts downward pressure on the federal funds rate. When reserves rise at banks, more loans can be extended. Open market sales by the Fed drain reserves from the banking system, forcing the federal funds rate upward. In the short run, lower interest rates may have the affect of stimulating the economy because it is easier for individuals and businesses to borrow, and higher rates tend to curtail economic activity, because it is more expensive to borrow. In the long run, however, low and stable inflation creates the best economic condition for sustainable economic growth.

A rise (or fall) in the fed funds rate can trigger a chain of events that will lead to a rise (or fall) of other interest rates. The fed funds rate is a low, base rate relative to other interest rates. Often other rates tend to follow the direction of fed funds rate. So, when you hear that the Fed has raised the fed funds rate, interest rates for loans may be rising soon, and interest rates paid to savers could rise. Conversely, when you read the announcement that the Fed has lowered the fed funds rate, interest rates for loans may decrease, and interest rates on savings accounts may fall.

RESERVE BANKS

The Fed has twelve Reserve Banks located around the country. Each Reserve Bank has a board of nine directors, representing banks and businesses within the district. The directors set their district's discount rate, subject to Board approval, and appoint the Bank's president. The duties of the Reserve Banks are to:

• Provide financial services for the U.S. government
• Supervise state-chartered member banks and bank holding companies in their districts
• Supply coin and currency to banks
• Collect and process checks
• Hold cash reserves of banks
• Make short-term advances to banking institutions

Each Reserve Bank also has an economic research staff and produces a wide variety of economic and monetary publications and Web-based material. Many Reserve Banks have branches to serve geographical zones within their district.

Monetary Trivia!

Whose Portrait Was Featured on the Largest Bill Ever Printed? What Was the Dollar Amount?

The $100,000 gold certificate featured the portrait of Woodrow Wilson, the U.S. president who signed the Federal Reserve Act into law. The U.S. Bureau of Engraving and Printing issued the $100,000 gold certificate, dated 1934. The $100,000 certificates were issued by the Department of Treasury to Federal Reserve banks against an equal amount of gold bullion held by the Treasury. These notes were used only in banking transactions between Federal Reserve Banks, and not circulated in the public.

Fast Fed Facts

• Princeton economics professor and former Chairman of the President's Council of Economic Advisers Ben Bernanke was sworn in as Fed Chairman and a member of the Board of Governors on February 1, 2006. Bernanke was appointed as a member of the Board to a full 14-year term, which expires January 31, 2020, and to a 4-year term as Chairman, which expires January 31, 2010. He can be reappointed as Chairman for subsequent 4-year terms until his Board term expires.

• Of the three main tools of monetary policy—open market operations, reserve requirements, and the discount rate—the most frequently used is open market operations. Such operations refer to the Fed's buying and selling treasury securities in the secondary market in order to affect bank reserves.

• The twelve Federal Reserve banks are located in Boston (1A), New York (2B), Philadelphia (3C), Cleveland (4D), Richmond (5E), Atlanta (6F), Chicago (7G), Saint Louis (8H), Minneapolis (9I), Kansas City (10J), Dallas (11K), and San Francisco (12L). If you look on a $1 Federal Reserve Note you will see a seal and the corresponding number and letter of one of the twelve Banks.

- The Board of Governors in Washington, DC, has about 1,850 employees.
- Over 3,000 U.S. banks are members of the Federal Reserve System. National banks are required to join, while state banks have the option of joining. Member banks are stockholders of the Reserve Bank in their district, and they receive stock dividends. Unlike a publicly traded corporate stock, however, member banks are not allowed to sell their stock.
- Three main advisory councils meet several times each year with the Board of Governors to discuss current economic issues unique to their interests. Advisory council members come from each of the twelve Fed districts. The Federal Advisory Council is traditionally composed of commercial bankers, the Consumer Advisory Council represents the interest of consumers, and the Thrift Advisory Council has representatives from savings banks, credit unions, and savings and loans.

Since 1913, America's central bank, the Fed, has been skillfully guiding the financial health of the U.S. economy. Through a highly complicated, but well-tuned structure, the Fed balances the nation's money supply in order to promote sustainable economic growth, full employment, and low inflation. As the Fed nears its 100-year anniversary, it is set to manage the challenges of our ever-changing $13 trillion economy.

Key Fed Facts

The Federal Reserve, the nation's central bank, affects the economic actions of every American. Getting a great bank loan? Choosing a safe financial institution? Spending a bank note? Those are all actions in which the Fed has a sizeable role. Dawn Conner, senior economic education specialist at the Federal Reserve Bank of St. Louis, talked about some Key Fed Facts. A Fed education expert, Conner's responsibilities include conducting programs for teachers and students, and producing economic and personal finance materials for the classroom.

What are typical careers at the Fed for recent college graduates?

Two positions found at most Federal Reserve Banks are research analyst and assistant examiner. A research analyst is responsible for assisting Federal Reserve economists by performing advanced econometric, computational, and analytical research, and reviewing economic and financial data. An assistant examiner observes bank examinations, and studies and practices methods and procedures related to bank examinations.

What Does the Federal Reserve Do?

The Federal Reserve's duties include:

1. Conducting the nation's monetary policy.
2. Supervising and regulating banking institutions.
3. Maintaining the stability of the financial system.
4. Providing financial services to depository institutions, the U.S. government, and foreign official institutions.

What is the Fed's role in circulating and shredding currency?

The Federal Reserve places an annual printing order for currency with the Department of the Treasury's Bureau of Engraving and Printing and pays the bureau for the cost of printing. The Federal Reserve Board then coordinates shipments of currency to the Reserve Banks around the country. The Reserve Banks issue the notes to the public through depository institutions. When currency flows back to Reserve Banks, each deposit is counted, verified, and authenticated. Notes that are too worn for recirculation (unfit notes) are destroyed by Reserve Banks on behalf of the Treasury.

Where can I find out more about the Federal Reserve?

To learn more about the history and structure of the Fed, how the Fed conducts monetary policy, or what CAMELS has to do with banking supervision, go to www.FederalReserveEducation.org and click on FED101.

Lesson 2

Big Production

"Consumption is the sole end and purpose of all production..."
—Adam Smith, (1727–1790), *The Wealth of Nations*

When economists want to take a quick pulse of the economy, they turn to Gross Domestic Product (GDP). This impressive indicator provides a gauge of both the size and health of the U.S. economy. GDP measures an economy's output, or production, by totaling the dollar value of all final goods and services produced within a nation's boundaries for the year. It is a huge statistical job! That is a lot of fast food, clothes, cars, groceries, doctor visits, and haircuts—to name just a few—to count.

When you went to the mall last weekend, perhaps you did not think about increasing the production of the economy, but the $20 haircut you had is now part of GDP. You are helping the economy grow. Your new $250 mountain bike added an even bigger punch. Even the $1 cola you just bought contributes. If we add together all the purchases made in the United States during the year, they total more than a whopping $13 trillion.

In order to avoid double counting, or counting more than once, only the final sale is totaled. A final good is one that has reached its final customer; intermediate goods are used to make other products. Consider your mountain bike: the tires, steel, paint, and frame, are all intermediate products. The value of the component parts are figured into the total value of the mountain bike, and thus should not be totaled in the intermediate stages of making the bike.

HERE'S A TIP! DON'T CALCULATE THESE TRANSACTIONS IN GDP

Sales of used goods. The total dollar amount of used merchandise sold each year is plentiful. Think of all the previously used items like cars, houses, boats, tractors, and computers that are resold. The initial transactions were tabulated in prior years, so the television you just purchased at the thrift store will not be counted in this year's total. This sale is not due to the current year's production, but simply transferred ownership of the television.

Financial transactions. Buying and selling of stock, bonds, and land is not included in the GDP calculation. These financial exchanges are merely transfers of assets because nothing is added to current production. The stock, for example, just changes ownership. There is no value added, or production, as a result of an actual trade. Commission fees paid to brokers to initiate trades are included in GDP. A broker works for his or her fees, thus providing a service. So if you got a great deal and paid only $7 for a stock trade online, the $7 commission fee represents economic activity.

Transfer payments. Money provided from the government to households is a transfer of funds between entities. Examples of transfer payments include Social Security, unemployment, welfare, and disability payments. They are transfers of funds for which current economic activity is not provided, so they don't fall in the GDP definition.

How to Remember Gross Domestic Product

Gross means the entire amount (it does not deduct depreciation of the capital stock).

Domestic is produced within the U.S. borders.

Product represents the final goods and services produced in a year.

The GDP number measures output produced within the United States' borders during the year, regardless of the nationality of the person producing it. If an American citizen and a foreigner work at businesses within the United States, both individuals are contributing to GDP. Visually trace the borders of the country in your mind; all final economic activity going on within the boundaries is calculated in the output figure. But if an American is working at a company outside the United States, the production total does not fall in GDP. Why? Here's the lowdown.

As early as 1942, the Department of Commerce developed annual estimates of Gross National Product (GNP) to show how income was generated, received, and spent by various components of the economy. GNP measures the total value of all goods and services produced by U.S. citizens no matter where they produce it. In other words, an American could be working in the United States or another country and that output would be totaled in GNP—it doesn't matter as long as they are U.S. citizens. For nearly 50 years, the use of GNP as the lead output measure served the country well. The difference between the dollar amounts of GDP and GNP is relatively small. But in 1991, the Bureau of Economic Analysis (BEA), the agency within the Department of Commerce that now handles production measurements, changed the official measurement of production from GNP to GDP to follow the practice of other countries. The reason for this change was to make it easier for government officials and economists to make comparisons internationally of economic activity with other countries.

The BEA, a Washington, DC, government agency, is one of the world's leading statistical agencies. BEA produces a host of other stellar economic statistics, which are a great source for economists, policymakers, business leaders, investors, and interested students. The numbers provide a detailed picture of economic activity in the United States, and they are utilized in tax and budget projections, monetary policy decisions, investment plans, and economic research. The BEA announces GDP on a yearly basis, but estimates are made quarterly as more comprehensive data is collected.

The quarterly GDP numbers consists of three statistics: an advance estimate, followed by a preliminary estimate, and a final figure. The advance estimate, which is an early peek into the economy, is published the month after the quarter ended; revisions are posted at the end of the following 2 months. Because GDP measures the state of the economy, its announcement is big news! It is widely reported by television, radio, print, and online media the day of and the day following the release of GDP results.

If you miss the GDP report on the news the day of its release, check out one of the following sources:

• The Bureau of Economic Analysis Web site at www.bea.gov.

• The monthly *Survey of Current Business*, published by the U.S. Department of Commerce.

• E-mail alerts. Sign up for the free e-mail subscription service by the Bureau of Economic Analysis at www.bea.gov (on the left side of the main page click E-mail Subscription). You may choose to receive, via e-mail, economic indicators including GDP, and even GDP by state.

• Phone summary. To hear a recorded message of GDP estimate and its principle components, call (202) 606-5306.

CALCULATING GDP

There are two major approaches to calculating Gross Domestic Product, according to the National Income Accounting formulas utilized by the BEA. The first is called the income approach, in which all the income received by those producing the goods and services is added together to arrive at GDP. Total employee compensation, self-employed income, rent, corporate profits, and interest—plus returns to government (examples include sales tax, property taxes, and special assessment taxes) and depreciation are all included in the calculation.

The other approach economists can utilize to tally GDP is called the expenditure approach. This method adds all the spending on final goods and services for the entire year. One side is buying the goods and services produced (expenditure approach), while the other is receiving income from those who spend it (income approach). Income will always equal expenditure for an economy because every dollar of spending by someone is a dollar of income for someone else. And the income approach and the expenditure approach will always balance—to the penny—due to statistical discrepancy adjustments by the BEA. The expenditure source data is thought to be more reliable, so let us view the calculation of GDP with the spending approach.

The expenditure method consists of totaling the following groups to calculate the monster GDP number:

Personal Consumption Expenditures (C): Total spending by consumers on durable goods, nondurable goods, and services. Durables are goods that have a lifetime over 1 year, and include such things as cars and washing machines. Nondurables have a lifetime use under 1 year; these include food and household supplies. Services include things like medical examinations, movies, accounting services, and piano lessons.

As you can see from Table 2.1, GDP and its Components, personal consumption expenditures amount to roughly two-thirds of entire spending in the

Table 2.1 GDP and Its Components (In Billions of Current Dollars on an Annualized Basis) First Quarter 2007 (Advance)

		Percentage
Consumption (C)	$9,589.8	70%
Investment (I)	$2,136.7	16%
Government Spending (G)	$2,618.3	19%
Net Exports (X-M)	$−712.2	−5%
Total	$13,632.6	100%

Source: U.S. Bureau of Economic Analysis.

economy. Consumer buying significantly impacts the economy and individuals directly influence economic fluctuations. When consumers are buying goods and services and consumption rises, output is stimulated and it is great for business. On the flip side, depressed spending by consumers will be bad news for business and can lead to an economic slump. Your spending power is a strategic element in the economic system.

Gross Private Domestic Investment (I): Investment expenditures by the business sector; consists of fixed investment and change in private inventories. Fixed investment includes spending on residential structures (e.g., houses and apartments owned by businesses and rented to tenants), nonresidential structures (e.g., new construction on factories, hotels, or office buildings), and equipment and software (e.g., machinery, office equipment, and computer software). Change in private inventories is the shifting of physical volume of inventories, tallied as the change in dollar value of those inventories. Investment is an important component of GDP to watch because such expenditures, designed to produce new capital goods, signal future production capabilities in the economy.

Government Spending (G): Federal, state, and local government spending. For example, national defense, highways, and police department expense fall in this category. At one-fifth of GDP, the government is an important player in the economy. This spending does not even include government transfer payments such as welfare, unemployment, and Social Security.

Net Exports (X-M): The difference between what a nation sells abroad or exports (X) and what it purchases or imports from other countries (M). This is characteristically a negative number as the United States, while a large exporter, imports an even larger amount of goods. Exports bring money into the U.S. economy, which increases the GDP. Conversely, when the U.S. imports goods, money leaves the economy, and goes to the exporting country, thus decreasing the U.S. GDP.

Calculating GDP is a huge job and economists at the BEA must make use of all available data. Yet GDP does not measure all production in the economy. There are a multitude of productive activities that are left out of the calculation because money does not enter into the transaction or the activity is "under the table."

Remember, GDP does not include these activities:

• *Household chores.* Your mom or dad may work hard doing the laundry, cooking, and cleaning the house. Although it is work, no financial exchange takes place for the work, and is thus not counted in GDP.

• *Volunteer work.* Since no money changes hands and the work is done to assist others, volunteering does not count toward GDP.

• *The underground economy.* The only way the BEA can calculate GDP is to use available government tax, sales, and monetary data. However, there is a tremendous amount of activity that is difficult to measure. For example, flea markets, bookies, or illegal gambling are big activities and generate substantial production. Economists have made ballpark estimates that the underground economy could be near $1 trillion a year. That is a lot of unreported income. But any person who fails to report under-the-table cash transactions as income on their taxes to the IRS is generally outside the statistical radar.

What State Has the Biggest Gross Domestic Product?

Answer. California. California has the largest economy of any of the states at $1.7 trillion (advance estimate, current 2006 dollars). Contrast this to the U.S. output for the year at $13.2 trillion and the smallest economy, Vermont, at just $24.2 billion.

Source: U.S. Bureau of Economic Analysis.

Economist In Action

Late each month, the Bureau of Economic Analysis (BEA) announces a stream of vital economic numbers. There are about 400 staff economists and accountants at the BEA who calculate the crucial statistics—national, international, regional, and industry data—using National Economic Accounting. Hands down, the GDP announcement is the most widely anticipated figure. Shelly Smith, Senior Economist at the BEA, is part of the NIPA (National Income Product Account) review team that works on compiling GDP—how final expenditures on goods and services $[C + I + G + (X - M)]$ aggregate together. Because financial markets are so sensitive to the GDP number growth rate, Smith and a small group of economists are sequestered in a secure conference room to spend the day reviewing the figures behind the big number. To make sure the number is kept under wraps, the economists in the room do not even say the number out loud, referencing data by line number only during their discussions.

Macro-economist Smith gives the lowdown on this highly watched number.

You contribute to GDP. Young people contribute to GDP by their purchases. Whenever you buy clothes, shoes, food, and athletic equipment, the purchase goes into GDP as part of personal consumption expenditures

(PCE). PCE are roughly 70% of GDP, so buying makes a huge impact on the number. Going to school also contributes to GDP because you are consuming educational services.

BEA collects data from a number of government agencies and private trade sources. In order to total the GDP, the BEA collects data from government agencies including the Bureau of Labor Statistics, Census Bureau, Internal Revenue Service, as well as private trade sources. Economists from both the Census Bureau and the BEA also collect data from companies on their international operations and investments for the foreign trade component.

GDP is the most important measure of the economy. There is an abundance of information provided in this one number. GDP is the most comprehensive measure of output we have. You can get an idea of what types of goods and services are being produced and who supplies the goods and services. When you want a quick reading of how the economy is doing, look at GDP and its growth rate.

The growth rate of GDP is the most essential number. What matters most is the growth in GDP from one period to another. In order to tell if an economy is growing, look at how the level of GDP—adjusted to remove any effects from rising prices—has changed. (Note: A growing number means the economic activity is rising—more jobs, larger incomes, and expanded production. A negative number suggests the economic activity is faltering: unemployment, depressed income, and fewer goods and services to go around.)

Smith notes it is important to watch GDP, because the "... number affects everyone's life." Consumers make financial decisions, such as saving or investing, based on economic data. For example, the GDP growth rate affects the Federal Reserve's decision on monetary policy, raising or lowering interest rates. Most Americans hold some form of loan instrument affected by these rates—home, business, or personal loan—or at the very least a credit card. So when your credit card interest rate is increased, borrowing costs rise and you have a tendency to watch your spending. But if the Fed lowers rates, Americans rev up the borrowing and spend, spend, spend!

NOMINAL VERSUS REAL GDP

The BEA provides two measures of GDP—nominal and real. Nominal GDP measures production in current prices and is also referred to as current-dollar GDP. The dilemma is that nominal GDP has not been adjusted for price changes. With nominal GDP, the number can increase because of producing more goods and services and/or rising prices. So if you want to measure production not affected by price changes, use the real measure, which adjusts for inflation. Economists and policymakers often utilize real GDP for statistical analysis because it provides the best picture of true economic growth. Real GDP measures production at constant prices, with prices existing during a base period. The year 2000 is the base year and will be updated to 2005 in 2009. It is also referred to as constant-dollar GDP. Holding prices fixed, real GDP reflects only changes in the amounts of goods

Table 2.2 GDP in Billions of Chained 2000 Dollars (Selected Years)

Year	Real GDP	Real GDP Growth Rate (Percent Change at an Annual Rate)
1996	$8,328.9	3.7
1997	$8,703.5	4.5
1998	$9,066.9	4.2
1999	$9,470.3	4.5
2000	$9,817.0	3.7
2001	$9,890.7	0.8
2002	$10,048.8	1.6
2003	$10,301.0	2.5
2004	$10,703.5	3.9
2005	$11,048.6	3.2
2006	$11,415.3	3.3
2007	$11,549 (Q1-prelim)	1.9

Source: U.S. Bureau of Economic Analysis.

and services produced. When measuring the economy's production over time, real GDP is the ideal measurement. The GDP number you hear reported on the news is typically real GDP. The nominal GDP of the economy may be roughly $13.6 trillion, but after an adjustment for inflation, real GDP measures just $11.5 trillion, according to the first quarter 2007 advance estimate.

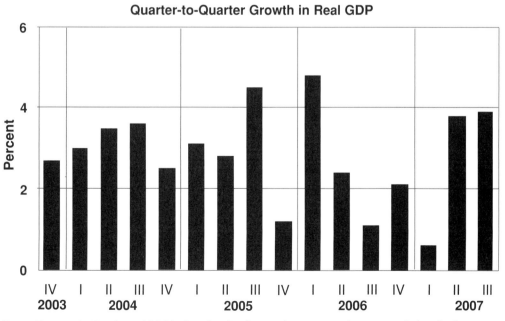

Gross Domestic Product (GDP) Graph, displaying low to modest growth levels for 2003 (IV)–2007 (III). *Source:* The Bureau of Economic Analysis.

Table 2.3 GDP Per Capita (Purchasing Power Parity) (Advanced Economies: 2008 Estimates)

Canada	$38,149
France	$33,123
Germany	$33,345
Italy	$32,717
Japan	$35,377
United Kingdom	$38,131
United States	$47,049

Source: IMF World Economic Outlook Database, April 2007.

While you may hear the GDP figure with details on the business news, the popular news media tends to report only the growth rate in real GDP. Annual real GDP growth has been respectable, averaging just over 3% in the last decade. Growth ranged from a high of 4.5 in 1999 to a paltry low of 0.8 in 2001 (see Table 2.2). Strong growth signals that the economy is booming and is a sign of good things to come. But a pattern of low growth suggests a slump and the economy may be in for hard times. When you hear the newscaster announce that GDP grew by 3%, you know that the reporter is really saying the real annual growth rate of GDP is 3%.

PER CAPITA GDP

Real GDP per person, or per capita GDP, is calculated by taking real GDP divided by the country's total population. GDP per capita is a rough estimate of a nation's strength. Think of totaling all the country's production for a year and giving each person living in the United States an equal dollar amount. Okay, so it really doesn't work that way. But economists do like to view GDP per capita for international comparison because it provides a vision of the living standards of an average person in a country (see Table 2.3).

The standard of living in the United States is high. The International Monetary Fund (IMF) estimates 2008 GDP per capita at $47,049 (in nominal, or non inflation-adjusted dollars) for the United States. It is the highest among the seven advanced economies. Contrast this to per capita estimates of just $3,393 for the high-unemployment economy of Honduras, or $1,087 for tourism-dependent Dominican Republic. The economic strength of the United States provides its citizens with educational, business, and health opportunities unparalleled elsewhere in the world. The prosperity of the United States and the well-being of the average American continues to grow by leaps and bounds.

Lesson 3

Government in Action

"The people's right to change what does not work is one of the greatest principles of our system of government."
    —Richard Nixon, thirty-seventh President of the United States of America

Jennifer was gazing out the window of her high school civics class, the last class of the day. The lesson had just concluded and Jennifer was thinking about her plans with Sam for the weekend; but her teacher, Mr. Koch, was already talking about what they planned to cover on Monday. This was not unusual; Mr. Koch so enjoyed teaching that he was always excited about new topics. Out of one ear she could hear Mr. Koch cheerfully ramble on about the upcoming chapter—the different levels of government and the services they provide. Mr. Koch suggested each student keep a diary of their weekend activities to see if they utilized any government goods and services. Finally the bell rang and Jennifer made a quick exit out the main door of the high school.

Sam was waiting for Jennifer outside the building. The two had been inseparable since middle school, and spent most weekends together. Sam suggested they spend the next day exploring different places around town. Jennifer was up for a road trip because she enjoyed travel, even around her hometown. The two set the time of departure for 8 A.M. Saturday morning, and then went their separate ways.

Early Saturday morning, Sam turned on the TV to hear the local weather forecast, provided by the National Weather Service. Sunny skies with intermittent scattered rain showers were predicted. Sam theorized that if he brought an umbrella, it might keep the rain away. So just before the hour, with umbrella in tow, Sam drove 6 miles on the sleek, newly constructed highway to reach Jennifer's house.

Upon arrival, Jennifer quickly jumped into the car. After a busy week at school she was looking forward to a fun day of adventure. The duo started to drive down Main Street but quickly noticed a fleet of fire trucks. There was a small fire in one of the town's older homes and it was causing quite a stir in the historic area. Minutes later, police were rerouting traffic and the pair was on their way.

Drive was the name of the game. The goal was to stop at every place that looked interesting. Their first stop: the city's art museum. Jennifer and Sam had not been there since they were kids and had a blast. They spent most of the morning going through the masterpiece art collections and exhibits they remembered as children.

Back in the car for just 5 minutes, Main Street Library was the next destination. Jennifer had been entranced by the artwork at the museum and checked out a super book on art history.

Next door to the library was the U.S. Post Office. Sam had been carrying around a letter in his car for a couple days. His older brother was serving overseas in the military, and with no access to e-mail, Sam reverted to old-fashioned letter writing. He dropped it into the mailbox and knew the letter would be on its way around the world.

It was time for lunch. Although it had drizzled just a bit—the National Weather Service forecast had been right—by lunchtime the weather was sunny. Jennifer and Sam chose to eat at the outside deli at Union Station. The city's remodeled train station served as a huge restaurant and retail draw. Jennifer and Sam split the cost of the deli meal, $10 total. Each paid with a crisp, $5 Federal Reserve Note. A bit of window-shopping at the array of trendy stores impressed both of the super shoppers. The city had been very successful in attracting first-class retail stores.

With the sun shining, Jennifer and Sam decided to spend the afternoon at the nearby 100-acre state park. Although it was a 45-minute drive, the sunshine, hiking, and paddle boating proved well worth the effort. When the sun set, the two decided to call it a day. In the car on the way home, Jennifer jotted down all the government-related places and things she and Sam had done that day. She even copied down the weather report and the various roads and highways they used because she knew Mr. Koch liked accuracy. Jennifer put the piece of paper in her purse and was glad to have her homework done for the weekend.

Jennifer pulled the wrinkled piece of paper out of her purse during Monday's civics class. She was proud her list was the most detailed. Mr. Koch used it as an example and copied her list on the board—he called it Jennifer and Sam's Road Trip. He then made a list of all the government uses with the government provider next to each activity. Jennifer was surprised to see that virtually everything they had done on Saturday was a government good or service, and further, there were three levels of government in the list: federal, state, and local. Her class realized the government provides some pretty important things. Jennifer was definitely going to tell Sam their trip was used as the class example, and a good one at that. Sam was going to be in Mr. Koch's class next semester and would appreciate the heads up (see Table 3.1, Jennifer and Sam's Road Trip).

Table 3.1 Jennifer and Sam's Road Trip

Service	Provider
The National Weather Service	Federal
Highway	Federal/State
Fire Protection	Local
Police	Local
Art Museum	Local
Library	Local
U.S. Post Office	Federal
Union Station	Local
State Park	State
Federal Reserve Note	Federal

The road trip highlighted the many government-provided goods and services in our society. And there are many government players: 87,576 to be exact—one federal, fifty states, and 87,525 local governments, according to 2007 statistics. The local level includes cities, towns, villages, counties, school districts, and special districts. All levels of government in the United States employ over 23 million people—over 4 million at the federal level and over 19 million at state and local governments. The government spends not only on goods and services—like highways, education, police, and national defense—but also on transfer payments. Transfer payments are payments for which no good or service is currently provided: Social Security, welfare, and unemployment, for example. And the government's pockets are deep. The federal, state, and local entities dip down in their pockets to the tune of nearly $5 trillion a year—and that does not include transfer payments.

THE ROLE OF GOVERNMENT

Every country must decide how much of their goods and services should be provided by the government and how much must be provided by individuals and businesses in the private sector. The specific obligations of government and associated spending choices are a hotly debated topic among Americans. Many believe our government has grown too big in an attempt to provide too much for too many.

Regardless of one's stance on the size and complexity of government, there are four major roles for government in our society.

1. *Regulator*—Government sets the rules and procedures that regulate business, and thus economic activity. Regulation is accomplished by passing laws that guide business activity.

2. *Provider*—The government provides essential goods and services that are difficult to secure via the private market.

3. *Reallocator*—The government works to improve the economic well-being of its citizens. By taxing, government can then shift, or reallocate tax revenue through social programs.

4. *Stabilizer*—Government implements policies to promote employment, economic growth, and price stability. The objective is to stabilize the economy and keep it on a healthy path.

What Is A "Fiscal"?

Fiscal refers to government spending, taxation, and debt, and/or to finances. A fiscal year refers to a financial time frame, a 12-month accounting period for an organization. An organization's fiscal year will not necessarily match the calendar year. The federal government's fiscal year runs from October 1 to September 30 each year. As an illustration, fiscal year 2010 actually begins in 2009—October 1, 2009. The fiscal year 2010 ends September 30, 2010. Congress passes appropriations legislation to keep the government funded every fiscal year.

Table 3.2 Federal Government Receipts (Fiscal Year 2008 Estimates) (In Billions of Dollars)

Individual Income Taxes	$1,246.6	47%
Social Insurance and Retirement Receipts	$927.2	35%
Corporation Income Taxes	$314.9	12%
Other	$173.7	6%
Total	$2,662.5	

Source: Department of Treasury and Office of Management and Budget.

GOVERNMENT INCOME

You may be asking yourself where the government gets close to $5 trillion to spend. That is an extremely large allowance. Most government funds come from taxes, which are paid by individuals and businesses.

Table 3.2 displays the receipts, or where the money comes from for the federal government. During fiscal year 2008, the government is projected to take in roughly $2.7 trillion. Let's review exactly how the federal government is earning its change.

Close to half, or 47%, of the federal income comes from individual income taxes. In 1913, the Sixteenth Amendment to the Constitution gave our federal government the right to collect income tax, and individual income taxes are, historically, the largest source of federal money. The system is progressive in nature; tax rates rise as income gets bigger. People with high incomes not only pay more in taxes, but they also pay a higher tax rate.

Social insurance and retirement receipts, at 35%, make up the second largest source of federal government funding. Employees are mandated to pay 0.0765 of their salaries, up to a certain level, to Social Security. Their employers match this same level, and the money is invested in Social Security trust funds. Social security is a federally managed retirement program and when U.S. workers retire, they qualify for benefits based upon age, dollar amounts paid in, and the number of years employed.

Corporate income taxes account for roughly 12% of federal income. Businesses must share their profits with the federal government, so the net earnings of corporations are taxed.

Other revenue items account for 6% of federal income and include excise taxes (e.g., taxes on gasoline, cigarettes, alcohol, and a number of other goods), custom duties on imported goods, estate and gift taxes, and miscellaneous.

GOVERNMENT SPENDING

What kinds of things does the federal government buy? Table 3.3 gives an overview of national spending. Providing Social Security checks to retirees is historically the largest expenditure, making up 21% of spending. National defense of our country, also at 21%, runs a close second. Third is Medicare, which is a federal program that provides health coverage if you are over age 65 or have a disability, at 14%. Next in line is income security—welfare payments and unemployment compensation—at 13%. Other expenses, at 11%, rank fifth and include

Table 3.3 Federal Government Outlays (Fiscal Year 2008 Estimates) (In Billions of Dollars)

Social Security	$612.5	21%
National Defense	$606.5	21%
Medicare	$391.6	14%
Income Security	$380.8	13%
Other	$332.3	11%
Health Programs	$280.6	10%
Net Interest	$261.3	9%
International Affairs	$36.1	1%
Total	$2,901.9	

Source: Department of Treasury and Office of Management and Budget.

such purchases as foreign aid and veterans benefits. Following that, in order of expenditure, are health programs at 10%, net interest payments on the federal debt at 9%, and international affairs at 1%.

The federal government anticipates annual spending to be $2.9 trillion in 2008 and expects to earn around $2.7 trillion. You are astute if you noticed these two amounts don't balance. How does the federal government make up the difference when they want to provide more goods and services but do not have enough money? They borrow. A government budget deficit occurs when outlays are greater than revenues. A budget surplus occurs when revenues exceed outlays. The debt is tabulated by adding up all the annual deficits and subtracting any surpluses.

From the previous two tables, you can see the government receipts of $2,662.5 billion, less outlays of $2,901.9 billion, equals a negative $239.4 billion. In other words, a deficit of $239.4 billion is estimated for the year. The U.S. federal government is expected to spend $239.4 billion more than it takes in from revenues in fiscal 2008.

During the 1940s, the federal government started to provide more substantial goods and services with the social programs that developed out of the depression years and wartime spending. The year 1942 was marked with a big yearly deficit for that time at $20.5 billion. The deficit trend began, and today the federal government usually runs budget deficits. The deficits have added up over the years—nearly $9 trillion, creating a large debt. This is money that the government borrows in the form of bonds and securities. It is essentially an I.O.U. by the federal government. The federal government pays investors back with a respectable interest rate for the use of their funds—to the tune of a whopping $263.1 billion per year.

Pork, Pork, Pork!

Most government spending is for useful goods and services for our nation. However, not being a good steward of government money is certainly a serious issue. "Pork barrel spending," sometimes called a pork project, or simply pork, is government funding of a project that is designed to benefit a particular locale, whose sponsoring politician will win votes. Each year, the Citizens against Government Waste, a private, nonpartisan, nonprofit organization, exposes the pork in its annual *Congressional Pig Book*. Congress hit an all-time high in fiscal 2006 as the government passed $29 billion in wasteful spending. Check out some of the most piggy projects:

Piggy Projects of Fiscal 2006
• $13.5 million for the International Fund for Ireland, which includes funding for the World Toilet Summit.

• $5 million for the Capitol Visitor's Center.

• $6.4 million for Wood Utilization Research.

• $1 million for the Waterfree Urinal Conservation Initiative.

• $550,000 for the Museum of Glass in Tacoma, Washington.

• $500,000 for the Sparta Teapot Museum in Sparta, North Carolina.

• $450,000 added by the House for plantings on the eastern front of the Capitol.

• $250,000 for the National Cattle Congress in Waterloo, Iowa.

Source: Citizens against Government Waste.

STATE AND LOCAL INCOME AND SPENDING

State and local governments take in nearly $2 trillion a year and spend slightly more. State and local governments issue debt as well, although not nearly as much as the federal government. The overwhelming majority of state and local debt takes the form of long-term debt, at around $1.9 trillion outstanding. They carry just $38 million in short-term obligations.

Table 3.4 shows where state and local governments obtain their funding, and where they spend it. Under revenues, the "Other" category is highest at 28% and includes other taxes and charges, plus miscellaneous revenues. Second, there is a huge transfer of funds from federal to state and local governments—Revenue from the Federal Government—at 23% of receipts. Third is sales and gross tax receipts. This group includes general sales and selective sales tax receipts like fuel, alcohol, tobacco, and public utilities, tallying 19%. Next in line are property taxes at 17%; individual income taxes at 11%; and corporate income taxes at just 2%.

At 34%, the largest expenditure for state and local governments is education. Public welfare comes in second at 18%, and highways rank third at 6%. Because the services provided by state and local governments are so expansive, the list goes on and on. The "Other" category is huge at 42% and includes spending for public libraries, hospitals, health, employment security administration, veterans' services, air transportation, water transport and terminals, parking facilities, transit subsidies, police protection, fire protection, correction, protective inspection and regulation, sewerage, natural resources, parks and recreation, housing and community development, solid waste management, financial administration, judicial and legal, general public buildings, other government administration, interest on general debt, and general expenditures.

Table 3.4 State and Local Government Revenues and Expenditures (Fiscal Year 2003–2004)

Revenues	
Corporation Net Income Taxes	2%
Individual Income Taxes	11%
Property Taxes	17%
Sales and Gross Receipts Taxes	19%
Revenue from the Federal Government	23%
Other	28%
Total	100%
Expenditures	
Highways	6%
Public Welfare	18%
Education	34%
Other	42%
Total	100%

Source: Department of Commerce, Bureau of the Census.

GOVERNMENT AS REGULATOR

Governments set rules to determine the relationships between businesses and consumers, and thus they affect economic activity. Regulation is accomplished by passing laws that guide business activity. People need to know the rules in order to conduct business, so it is the responsibility of local, state, and federal governments to provide the structure. In order to manage business activities in a complex economy, governments have created numerous rules and regulatory agencies. Regulations typically fall into two main categories: economic regulation and social regulation.

Economic regulation involves regulating prices, both directly and indirectly, and regulating financial markets. Direct regulation usually occurs in relationship to industries that have been granted the right to function as a monopoly by the government. In these situations, the government has decided it is more efficient for an organization to operate as a monopoly and allow it to take advantage of economies of scale. Economies of scale are decreases in cost as a result of increases in volume. Because it is now a sole producer of a service, the government regulates the company to ensure prices remain at acceptable levels. Examples of organizations granted monopolies include the United States Post Office (USPS), public utility companies, and local water providers.

States and the federal government often have agencies overseeing industries in which there are monopoly providers. One example is the Federal Energy Regulatory Commission (FERC), which regulates electricity and natural gas.

Indirect price regulation involves antitrust policy, which prohibits practices to fix prices in an industry or reduce competition. Regulation of financial markets is designed to protect the public. An example is the Securities and Exchange Commission (SEC), which regulates the nation's securities markets.

Social regulation is concerned with protecting workers, firms, and the environment. Examples of social regulatory groups include Consumer Products Safety Commission (CPSC) to protect the public against unreasonable risks associated with consumer products; Occupational Safety and Health Administration (OSHA) charged with the enforcement of legislation designed to keep workers safe; and the Environmental Protection Agency (EPA), which protects human health and the environment.

Naturally, social regulation adds costs to conducting business. But society, as a whole, has decided that such costs provide benefits in the form of greater health and safety.

GOVERNMENT AS PROVIDER

The U.S. business sector is a well-run machine and provides topnotch quality goods and services. Why then do we even need a government to provide goods and services? The government can often improve the economy by providing certain goods that are essential to our well-being. What goods and services? Let's look at the difference between a public and a private good to see why government provides select goods and services.

A public good or service is both nonrival (when consumed or used by one person, it does not deprive others from use) and nonexcludable (it is impossible to exclude people from the good's consumption). Examples of public goods include national defense, the legal system, and air quality. Since it is impossible to exclude people from using public goods, they are not supplied by the private market. To illustrate the concept, let's examine one public good provided by the federal government: national defense. Imagine if a private firm provided national security and attempted to protect only those who paid for the service. There would be many people who would not pay, knowing they would still receive protection; hence the term free rider—letting someone else pay for a good or service. Therefore, the government steps in and pays the tab, essentially making everyone share part of the expense of national defense through the tax system.

A private good, in contrast, is both rival and excludable. In economics, rival means when consumed or used by one person, it diminishes use by another person. Excludable means you can exclude others from consumption. Examples of private goods are food, housing, and computers. When you drink a soft drink it is no longer available for others to drink. And you can also exclude someone from consuming if they cannot pay for the soft drink. Most ordinary goods are private goods and are provided by the market for a profit.

The government also provides a host of goods and services that lie somewhere between public and private goods, termed quasi-public goods. They tend to share some characteristics of both public and private goods, but the government thinks it is important to supply these goods to its citizens. These goods are partially nonrival and partially nonexcludable. For example, people using a park do not reduce the amount of enjoyment by others until the attendance numbers skyrocket. You may be able to exclude others from the park by charging an admittance fee. The majority of goods and services provided by the government are technically

The government provides many quasi-public goods for Americans to enjoy like the Acadia National Park in Bar Harbor, Maine. *Source:* National Park Service.

quasi-public; examples include education, beaches, parks, roads, highways, and public housing.

The Power of the Purse

The term "power of the purse" is usually used in reference to a group with power to control actions of another group, due to their ability to control money. The Constitution provides Congress the power of the purse to raise and spend money. This power of the purse does give Congress the power to hold certain programs ransom to get what it wants, or to add certain funding stipulations to bills in order to get them passed. Our Congress approves the spending and revenue bills, which are signed by the president. But the president can reject or veto most budget bills. So Congress and the president must work together to pass a budget. The process is usually arduous and combative, and the annual budget consideration is big work because if they don't pass the budget, the federal government will shut down. So Congress and the executive branch of government have a huge incentive to work together to get the budget passed.

Think Tank Talk

The Heritage Foundation is a Washington, DC, public policy research institution, otherwise known as a think tank. It publishes papers and works with Congress and the White House for free markets, individual freedom, limited government, traditional values, and a strong national defense. Founded in 1973, this conservative think tank is regarded by many as the premier public policy research institute. The organization operates by private donations and does not receive funding from the government.

Brian Riedl is Heritage's senior policy analyst, and Grover M. Hermann Fellow in Federal Budgetary Affairs. Riedl's budget research is topnotch, having been featured in editorials in *The New York Times*, *The Wall Street Journal*, *The Washington Post*, and *The Los Angeles Times*. He has appeared to discuss the federal budget and other topics on NBC, CBS, CNN, FOX News, CNBC, C-Span, and PBS. Clearly, Riedl knows how to analyze and explain the complicated federal budget in a way people can understand.

Riedl shared some insightful responses into the complex world of government spending and taxation.

Why is it important to monitor government spending?

How Washington taxes and spends your income has a large impact on your life. During your lifetime, about 20% of your income is paid in federal taxes (plus 10% more on state and local taxes), and the things it is spent on—protection from foreign invaders, criminal justice, antipoverty programs, or highways—affect you.

How can tax policy affect economic growth?

Tax policy affects economic growth because if you tax something, people will do, or use it, less. Working, saving, and investing all create economic growth. Yet most taxes are levied on those three activities, which reduce incentives by making them less profitable. The corresponding reduction in working, saving, and investing means less wealth is created and the economy grows more slowly.

What is the breakdown on spending and taxation?

It is easiest to look at federal spending and taxation on a per household basis. The government spends about $24,000, and taxes about $22,000 per household. What's left is a deficit of around $2,000 per family, and that money must be borrowed.

What are the most outstanding examples of government waste you have seen?

There are many examples of pork projects and government waste. Some of the most memorable were $50,000 for tattoo removal; $200,000 for The Rock & Roll Hall of Fame; and $250,000 for a program to combat teen Goth culture.

GOVERNMENT AS REALLOCATOR

A third role of government comes in the shifting, or reallocation of income. Government takes income from tax dollars and then reallocates the money. In our progressive federal personal income tax system, this means taxing more from proportionally high earners. Some of that money is then transferred from the well-to-do to those that are less fortunate via transfer payments. A transfer payment does not involve any current exchange for work and is part of the process of redistribution of the economy's output. Income transfers include direct cash payments to individuals, such as Social Security, welfare, unemployment compensation, and Federal Emergency Management Agency (FEMA) disaster assistance. In-kind benefits involve a transfer of goods and services such as food stamps, housing assistance, Medicaid (health insurance program for the poor), and Medicare (health insurance program for the elderly).

GOVERNMENT AS STABILIZER

The goal of government stabilization policies is simply to stabilize the economy, or smooth out the business cycle by fostering employment, economic growth, and price stability. Former Federal Reserve Governor Edward M. Gramlich commented in a speech before the Wharton Public Policy Forum, "In domestic macroeconomic theory either fiscal or monetary policy can be used to stabilize output and employment around their trend levels, and hence prevent booms or recessions from getting out of hand" (Gramlich, 1999, p.1). The experienced Fed board member hinted at the complicated strategies involved with stabilization policies. "Economists and others have debated these questions of stabilization policy strategy for years, with many issues still unresolved" (Gramlich, 1999, p.1). Let's untangle the complicated process and put it in plain speak.

Fiscal policy is a government's use of spending and taxation—the two components of the government's fiscal budget—to affect the health of the overall economy. Monetary policy is how a central bank uses money supply, interest rate targets, and credit, to influence broad economic goals such as growth, inflation, and employment. Although two different policymakers practice stabilization, the goal of both monetary and fiscal policies is to influence overall economic activity.

Stabilization policies can be either expansionary, if the economy is dragging, or contractionary, if the economy is wound too tight. An expansionary fiscal policy entails an increase in government spending and/or a decrease in taxes. These expansionary tactics cause spending to increase and the job level to rise, which stimulates the economy. A contractionary fiscal policy involves a reduction in government spending and/or an increase in taxes. These contractionary tactics dampen economic activity and reduce prices.

Expansionary monetary policy means an increase in money supply. As more money is available in the economy, interest rates will fall. Economic activity will rise as consumers and businesses borrow more, spend more, and create more jobs. Contractionary monetary policy is a decrease in the money supply. As the quantity of money decreases, competition will force banks to make higher interest rate loans. Consumers and businesses will borrow less and spend less, reducing inflation.

Although stabilizing a $13 trillion plus economy is a complex matter, government policymakers should be given high marks. The United States largely maintains respectable GDP growth, stable prices, and low unemployment year after year. Stabilization policy, designed to smooth out the fluctuations in our economy, is yet another example of our government in action.

Lesson 4

The National Credit Card

"The debt is like a crazy aunt we keep down in the basement. All the neighbors know she's there, but nobody wants to talk about her."
—Ross Perot, *United We Stand: How We Can Take Back Our Country* (1992)

Do you or your parents have a credit card? Or perhaps two, three, or more cards? If you have four credit cards, you are average, according to a recent study by Experian Consumer Direct. If you carry eleven or more, you fall within 14% of the U.S. population that have more than ten credit cards (Experian, February 15, 2007). Wow! That is a lot of credit exposure! The use of credit is a lifestyle choice Americans have become increasingly comfortable with, and the U.S. Government is no different. The size of the credit card debt is the only difference. Consumers carry an average of four credit cards with balances in tens, hundreds, or thousands of dollars. The government, in essence, carries only one credit card, but it has an outstanding debt balance of nearly $9 trillion. To get a feel for just how large this number is, picture $9,000 billion, or a $9 followed by twelve zeros— $9,000,000,000,000.

The huge and growing size of this debt is a political hot topic. Most citizens know the number is large, but don't really understand the complexities behind the debt issuance of the U.S. government. People generally support reducing the debt, but tend not to favor either of the two methods used to accomplish this feat: increasing taxes and/or reducing government spending. Let's explore the details of the gigantic debt by looking at the types of government budgets, history, composition, and the major issues surrounding the government debt.

What's A "Gross" Debt?

There are many different names for the government's debt including federal debt, public debt, national debt, and gross debt. In this case, "gross" does not suggest a debt that is disgusting, icky, or nasty. Gross debt simply means overall or total debt. The gross federal debt is about $8.8 trillion as of this writing.

TYPES OF BUDGETS

How does the federal government amass such a huge credit card balance? When the government spends more money on goods and services (like Social Security, welfare, Medicare, national defense, interest, health, and education) than it takes in (largely from taxes), it must borrow money. The $9 trillion debt is the total amount of outstanding debt for the government. When the government spends more money than it collects, the budget has a deficit. If however, the government collects more than it spends, it has a budget surplus.

For fiscal year 2008, the government is expected to take in about $2.7 trillion ($2,662.5 billion) in revenue and spend about $2.9 trillion ($2,901.9 billion). This results in a negative balance of $239.4 billion. In other words, a deficit of $239.4 billion is estimated for the year. So that means the government's "credit card balance" will increase.

Deficit spending causes concern because the government must borrow money to pay for its credit card free-for-all spending. And just like your credit card company, which charges interest on the borrowed money until it is repaid, the government is charged interest on the money it borrows until repayment. The government sells secure, risk-free instruments so the interest rate on the debt is low; but pennies it is not. The total interest charge is estimated at $261.3 billion for fiscal 2008.

$29,000

The U.S. per-person liability of the national debt.

HISTORY OF THE DEBT

The debt started at a mere $75.5 million in 1790, when the federal government assumed all war obligations of the Continental Congress. Since that time, the debt has risen and fallen; yearly deficits increased the amount and sometime surpluses pushed the total down. The lowest point of government debt was in 1835, when the national debt fell to just $33,733. It is common to see the debt rise sharply during war periods due to high defense spending. A major rise in government debt occurred during World War I; the national debt rose from $5.7 billion in 1917, to $27 billion in 1919. Then came World War II and by 1945, the debt stood at $259 billion. The Korean conflict in the early 1950s saw the debt jump to $266 billion and the Vietnam War in the mid-1960s pushed the debt to the half-trillion mark. In 1982, the debt topped $1 trillion and it has been skyrocketing ever since. Recent defense spending has burgeoned because of costs associated with the fight against terrorism, and the cost of military operations in Iraq and Afghanistan. Table 4.1, Historical Debt Outstanding, shows the 8-fold increase during the 25-year period.

Table 4.1 Historical Debt Outstanding (Fiscal Year Begins October 1)

09/30/2006	$8,506,973,899,215.23
09/30/2005	$7,932,709,661,723.50
09/30/2004	$7,379,052,696,330.32
09/30/2003	$6,783,231,062,743.62
09/30/2002	$6,228,235,965,597.16
09/30/2001	$5,807,463,412,200.06
09/30/2000	$5,674,178,209,886.86
09/30/1999	$5,656,270,901,615.43
09/30/1998	$5,526,193,008,897.62
09/30/1997	$5,413,146,011,397.34
09/30/1996	$5,224,810,939,135.73
09/29/1995	$4,973,982,900,709.39
09/30/1994	$4,692,749,910,013.32
09/30/1993	$4,411,488,883,139.38
09/30/1992	$4,064,620,655,521.66
09/30/1991	$3,665,303,351,697.03
09/28/1990	$3,233,313,451,777.25
09/29/1989	$2,857,430,960,187.32
09/30/1988	$2,602,337,712,041.16
09/30/1987	$2,350,276,890,953.00
09/30/1986	$2,125,302,616,658.42
09/30/1985	* $1,823,103,000,000.00
09/30/1984	* $1,572,266,000,000.00
09/30/1983	* $1,377,210,000,000.00
09/30/1982	* $1,142,034,000,000.00

* Rounded to millions.
Source: U.S. Department of Treasury, Bureau of Public Debt.

A poster used to promote the buying of government issued Liberty Bonds to finance the war effort during World War I: "Clear The Way!! Buy Bonds." Fourth Liberty Loan. Color poster by Howard Chandler Christy, 1918. *Source*: The National Archives.

The poster asks for patience by those that took part in the war bond drive. "If there is a Delay in the Delivery of your Savings Bond—be Patient! The Federal Reserve Banks are swamped with Work." Approximately 1942 or 1943. *Source*: The National Archives.

The Debt Scoop

The federal debt is also called the national debt, public debt, or sometimes just plain debt. At near $9 trillion, there is a lot of misinformation on this growing figure and the details behind it. The Bureau of Public Debt is responsible for financing, accounting for, and reporting the debt in accord with statutory guidelines. Peter Hollenbach, Director of Public Affairs at the Bureau of Public Debt, set the record straight on some of the fascinating complexities of the borrowing power of the federal government.

Why does the federal government issue debt?
The government issues debt to pay the government's bills. Congress decides how much the government will spend. How much is spent doesn't always agree with revenue, so when a deficit occurs, the government sells securities.

What year did the U.S. debt begin?
The debt actually began in 1790, when one of the first duties of the new federal government was to assume the revolutionary war debt of the states.

Why is the debt so large?
The government started with a sizable debt. We have been issuing debt since 1790, so it adds up. The first recorded debt was reported on the books

January 1, 1791, for $75,463,476.52. One of the first things the government did after the constitution was ratified was to issue debt to pay the president.

How often do you update the debt total?

We update the totals for debt once each day, which is reported in the Daily Treasury Statement. At any point in time you can know the government's financial position. You can see the outstanding balance on the Web site—www.treasurydirect.gov under Debt to the Penny. Today the total is $8,835,268,597,181.95. The total can go up one day as we borrow money and down the next, as we need to redeem securities; this daily fluctuation happens in both deficit and surplus situations. We increase debt when we sell securities and reduce debt when we pay off securities.

How can people participate in financing the debt?

One way people can participate in the financing is to lend their money to the government. Individuals can help by holding Treasury notes, bills, bonds, or savings bonds. People lend money to the government because these are safe instruments and you are assured of getting your money back.

So if you are thinking of investing some of your extra hard-earned money, consider a savings bond—an extremely low-risk investment. The added plus: you can help your government pay its bills!

A 1943 poster used to promote the buying of government bonds to finance the war effort during World War II: "The Best Present for the Best Future!!!" Sketch by Charles Henry Alston. *Source*: The National Archives.

Table 4.2 Total Public Debt Outstanding (May 31, 2007)

	(Millions of Dollars)
Debt Held by the Public	$4,980,871
Intragovernmental Holdings	$3,848,121
Total	$8,828,992

Source: Bureau of the Public Debt, Monthly Statement of the Public Debt of the United States.

COMPOSITION OF DEBT

In reality, of course, the government does not carry one big credit card, but the borrowing function is the same. The government obtains needed cash by selling treasury securities and savings bonds, and in turn, paying off old issues as they mature. The total treasury securities and savings bonds outstanding is the national debt. The gross debt of $8.8 is divided into two categories: intragovernmental holdings and debt held by the public.

Viewing Table 4.2 shows $3.8 trillion of the debt is held internally by government agencies. Holdings include securities held by numerous government trust funds, including the huge Social Security Administration trust funds, Unemployment Trust Fund, and the Civil Service Retirement and Disability Fund. Also on the long list are lesser-known funds such as the Leaking Underground Storage Tank Trust Fund, Oil Spill Liability Trust Fund, and the Vaccine Injury Compensation Trust Fund. Most federal trust funds invest surplus funds in government securities. It also includes other government holdings: revolving funds, special funds, and Federal Financing Bank (government-owned corporation established to centralize and reduce the cost of government borrowing) securities. Most of the securities held by government accounts fall in the nonmarketable category—they cannot be traded.

The net debt includes the other roughly $5.0 trillion the government borrows—from the public. This total includes all the federal debt held by people, businesses, corporations, state and local governments, and foreigners. The securities sold to the public fall within two categories: marketable and nonmarketable. Marketable securities, once originally sold by the Treasury, can be sold in the financial marketplace. They include Treasury bills, Treasury notes, Treasury bonds, and Treasury Inflation-Protected Securities (TIPS). Their prices will fluctuate slightly, depending on supply and demand conditions in the credit market. They can be purchased from the Treasury or on the secondary market for as little as $1,000. If you want to buy a security at original issue, contact the U.S. Treasury, one of the Federal Reserve Banks, a financial institution, or a government securities dealer. Nonmarketable securities, such as savings bonds, cannot be traded and can only be redeemed by the government. Savings bonds and Treasuries are backed by the full faith and credit of the U.S. government; they are exempt from state and local income taxes, and pay a respectable interest rate. Here's a quick glimpse at a few details of the main securities offered by the Treasury.

Treasury Bills

T-bills are short-term securities with maturities ranging from a few days to 1 year. Bills are sold at a discount from their face value; the investor receives the full face value when the bill matures. Investors make their money, or interest, on the difference between the discount price and the face value. So an investor may pay $975 for a T-bill and receive $1,000 on maturity. The interest earned is $25.

Treasury Notes and Bonds

T-notes have fixed maturities of 1 to 10 years; the Treasury currently issues T-notes with 2-, 5-, and 10-year maturities. T-bonds have maturities that range from 10 to 30 years, 30-year bonds being the current standard issuance. T-notes and T-bonds pay a fixed rate of interest every 6 months. Upon maturity, the investor receives the full face value of the issue.

Treasury Inflation-Protected Securities (TIPS)

A unique type of Treasury security linked to the inflation rate, TIPS were first issued in 1997. Every 6 months, the principle value of the security is adjusted to the Consumer Price Index (CPI). The securities are offered in 5-year, 10-year, and 20-year maturities. Every 6 months the investor receives fixed-rate interest payments based on the inflation-adjusted principal. Upon maturity, the investor will receive the greater of the inflation-adjusted principle amount or its original par value.

Savings Bonds

Savings bonds are registered securities and cannot be traded with other investors. Savings bonds are good investments for the small investor, as the minimum investment for a savings bond is only $25. Interest on savings bonds accrues monthly, but compounds semiannually. Savings bonds can be purchased from over 40,000 financial institutions, through payroll deductions administered by companies, or online with the U.S. Treasury's program, Treasury Direct at www.treasurydirect.gov. Currently available are Series EE bonds and Series I bonds.

Series EE bonds earn a fixed rate of interest, which remains constant for the 30-year life of the bond. Series EE are purchased at a 50% discount. For example, you pay $25 for a $50 face value bond. When the bond is cashed in, you will receive the purchase price of the bond plus accrued interest. At a minimum, the U.S. Treasury guarantees that an EE bond's value will double after 20 years, its original maturity, and it will continue to earn the fixed rate unless a new rate or rate structure is announced.

The I bond is inflation-indexed and designed to protect investors from inflation. Series I bonds are issued at face value; for example, you pay $100 for a $100 face value bond. Its earnings rate consists of a fixed rate that remains the same for the life of the bond and a semi-annual inflation rate. Interest accrues over the life of the bond, up to 30 years, and is paid upon redemption.

Over $13 Billion

Dollar amount of savings bonds that have stopped earning interest but have not been cashed in to the U.S. Treasury Department, Bureau of Public Debt.

MAJOR ISSUES SURROUNDING THE DEBT

Back in 1917, an insightful Congress, concerned about the rising debt, approved a debt ceiling. Also referred to as a statutory debt limit, the ceiling limits the amount of debt the government is allowed to borrow. The design of the debt ceiling was to force Congress to scrutinize the budget closely before raising the limit. When the government reaches the debt ceiling, the Treasury must ask Congress to give the okay before borrowing additional funds. Without funding approval, a government shutdown occurs, where the government discontinues nonessential services. It is actually only a partial shutdown. In September 2007, Congress increased the debt limit to $9.815 trillion—that's $9,815,000,000,000! With a total debt outstanding of $9 trillion, the country will soon be in need of another increase, or face the possibility of a potential shutdown.

Think it doesn't happen? Not many years ago, the second fiscal year 1996 shutdown, the longest government shutdown in history, occurred from December 16, 1995, to January 6, 1996. Then-President Clinton and Congress took some time to reach an agreement on government-funding measures. Major sections of the government—those considered nonessential—were shut down for 3 weeks. These are just a few of the outcomes of that shutdown: over 3,500 federal bankruptcy cases were suspended; 200,000 U.S. passports were unprocessed; 368 National Park Service sites were closed; the hiring of 400 border control agents was cancelled; and toxic waste pickup ceased at 609 sites.

DEBT

Deficit Spending!
Enormous expenditures!
Bureau of the Public Debt!
Treasury bills, notes, and bonds!

The issuance of debt is not a clear-cut issue. On one side of the coin are policymakers and economists who believe the benefits from deficit spending, and hence the national debt, outweigh the costs. The other side of the coin has policymakers and economists who believe the costs of deficit spending and the rising national debt outweigh the benefits. Take a brief look at some of the main issues surrounding the U.S. debt, both the pros and the cons.

Arguments against National Debt

1. Foreign and international investors hold roughly 44% of the public debt. If their willingness and ability to buy U.S. debt falls, domestic investors will be needed to cover this amount. Furthermore, a large amount of money in interest payments is going out of the country to service this debt. This money goes to other countries rather than into the pockets of Americans.

2. Interest payments on debt are roughly 9% of the federal budget. Interest is a hefty portion of the government's yearly budget and one from which you receive no goods and services. This forces the government to reduce spending on other highly worthy activities such as education, medicine, and public works.

3. Businesses and individuals are crowded out of the lending market by the government. The government borrows a great deal of funds and may offer higher interest rates in order to get investors to buy securities. The government is able to pay a market rate of interest. Businesses and people may want to borrow too, but at some point they will be unable to afford the borrowing costs and will be crowded out.

4. Too much deficit spending can lead to inflation and economic problems. Fiscal policy is the adjustment of government spending and/or taxation for the purpose of affecting the economy and the rate of its growth. Increasing federal spending and/or reducing taxes can promote more employment and output, but these policies also put upward pressure on price levels and interest rates.

Arguments in Favor of National Debt

1. One way to view the size of a person's debt is to compare it to what he or she earns in income. For the nation, we can do this by looking at public debt compared to the nation's earnings or output—Gross Domestic Product (GDP). The United States publicly held debt of $5 trillion represents roughly 38% of its $13 trillion GDP. A 38% debt ratio is far below the 1946 peak—a whopping 108.6% of GDP. And estimates suggest the debt-to-GDP ratio will fall further, to 32.1% by 2012. So the national debt as a percentage of GDP has remained fairly stable recently and is low compared to the post-World War II period.

2. Treasury securities and savings bonds are an important savings vehicle in the economy. Treasuries also allow the Federal Reserve, the vehicle with which to conduct monetary policy.

3. Government spending has contributed to stellar economic growth; more jobs are created and output rises. Increases in government spending, and hence deficit spending, has pulled the country out of many recessions and the associated economic difficulties.

4. The government provides essential goods and services for our nation. Social Security, education, defense, and health programs are all critical to a socially good and prosperous market economy.

What do you think? Try thinking like an economist and analyze whether the benefits of the debt outweigh the costs. Or do the costs outweigh the benefits? It is in your hands, because future generations bear the burden of managing and paying off the debt.

Lesson 5

Money, Money Everywhere

"The pieces of green paper have value because everybody thinks they have value."
—Milton Friedman, *Money Mischief* (1992)

Every time Jack ate dinner at his friend Abby Morrison's house, Mr. Morrison had a "question of the day." Their table discussions were an interesting change of pace for Jack. He had six siblings and there was mainly eating—first come, first served—at Jack's family table. Abby was an only child and got a lot of individual attention from her parents. Mrs. Morrison was a homemaker and Mr. Morrison was a high school social studies teacher who was big on thought-provoking discussions.

As Jack sat down to eat Mrs. Morrison's delicious chicken bake, he couldn't help but wonder if he would be able to answer the question of the day. It was summertime and Mr. Morrison was on break, so Jack figured he would have extra time to come up with a super-difficult question. The big question usually centered on business, politics, or economics. Some of the recent ponders included, "What are the advantages of a corporation?" "Should the president veto the defense spending bill?" and "What are the implications of the growth of the federal debt?" No sooner had Jack taken his first bite, than the question was thrown out: "What is money?"

This sure seemed simple enough to Jack. He felt himself relax and as soon as he'd swallowed, he quickly answered, "The 10 bucks I have in my wallet plus the 55 cents in change out in my car, sir."

Mr. Morrison added a simple, "And?"

"The 89 dollars I have in my checkbook," responded Jack.

"And?" continued Mr. Morrison.

"Okay, the $1,000 I have in my savings account," said Jack.

"And?" Mr. Morrison pressed.

"How about the $3,000 balance I have on my maxed-out credit card?" asked Jack.

"No, you should have stopped with the savings account," chuckled Mr. Morrison.

Mr. Morrison explained that there are many forms of money. The most basic form is liquid and can be spent immediately, like cash (bills and coins) and checkable deposits. There is another group of assets still counted as money by economists. This group includes savings account funds because, even though you can't write a check on your savings account, you can easily withdraw the money in cash. Why isn't the credit card a form of money? It is simply an obligation to pay the credit card company every month when you get your statement. Jack couldn't help but think that Mr. Morrison was a walking encyclopedia.

FUNCTIONS OF MONEY

Money has three distinct functions: a medium of exchange, a store of value, and a unit of account. Put all three functions together and you can see how the dollar bill functions as money. Money as a medium of exchange is anything that is generally accepted in exchange for goods and services. It is common practice to quote prices in terms of the accepted monetary unit; in the United States it is the dollar.

People have jobs that allow them to earn money to pay for the goods and services they desire. If they didn't, they would need to go back to old-fashioned bartering for goods and services. In a barter system, there must be a double "coincidence of wants" before two people can exchange. Bartering makes it extremely challenging for goods and services to move freely. Both people must want exactly what the other is offering (and both must expect to feel better off after the exchange) before a bartering event can take place. A medium of exchange is an intermediary used to buy goods and services and avoids the difficulties of the bartering system.

Money is a store of value, although during periods of high inflation it may not be the best store of value. Money is not unique in this function. Many assets store value, such as gold, land, buildings, bonds, and art. Some are better than others at retaining value. Think if you put away $10 and plan to pull it out 20 years from now. Today you can get a nice lunch for that price, but in 20 years you may be doing well to get a soda. On the other hand, the one-acre lot your Uncle Bill bought for $10,000 may double, triple, or quadruple in price in the next 20 years. So although money is not the best source of value, it certainly retains some value and it is convenient. You can store purchasing power in currency, a checking account, or a savings account until it's needed.

Money also serves as a unit of account—a benchmark for comparing values of goods and services with one another. As a unit of account, money provides a common measure of the value of the goods and services being exchanged. The monetary unit is set by a country's government. Goods and services in the United States are priced in dollars, but in England it's the pound, in Japan the yen, and in Mexico the peso. Knowing the value of an item helps buyers and sellers conduct business.

KINDS OF MONEY

Commodity money takes the form of a commodity with an intrinsic value—like gold, cigarettes, or corn. This means that the commodity has a usefulness or utility even if it were not used as a medium of exchange. An example of commodity money is cigarettes in a prisoner of war camp, where cigarettes have functioned as a medium of exchange, by both smokers and nonsmokers. Corn was traded by the colonists as money, but could also hold value simply as a food product. Gold is a common example of commodity money, and coins containing the precious metal have been traded throughout history. The coins that traded did so because they held value based upon the amount of gold contained in the coin.

Workman punching out blank coins at the U.S. mint in New Orleans, 1897. *Source:* Library of Congress.

Representative money is typically a certificate that is not intrinsically valuable itself, but represents a commodity. The certificate can be exchanged for a specific commodity, such as tobacco or gold coins. In the early 1800s, Tobacco Notes became a medium of exchange in Virginia and were used throughout the century. The note, easier to transport than the tobacco leaves, could be converted to a certain amount of tobacco held in a warehouse facility. The gold certificates that circulated in the United States prior to their withdrawal in 1933 were redeemable in gold; you could redeem them at the Treasury for gold.

Today, all the money in the United States is fiat money. Fiat money is given value only by government fiat, or decree. Fiat money does not have intrinsic value. Federal Reserve Notes are an example of fiat money. You accept a Federal Reserve Note as payment because it is legal tender and you know it will be accepted elsewhere.

We all are quite familiar with the paper money we use today, the Federal Reserve Note. In fact, Americans have such a close feeling for their money that nicknames for the dollar are plentiful. A buck, referring to a dollar, traces it origins to when early colonial traders used deerskins, or buckskins, as a medium of exchange. Greenbacks, another common reference to the dollar, originated with the issue of the Demand Notes of 1861, which were printed on one of the sides with green ink. Of course, everybody wants the Benjamins, referring to the $100 bill with Ben Franklin's portrait. A C-note is equally good because it denotes $100, too. It is derived from the Roman numeral C, which represents 100. And if you have a grand, you are sitting on $1,000.

HISTORY OF MONEY

Over time in the United States, people have used some items for exchange we may consider unusual. Native Americans would use wampum, a string of beads fashioned from polished shells. Colonists used a mixture of wampum, their own

The U.S. Mint is responsible for the country's coin production, producing between 11 billion and 20 billion coins annually. *Source:* Federal Reserve Bank of Chicago.

notes, foreign currency, tobacco, animal hides, corn, and livestock as mediums of exchange. There was a shortage of specie, gold, and silver coin, in the new colonies. So out of necessity in 1690, the Massachusetts Bay Colony became the first colony to issue notes, to pay expenses for an ill-fated border war with French Canada. In time, all thirteen colonies had issued some form of paper currency. Most of the Colonial notes could not be redeemed in specie and thus depreciated quickly and became worthless.

The first printing of bills by the new republic began in 1775 when, to help finance the Revolutionary War, Congress authorized the printing of currency. But there was counterfeiting and inadequate specie backing, so the Continentals, as they were called, quickly became worthless. Ultimately, 6% interest-bearing bonds were provided to people who turned in their Continental currency, at the rate of $1 for every $100.

After the failure of the Continentals, the U.S. government quit printing paper money until 1861. The distrust of paper money was too severe after the first bad experience.

In 1792, Congress passed the Coinage Act, which set the dollar as the U.S. monetary unit. A national mint was established in the nation's capital, Philadelphia, with responsibilities for the nation's coinage. The first coins of the new republic were issued in 1793, at the Philadelphia Mint. Today the United States Mint maintains headquarters in Washington, DC, facilities in Philadelphia, Denver, San Francisco, and West Point, and a bullion depository in Fort Knox, Kentucky.

The years from 1793 to 1861 are often called the Wildcat Banking Era, or free banking. Banks were free of federal regulation and left to be regulated by individual states. States granted the bank charters, and in turn, these banks were authorized to print their own currency. The United States became saturated with private bank notes from state banks, and even railroads, insurance companies, and main street apothecaries. Tens of thousands of bank notes covered the United

States, many issued with little or no specie backing the paper. Although some were sound issues, many of the notes traded at deep discount or became worthless paper. This widespread but flagrant private note issuance further exacerbated negative feelings about paper money.

In 1861, desperate to pay for the Civil War, the government permitted the U.S. Treasury Department to issue paper currency. The money took the form of noninterest-bearing demand notes, nicknamed greenbacks. The next year Congress retired the demand notes and issued U.S. notes called legal tender.

Then in an effort to build stability in the U.S. monetary system, in 1863 and 1864, the government passed the National Banking Acts. They established a system of federally chartered national banks alongside the state chartered banks. The national banks were permitted to issue a uniform currency. The currency, national bank notes, were backed by bank-owned U.S. government securities, and thus provided some degree of control over the monetary system. The government imposed a 10% tax on any outstanding state bank notes and effectively forced all state bank notes out of circulation; later the issuance of private bank notes was forbidden. These were giant steps that brought back some level of trust to the use of paper money.

The National Banking system, although a positive move in strengthening the U.S. monetary system, experienced numerous financial crises. There was still no stable method to regulate the level of money in the economy. In 1913, Congress established a central authority, the Federal Reserve, to do just that. The Federal Reserve System—also known as the Fed—was created to provide a safer and more stable monetary and financial system. In 1914, the Fed began issuing Federal Reserve Notes, today the only paper currency manufactured by the Bureau of Engraving and Printing. The Federal Reserve Notes and National Bank Notes circulated side-by-side for a time, but the last series of National Bank Notes were printed in 1929.

The Federal Reserve pays the cost of producing the notes, with the average note costing just under 6 cents to produce. Once paid for, the notes become liabilities of the Federal Reserve Banks and obligations of the U.S. government. Federal Reserve Notes do not have any specie, gold, or silver, backing the notes. In 1933, the country went off the gold standard domestically. Under the gold standard, if you held a Federal Reserve Note you could demand that amount of paper currency in gold. So in 1934, the U.S. moved from the gold standard to a fiat currency. Today there is nothing that backs the money—only the full faith and credit of the U.S. government. Federal Reserve Notes are fiat currency with: "This note is legal tender for all debts, public and private," printed on each bill. You accept a Federal Reserve Note as payment because you know it will be accepted elsewhere.

Money Matters

The Bureau of Engraving and Printing (BEP), which comes under the Department of the Treasury, prints billions of Federal Reserve Notes each year. It is the only U.S. paper currency manufactured today. The Federal Reserve Notes are printed at the BEP's facilities in Washington, DC, and Fort Worth, Texas. A spokesperson for the BEP's Washington, DC, facility

$1,000,000 in $1 currency notes. A woman poses with stacks of packages of $1 silver certificates at the Bureau of Engraving and Printing, Washington, DC. *Source:* Library of Congress.

provided some intriguing facts about this agency, which began in a single room in the basement of the main Treasury building in 1862.

What is money?
Money is the legal tender of the United States, or any foreign country.

What does the BEP do and how many people does it employ?
The BEP produces paper currency and other government securities and documents. From the Federal Reserve, a yearly order of currency is taken and that is how we plan our work. We know how many $1s, $2s, $5s, $10s, $20s, $50s, and $100s to print for each of the twelve Federal Reserve Districts. About 95% are replacement notes.

There are 2,400 employees at the BEP—1,800 at Washington, DC, and 600 at Fort Worth. The two production facilities run 5 days a week with three shifts. We make certain there are two places that produce currency in the event of a natural disaster or terrorism.

Why is the currency being redesigned?
The main reason is to deter counterfeiting and to make the currency as safe as possible. Technology is growing by leaps and bounds and, in order to

stay ahead of counterfeiting, the currency will be redesigned every 7 to 10 years.

The first note of the newest currency designs, the $20 note, was issued in 2003; the $50 note issued in 2004; the $10 note began circulation in 2006. We expect the redesigned $5 note to be issued in early 2008. Subtle colors have been added to the redesigned currency. There are three security features—the watermark, the security thread, and the color-shifting ink.

What are some interesting facts about U.S. paper currency?

Many people don't realize there is no wood pulp in the currency. It is made of cotton and linen.

Many people also don't know that the $100 bill is now the highest denomination note printed. In 1969, the notes in denominations of $500, $1,000, $5,000, and $10,000 were retired. Although they were issued until 1969, they stopped printing them in 1945.

Security of the Newly Designed Bills

How can you tell if you have one of the bills newly designed to thwart counterfeiters? Three ways:

• First, look at the numeral in the lower right hand corner on the face of the bill, depicting the note's denomination. The color-shifting ink changes from copper to green when you tilt the note up and down.

• You can also hold the bill up to the light and look for the watermark, or faint image, similar to the large portrait of President Grant on the $50 note, President Jackson on the $20 note, and Treasury Secretary Hamilton on the new $10 note. The watermark is part of the paper itself and can be seen from both sides of the note. On the new $10 note in particular, a blank oval has been incorporated into the design to highlight the watermark's location.

• Lastly, hold the bill up to the light and look for the security thread running vertically through the note. If you look closely, you can see the words "USA TEN" printed on the $10 note, "USA TWENTY" printed on the $20 note thread, and "USA 50" printed on the $50 note thread. The security thread is visible from both sides of the note.

Source: Bureau of Engraving and Printing.

MEASURING MONEY

There are many financial assets in a sophisticated economy such as the United States: stocks, bonds, commercial paper, and repurchase agreements, to name just a few. All are important components of the burgeoning U.S. economy. But economists are particularly interested in the official measurements of money, the levels of M1 and M2—liquid assets available to readily buy goods and services. Together, M1 and M2 make up the money supply. The two measures of the money

Table 5.1 Money Stock Measures (In Billions of Dollars; Seasonally Adjusted)

	Amount	% of Total
Total M1	1,379.2	100%
Currency in Circulation	754.6	55%
Traveler's Checks	6.5	1%
Demand Deposits	306.7	22%
Other Checkable Deposits	311.3	23%
M2 =		
M1	1,379.2	19%
Plus: Savings accounts	3,820.2	53%
Small time deposits	1,175.4	16%
Money market mutual funds	854.2	12%
Total M2	7,229.0	100%

(Components do not add to total due to rounding.)
Source: The Federal Reserve (May 2007 data).

supply reflect the degrees of spending power available in the economy, M1 being the most liquid.

As you can see in Table 5.1, the narrowest definition of money, the basic classification is M1. Everything in M1 is liquid and easy to spend. M1 consists of currency held by the public, traveler's checks, demand deposits (funds in a bank account that you can access "on demand" by writing a check), and other checkable deposits (NOW accounts, automatic transfer service [ATS] accounts, credit union share drafts, and demand deposits at thrift institutions).

The other measure of money supply, M2, consists of everything in M1 plus balances in savings accounts, time deposits less than $100,000, and money market mutual funds.

These measures are easily converted into M1. You can usually transfer money from your savings account to your checking account; money market mutual funds usually carry limited check-writing privileges; and small time deposits often require a brief time period before funds can be withdrawn.

The main role of the central bank of the United States, the Federal Reserve, is to regulate the supply of money and credit in the economy, in order to promote the goals of high employment, sustainable growth, and stable prices. Through monetary policy, the Fed regulates the amount of money and available credit. There are three monetary policy tools: adjustment to the discount rate; adjusting the reserve requirement percentage; and open market operations. The most widely used tool of the Fed is open market operations, or the buying and selling of government securities.

The Fed can engage in easy money or tight money policies. A simplified scenario: In an easy money policy, the Fed would buy government securities. The funds it uses to purchase the government issues increase the amount of money in the economy. When the Fed makes more money available in the economy, interest rates will fall. Likewise, a tight money policy has the Fed selling government securities. The money it receives for selling the government issues is removed from the economy, thus contracting the money supply. Restricting money will limit credit and raise interest rates.

To effectively regulate, economists at the Fed must be keyed in to the amount of money circulating in the economy. The Fed therefore measures the money supply on a weekly basis. The Federal Reserve publishes weekly and monthly statistics on M1 and M2 every Thursday, unless Thursday is a federal holiday, in which case the release will be on Friday. Check out www.federalreserve.gov, click All Statistical Releases, and look at Money Stock Measures—H.6.

Do You Know Your Dollars?

You spend money daily, but how closely do you look at the dollars in your wallet? Try to name the person whose portrait is featured on each denomination of Federal Reserve Note. The Secretary of the Treasury is responsible for the selection of portraits that appear on the currency, and by law, only the portrait of a deceased individual may appear. A hint is provided for each bill.

$1 Bill   *(The first president of the United States.)*
$2 Bill   *(The third president of the United States.)*
$5 Bill   *(The sixteenth president of the United States.)*
$10 Bill   *(The first Secretary of the Treasury.)*
$20 Bill   *(The seventh president of the United States.)*
$50 Bill   *(The eighteenth president of the United States.)*
$100 Bill *(A statesman, inventor, and scientist.)*

Answers: $1—George Washington; $2—Thomas Jefferson; $5—Abraham Lincoln; $10—Alexander Hamilton; $20—Andrew Jackson; $50—Ulysses Grant; and $100—Ben Franklin.

Lesson 6

The Big Bouncing Economy

"The U.S. economy has experienced recurrent upswings and downswings, but of widely varying length, intensity, and frequency."
—Bradley R. Schiller, *The Macro Economy Today* (2006)

Right after the turn of the new millennium, you can remember newspaper headlines with big print: Unemployment Skyrockets in the City. This was also around the time your friend, Michael, was laid off from his part-time job delivering flyers for the local newspaper company. The flower shop his mom and dad owned still made money, but profits were down. Normally, Michael and his family took elaborate annual vacations—the Bahamas, Cayman Islands, or an Alaskan cruise. That summer Michael went for a weekend trip to the lake.

You ran into Michael at the mall last week and he told you about the fabulous trip he took with his parents to London, Paris, and Rome, and his other good fortune. He won't even graduate from college until spring but already has a job lined up at the bank in town, as a management trainee. And his parents' flower shop just opened a third location. Wow! You were happy for Michael, but couldn't help but wonder if there was something more going on here than good luck.

You are right. What was going on was the economy. It would be great to imagine the economy always operates at full force and everybody has a job, people earn fabulous paychecks, and businesses make huge profits. But sometimes the economy dips and layoffs occur, pay raises are halted, and businesses curtail production. The economy definitely has highs and lows, or as an economist would say—peaks and troughs. Sometimes the economy is booming and businesses struggle to keep up with consumer demand. That may be why Michael landed that bank job before he even graduated. But then hard economic times hit and even part-time jobs, like Michael had when he was younger, sometimes go by the wayside. The economy falls and then bounces back up, over and over again, the cycles akin to a big bouncing ball (see Figure 6.1).

WHAT IS A BUSINESS CYCLE?

If you have the idea that the business cycle is the cyclical highs and lows of the economy, you are correct. The business cycle is the rise and fall of economic activity relative to the economy's long-term growth rate, which is roughly 3% as measured by real GDP. Some cycles are long while others are brief. Regardless of the length and intensity of the business cycle, the economy will move through four distinct phases:

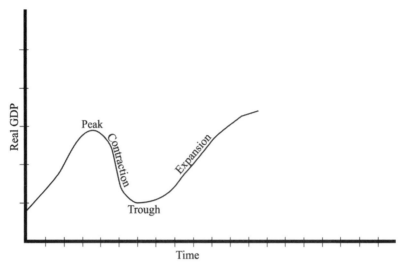

Figure 6.1 Peaks and Troughs.

Peak. The peak is the high point of an expansion, just before the downturn in economic activity begins. New businesses are opening, employment is high, and firms are operating at a high production level. It is followed by a contraction.

Contraction. The contraction (recession) is the period where business activity slows down. More business failures will occur with fewer startups, it will be harder to find a job, and firms will cut production.

Trough. The trough is the lowest point of the contraction phase of the business cycle, just before economic activity turns upward.

Expansion. The expansion phase is when the economy starts to turn upward and recover. The expansion continues until the economy hits another peak.

Take a look at Figure 6.1 to see the phases of the business cycle. The period from the peak to the trough is a recession, while the span from trough to peak is an expansion. Then the cycle starts all over again. Technically, fluctuations occur around the long-run growth trend. The long-run trend represents the direction of the economy over an extended period of years.

NBER BUSINESS CYCLE DATING COMMITTEE

In the media you will most often see the financial news refer to a recession as two consecutive negative quarters of real Gross Domestic Product (GDP). Real GDP is a measure of the overall economy, the inflation-adjusted market value of all final goods and services produced within the country in a given period of time. Real GDP has often been used as a simple means to identify a recession. This may be a quick, easy measurement for the public to know when the economy is in hard times, but it is actually much more complicated than that.

No one knows how long prosperity will last before it takes an ugly turn, or how long the bad times will run before a good stretch hits. However, the National Bureau of Economic Research's Business Cycle Dating Committee, a group of seven economists, keep a closer watch on the economy than the rest of us. The

National Bureau of Economic Research (NBER) was founded in 1920, and is a Cambridge (Massachusetts), nonprofit, nonpartisan research organization that promotes a greater understanding of how the economy works.

The Business Cycle Dating Committee dates recessions and expansions, and both the government and the public adopt their calls. According to the committee, "A recession is a significant decline in economic activity spread across the economy, lasting more than a few months, normally visible in real GDP, real income, employment, industrial production, and wholesale-retail sales." Most of the recessions classified by the Business Cycle Dating Committee do consist of two or more quarters of falling real GDP, but not each and every one. Because a recession impacts the entire economy and, to maintain some continuity with the business cycle chronology, the committee considers a wide range of indicators when dating recessions, not just GDP. The Framing the Big Picture sidebar gives more details on the process of dating business cycles.

Framing the Big Picture

Saying the U.S. economy is big is definitely an understatement. Producing $13.6 trillion dollars of new goods and services each year, it is the world's largest economy. With a total population of just over 301 million people interacting in this bustling economy, each person's share of output is a staggering $45,291, the highest of the advanced economies. The economic complexity of this leading industrial power is difficult to comprehend. Donna Zerwitz, Director of Public Information, at the National Bureau of Economic Research (NBER), a private, nonprofit research organization, provides some fascinating insight on how the Business Cycle Dating Committee frames the big picture of the burgeoning U.S. economy.

When did the NBER begin its work on business cycles?

If you think about the size of our economy, it's an enormous chunk of information, and it is hard to get your mind around it. That is partly why the process got started. The NBER began in 1920 in New York City, when a small group of economists who were interested in the idea of business cycles and other ways to measure an economy got together. Their on-site collaboration during the 1920s, 1930s, and 1940s at the New York office of the Bureau focused on measuring the business cycle and on developing leading, coincident, and lagging indicators.

The NBER has changed over the years and today has mostly a small residence staff. But researchers—over 600 academics who are leading scholars in their field—sit in offices at universities across the country doing work on many areas of the U.S. and global economy. These researchers come to the NBER on sabbaticals and to attend workshops, and their work is published in academic papers and books. The NBER provides studies and quantitative research, but does not make policy or forecast. One area that was never lost, a remnant of the past, is the work of the Business Cycle Dating Committee. The Bureau's main office today is in Cambridge, Massachusetts, with a small office remaining in New York City, and also one in Palo Alto, California.

What does the Business Cycle Dating Committee do?

The function of the committee is to decide when we have seen turning points in the economy, the peaks and troughs. In 1961, the U.S. Department of Commerce, Bureau of Economic Analysis asked the NBER to publish its business cycle dates in its *Business Conditions Digest*. This effectively made the NBER the official spokesperson of the cycle.

What is a cycle?

The cycle is the complete up and down of the economy. The business cycle will be the curves up and down around the economy's long-term growth trend line. The peak is the top of the mountain and the trough is the hole in the ground. The period from peak to trough is a recession and the period from trough to another peak is an expansion. A complete cycle is from peak to peak or trough to trough.

How is the committee's membership selected?

Since 1978, the president of the NBER appoints the members who include the directors of the macro and international economy programs and other members with specialties in economic fluctuations and growth. There are currently seven members of the committee. These include the president of the NBER, Martin Feldstein, and chair, Robert Hall, who heads the NBER's Research Program on Economic Fluctuations and Growth.

How often do the members of the committee meet?

The committee does not have a set schedule for meetings. They decide how often to communicate depending on what is going on in the economy. For the last 10 years they have not met formally in one physical location. They conduct business by e-mail communication and telephone conference calls.

What are some of the indicators the committee reviews when developing the business cycle chronology?

Because a recession influences the economy broadly, the committee emphasizes economywide measures of economic activity. The committee views real GDP as the single best measure of aggregate activity and places heavy weight on the estimates of real GDP (adjusted for inflation) by the Bureau of Economic Analysis (BEA). The BEA's estimates are only available quarterly. This results in a serious disconnect with monthly data, so the committee also looks at monthly estimates of real GDP like those prepared by Macroeconomic Advisers, a private consulting firm. The committee views monthly measures of activity across the economy—real personal income less transfer payments and employment. The committee refers to two indicators with coverage primarily of manufacturing and goods—industrial production and real manufacturing wholesale-retail sales.

This is one area where the academics don't use a computer program or software. There is no fixed rule about what other measures contribute to the process of dating business cycles. It is the judgment of a group of smart individuals. Members talk until they reach a consensus.

Table 6.1 Business Cycle Expansions and Contractions

Longest Contraction	(From October 1873 to March 1879)	65 months
Shortest Contraction	(From January 1980 to July 1980)	6 months
Longest Expansion	(From March 1991 to March 2001)	120 months
Shortest Expansion	(From March 1919 to January 1920)	10 months

	Duration in Months		
Average, all Cycles:	Contraction	Expansion	Cycle
	(Trough from previous Trough Peak from Previous Peak)		
1854-2001 (32 cycles)	17	38	55	56*
1854-1919 (16 cycles)	22	27	48	49**
1919-1945 (6 cycles)	18	35	53	53
1945-2001 (10 cycles)	10	57	67	67

*31 cycles
**15 cycles
Source: NBER. The NBER Business Cycle Expansions and Contractions Table at www.nber.org/cycles.html. Accessed July 28, 2007.

DURATION OF BUSINESS CYCLES

Mass data is available for economists to analyze economic fluctuations. The NBER has measured the duration of business cycles, along with peaks and troughs dating from December 1854 to current times. Some contractions have been fairly mild and short-lived, while others have endured to cause major slowdowns in the economy with huge job loss, widespread bankruptcies, and severe cuts in business production. Expansions, too, have varied in duration and long-term booms have brought economic prosperity, often due to heightened government spending during wartime. During war efforts, demand for goods and services rise; the job level and production rates boom. Military spending during World War II greatly increased the output level of the economy. Gross Domestic Product (current dollars) was just $101.4 billion in 1940, but had more than doubled in size to $223.1 billion by the end of the war in 1945.

You can view the duration of the longest and shortest contractions and expansions, along with average cycle data, in Table 6.1, Business Cycle Expansions and Contractions. Let us examine the extremes of the cycles to illustrate the varied effects and terms of fluctuating cycles.

Although the cycles are subject to different interpretations, several apparent details emerge. A clear observation from the data shows business cycles have varied durations. The longest contraction recorded was from October 1873 to March 1879, and lasted 65 months. A severe contraction is typically referred to as a depression, and this era certainly fits that description. From 1873 to 1879 the depression was spurred by a financial panic. Credit was limited and panicked banks demanded repayment of loans. This lead to mass business failure and resulted in a nationwide economic crisis.

The Great Depression, as it is typically called, ran from August 1929 to March 1933, 43 months long. It is the second longest recorded contraction in U.S. history, but was the worst economic collapse worldwide. At the end of 1929, the stock market crashed, precipitating bank failures, business closings, and forcing millions out of work. At the height of the crisis, which spread from the United States to the rest of the world, one-fourth of the U.S. workforce was without a job.

The shortest recorded contraction was just 6 months, from January 1980 to July 1980. It was brief and relatively mild. But after a short respite, the small recession turned into a serious 16-month contraction from July 1981 to November 1982. Inflation, double-digit interest rates, and skyrocketing unemployment plagued the country.

At one time the record holder for the largest expansion was from February 1961 to December 1969—106 months—and was heightened by spending associated with the Vietnam War. But then came the 1990s and everything seemed to turn to gold: jobs were plentiful, the stock market boomed, corporate profits took off, and technological advancement surged. The longest expansion in recorded history ran for 10 years, from March 1991 to March 2001. But the September 11, 2001, terrorist attacks halted an economy that was already beginning to develop economic challenges. As you can see, expansions can be brief, too. The shortest expansion in history ran from March 1919 to January 1920, just 10 months, a post-World War I boom.

The good news is that on average, recessions tend to be the shorter fluctuation and expansions the longer fluctuation. The most recent decision of the Business Cycle Dating Committee was its determination that the last contraction ended in November 2001. Since recorded business cycle history (1854–2001), there have been 32 cycles, the average contraction being 17 months and the average expansion 38 months. Other positive news is that since 1945, post-World War II (1945–2001), the average length of contractions has fallen to 10 months and expansions have averaged 57 months. Why? Some economists maintain that policymakers have fine-tuned monetary and fiscal policy actions to smooth out the fluctuations in the economy.

So while recessions and expansions will vary in length and intensity, the average postwar contraction is just under a year and expansion is just under 5 years. Remember, the typical condition of the economy is a prosperous expansion.

GET A CLUE!

Policymakers, economists, and investors all try to predict changes in the business cycle. Policymakers want to know the phase of the business cycle and where it is headed to plan for fiscal and monetary policies along with budgetary planning. Economists want to be ahead of the curve in order to prepare more accurate economic forecasts. Investors want to know about overall business activity in order to plan their financial and business strategies.

Anyone interested in the economy can get a feel for the direction of the overall economy by keying in on economic indicators. There are three statistics to watch: leading, coincident, and lagging indicators. Each provides a great clue to the direction of economic activity. Leading indicators are things that precede an economic change; coincident indicators coincide or match the economic trend; and lagging indicators follow an economic change. Statistics on all three major indicators are gathered monthly by The Conference Board, a nonprofit New York-based business membership and research organization. Founded in 1916, this premiere establishment has members from over 2,000 companies in 60 countries. The Conference Board publishes leading, coincident, and lagging indexes designed to signal peaks and troughs in the business cycle for eight other countries—Australia, France, Germany, Japan, Korea, Mexico, Spain, and the United Kingdom—in addition to the United States.

Here is a quick summary of the U.S. indexes that aid in anticipating the economy's highs and lows.

Leading Index—A group of ten indicators all rolled into one composite index. The upturns of the index precede the upturn of the economy; downturns of the index precede the downturn of the economy. The individual indicators are: state unemployment insurance claims (inverted); building permits; vendor performance (companies that are receiving slower deliveries); manufacturers' new orders for consumer goods and materials; manufacturers' new orders for nondefense capital goods; average weekly manufacturing hours; stock prices; index of consumer expectations; interest rate spread; and real money supply.

Coincident Index—Four indicators whose movements tend to correspond to the peaks and troughs of the economy. The individual indicators are: employees on nonagricultural payrolls; personal income less transfer payments; industrial production; and manufacturing and trade sales.

Lagging Index—A group of seven indicators measured in a single index, whose high points and low points occur after the economy hits its highs and lows. The individual indicators are: average duration of unemployment (inverted); inventories to sales ratio, manufacturing and trade; labor cost per unit of output, manufacturing; average prime rate; commercial and industrial loans; consumer installment credit to personal income ratio; and consumer price index for services.

CAUSES OF BUSINESS CYCLES

What causes such fluctuations in the economy? This is a question that holds serious debate in the economics profession. There are many theories offering explanations on these cyclical ups and downs, but no single theory seems to explain all the fluctuations. Often it is a combination of theories that may best explain the cycles. Also, one theory may be more pronounced at a certain time than another. As pioneering NBER business cycle economist Wesley C. Mitchell prophetically wrote, "As knowledge of the business cycle grows, more effort is required to master it. (Mitchell, 1927, p. 1)" Theories abound on the likely cause of economic fluctuations, but let us review four main postulates: investment spending, monetary policy, fiscal policy, and real business cycles.

Investment Spending—Heightened business investment can stimulate the economy, while a pullback on investment can contract the economy. If businesses have high hopes for sales, they will invest in new buildings, buy new capital equipment, increase employment, and expand inventories. Businesses may likely rev up borrowing to finance these new operations. These are all positive actions that will provide a stimulant for the economy. On the flip side, if businesses have concern that sales may be slowing, they will curtail spending on buildings and equipment, hiring will cease, people may be dismissed from their employment, and inventories will be reduced. Business owners won't be knocking on the local banker's door for new loans. These are all actions that will cause a contraction in economic activity.

Monetary Policy—The more money made available, the more businesses and people will borrow. America's central bank, the Federal Reserve, is in charge of monetary policy and, ultimately, the overall level of interest rates. By forcing more money into the economy, interest rates will fall; businesses will want to expand production, and people will want to buy homes, cars, and more. Constricting money and raising interest rates, on the other hand, may cause businesses to cut business plans and people will be more reluctant to borrow and spend. By controlling the amount of money and credit in the economy and raising or lowering interest rates, the Fed will affect contractions and expansions.

Fiscal Policy—Fiscal policy refers to changes in government spending and taxes to affect the economy. An increase in government spending or a reduction of the tax rate may cause a boom in economic activity. A cut in government spending or a rise in the tax rate may result in a business slump. For example, if the government raises taxes, consumers may curtail spending on consumer goods like furniture, cars, and clothes, thus causing the economy to contract. Conversely, if the government increases spending during war efforts, the economy will boom as military production increases. Firms will increase factory production and workers will have increased income, thus expanding the economy.

Real Business Cycles—Real business cycle theory maintains that business sector productivity levels drive the business cycle. The theory holds that changes in business productivity explain the cyclical fluctuations in the economy. Supply shocks, like a sudden rise in the price of oil, bad weather, or technological change, can create fluctuations in the productivity level. One example is the technology boom of the second half of the 1990s, based on new technology and computers, causing an increase in productivity growth and an economic boom.

Studying the business cycles provides knowledge about possible causes and duration of fluctuations, shedding light on how policymakers may best utilize monetary and fiscal policy to reduce the severity of recessions. But slowdowns and booms will always be an inevitable flow of people, businesses, and governments interacting in a nation's economic system. Fluctuations will always come and go. So when the economy enters a declining period, the good news is that prosperous economic times are right around the corner.

Appendix A: A Century of Major U.S. Monetary Events

1900—The United States adopted a gold standard—currency converted into gold at a fixed price.

1907—A financial panic triggered "runs" on banks throughout New York City, and spread across the country. Financier J.P. Morgan played a lead role in pumping money into the banking system and halting the panic.

1908—As a result of the banking panic of 1907, the Aldrich-Vreeland Act of 1908 was passed, authorizing emergency currency issues during times of crises. It also established the National Monetary Commission, which studied banking in Europe and North America. These report findings formed a basis for a central banking system for the United States, the Federal Reserve Act of 1913.

1913—Federal income tax on individuals and corporations introduced.

1913—The Federal Reserve Act signed into law by President Woodrow Wilson.

1914—The Federal Reserve Banks opened for business. Federal Reserve Notes—the only form of U.S. paper money in production today—first issued.

1914–1918—World War I.

1917—Three weeks after the United States declared war on Germany, the First Liberty Loan Act authorized the issue of $5 billion worth of government bonds. Liberty Loan Bonds and Victory Notes were issued during the World War I era to help finance expenses associated with the war.

1929–1933—On October 29, 1929, "Black Tuesday," the stock market crashed, marking the beginning of the Great Depression. A record volume of nearly 16.5 million shares traded, compared with the September daily average of just over 4 million. During the 4-year time frame, there was widespread banking failure with more than 9,000 banks failing. The most severe economic downturn occurred during the years from 1929 to 1933, but the Depression did not end in the United States until 1941.

1933—Congress passed the Banking Act of 1933, also known as the Glass-Steagall Act. This created the Federal Deposit Insurance Corporation (FDIC) as a temporary agency in response to the thousands of bank failures and in order to restore financial stability to the nation. This Act also separated commercial banking from investment banking, establishing them as separate lines of business.

The United States also abandoned the gold standard. President Roosevelt declared a 4-day nationwide bank holiday in which banks were closed to prevent the exportation or hoarding of gold or silver. The Emergency Banking Act required government inspectors to declare a bank financially sound before it could reopen its doors for business. The government continued to sell gold to foreign central banks and institutions.

1934—The Gold Reserve Act withdrew gold coins from circulation. Compensation was Federal Reserve Notes or other currency. The act also provided for the devaluation of the gold dollar and created the Exchange Stabilization Fund (ESF), for the purpose of contributing to exchange rate stability.

1935—The Banking Act of 1935 established the FDIC as a permanent agency of the government.

1939–1945—World War II.

1941—Japan bombed Pearl Harbor in Hawaii, forcing the United States into World War II. Large amounts of War Savings Bonds were sold to help with the vast cost of the war.

1944—Delegates from forty-five nations gathered at the Mount Washington Hotel in Bretton Woods, NH to attend the United States Monetary and Fiscal Conference. The Bretton Woods Conference, as it is commonly known, created the International Monetary Fund (IMF) to oversee the international monetary system and the International Bank for Reconstruction and Development (IBRD), to help Europe rebuild after the war.

1956—The Dow Jones Industrial Average reached the 500 milestone.

1968—Redemption of silver certificates for silver bullion ceased.

1969—Denominations higher than $100 were discontinued by the Department of the Treasury. Although issued until 1969, the $500, $1000, $5000, and $10,000 bills had not been printed since 1945.

1971—President Richard Nixon announced that the United States would no longer allow foreign governments the right to convert their dollars into gold.

1972—The Dow Jones Industrial Average reached the 1,000 milestone.

1974—President Ford repealed the 1933 ban on gold ownership by U.S. citizens.

1980—The Depository Institutions Deregulation and Monetary Control Act (DIDMCA) was enacted. This legislation raised deposit insurance, phased out interest rate ceilings, authorized NOW accounts nationwide, eliminated usury ceilings, extended uniform reserve requirements on all depository institutions, and expanded the powers of thrift institutions.

1982—Garn-St. Germain Act. This legislation authorized money market deposit accounts, expanded investment powers of thrifts, and allowed banks to buy failing banks across state lines.

1987—The "Black Monday" stock market crash occurred on October 19. The Dow fell 508 points, or 22.61%, the largest 1-day percentage drop in history.

The Federal Reserve, with Alan Greenspan at the helm, issued a one-sentence statement before trading the next day to calm the market: "The Federal Reserve, consistent with its responsibilities as the nation's central bank, affirmed today its readiness to serve as a source of liquidity to support the economic and financial system."

1991–2001—Longest expansion in U.S. history. The expansion began in March 1991 and ran for exactly 10 years, coming to a close in March 2001.

1999—The Dow Jones Industrial Average reached the 10,000 milestone.

2001—On September 11 the terrorist attacks destroyed the World Trade Center in New York City. Financial markets were disrupted and the NYSE closed for 4 days. On the day of the attack, the Fed issued a two-sentence statement showing its readiness to pump liquidity into the market: "The Federal Reserve System is open and operating. The discount window is available to meet liquidity needs." On September 12, bank borrowing from the Federal Reserve discount window to banks totaled $45.5 billion; this was more than 200 times the daily average for the previous month. By the end of September, discount window lending had returned to normal levels. The Fed had succeeded in dampening the effects of the terrorist attacks.

The Dow fell 684.81 points on September 17; this was the steepest point slide in history.

2003—Federal Reserve employed a change in discount window lending. Strong, well-capitalized banks would be extended primary credit on a short-term basis, at a rate above the federal funds. Reduced need for the Fed to review funding situations made the discount window a more favorable borrowing source for banks.

2007—The Dow Jones Industrial Average reached the 14,000 milestone.

Appendix B: Fascinating Financial Web sites

www.barrons.com
Barron's online is a definite must for your Favorites list. The online edition is free (although paying subscribers do have access to special articles) and jam-packed full of stories from the magazine as well as online exclusives. Check out Up and Down Wall Street Daily, Striking Price Daily, Tech Trader Daily, Weekly Stock and Mutual Fund Listings, and a must see—Barron's Economic Calendar with a heads-up on economic reports and the icing on the cake: report explanations.

www.bea.gov
The Bureau of Economic Analysis produces some of the most highly monitored economic data in the United States, including the benchmark Gross Domestic Product. For a quick look into the health of the U.S. economy, be sure to check out *U.S. Economy at a Glance.*

www.conference-board.org
The Conference Board is a business membership and research organization, known for its consumer confidence index and leading economic index. Check out indicators (U.S. and international), analyses, and forecasts. Scan "Management Knowledge" for an extensive array of information for the inquisitive, globally minded business executive.

www.federalreserveeducation.org
For economic and financial education, the Federal Reserve Web site is a must to visit. The best part—all of the curriculum, newsletters, booklets, and data are free of charge. A link to each of the twelve Federal Reserve banks is provided, along with the Board of Governors. A click on the Great Economist Treasure Hunt, American Currency Exhibit, and A Day in the Life of a FOMC, are all a must.

www.marketwatch.com
Marketwatch is packed full of up-to-date business and financial information. Take a look at some favorites: "Video" let's you watch business and economic news on the computer. A wide selection of business news, analyses, and commentary is available. Don't miss "Emerging Markets" for hours of reading on China, India, and more. "Personal Finance" is an insightful read and will help you manage and invest your money.

www.nber.org
The National Bureau of Economic Research, a private economic research organization, provides topnotch working papers from the lead researchers in the field.

Check out historical data on business cycle recessions and expansions. To further investigate recessions and their causes, view information from the NBER's Business Cycle Dating Committee on how it chooses turning points in the economy.

www.oecd.org
The Organization of Economic Co-operation and Development is an international organization managing the economic, social, and governance challenges of the global economy. It's widely known for its statistical data on comparable economic and social statistics for countries. Don't miss "Hot Topics" for a wide range of issues the OECD is currently studying.

www.treasurydirect.gov
This Web site is jam-packed full of helpful information. Here, among other things, you can buy U.S. Treasury securities online. You can further manage the securities online with an account history noting the value of your securities. Do you have savings bonds sitting in a box in your closet? Pull them out and check the Web site to calculate the value of your bonds and make sure they are still earning interest. You will find a daily history of "Debt to the Penny," adjusted late each morning, to help you monitor the rising national debt.

PREMIER PODCASTS

Do you like to listen to your economic information? Check out these great economics Web sites and listen, via your computer or download to your audio player:

www.chicagogsb.edu/multimedia/podcast/
Views on business and economics from the seat of one of the powerhouses of current thinking on the economy. The Chicago Graduate School of Business provides a podcast that will stimulate your intellectual curiosity. Listen to faculty members and professionals to broaden your global business perspective. Can't find a topic that interests you? Check out the extensive Chicago GSB Archive.

www.econtalk.org
For high-level economic topics, Russell Roberts, Professor of Economics and the J. Fish and Lillian F. Smith Distinguished Scholar at the Mercatus Center at George Mason University, hosts featured guests and professors on topics including current events, markets, and free markets. Listen in to increase your economics I.Q.

www.frbatlanta.com
Check out the Federal Reserve Bank of Atlanta Podcast Directory for featured economic interviews and commentaries. A favorite, speeches, podcasting high-level speeches by Atlanta Federal Reserve officials on events relating to the economy, finance, and banking.

www.npr.org
Always well done, listen to public radio for select business and economic reports. Over fifty public radio stations across the country work with NPR to provide podcasting. The NPR podcast directory makes it a breeze to pick your favorite

podcasts. Check out topic selections: Business, Economy, News, and Your Money to be "in the know."

www.radioeconomics.com
World famous economists are interviewed on a host of pressing economic issues. Check out Dr. James Reese, economics professor at the University of South Carolina Upstate. There are many attention-grabbing interviews with leading intellectuals.

Acronyms

AMEX—American Stock Exchange

APR—Annual Percentage Rate

BEA—Bureau of Economic Analysis

BEP—The Bureau of Engraving and Printing

CEO—Chief Executive Officer

CPI—Consumer Price Index

DPI—Disposable Personal Income

DJIA—Dow Jones Industrial Average

EIN—Employer Identification Number

EPA—Environmental Protection Agency

ECB—European Central Bank

EU—European Union

FACT Act—Fair and Accurate Credit Transactions Act of 2003

FDIC—Federal Deposit Insurance Corporation

FED—Federal Reserve System

FOMC—Federal Open Market Committee

FTC—Federal Trade Commission

GAO—Government Accountability Office

GATT—General Agreement on Tariffs and Trade

GNI—Gross National Income

GDP—Gross Domestic Product

GNP—Gross National Product

IBRD—International Bank for Reconstruction and Development

IMF—International Monetary Fund

IPO—Initial Public Offering

IRS—Internal Revenue Service

LEI—Leading Economic Indicators

NASDAQ—National Association of Securities Dealers Automated Quotations

NBER—National Bureau of Economic Research

NAFTA—The North American Free Trade Agreement

NYSE—New York Stock Exchange

OECD—The Organization for Economic Co-operation and Development

OPEC—The Organization of Petroleum Exporting Countries
OTC—Over-the-Counter
PPI—Producer Price Index
PPP—Purchasing Power Parity
REITs—Real Estate Investment Trusts
SEC—Securities and Exchange Commission
TIPS—Treasury Inflation-Protected Securities
WTO—World Trade Organization

Bibliography

A Guide to the National Income and Product Accounts of the United States. November 2006. *Survey of Current Business*. Available at www.bea.gov (Accessed May 21, 2007).

Analytical Perspectives of the FY 2008 Budget. Federal Borrowing and Debt, Office of Management and Budget, Table16-1, Economic Report of the President. Available at www.whitehouse.gov/omb (Accessed July 7, 2007).

Berman, J. February 2004. Industry Output and Employment Projections, *Monthly Labor Review*. Available at www.bls.gov/opub/mlr/archive.htm (Accessed October 1, 2007).

Bernanke, B. 2007. "Central Banking and Bank Supervision in the United States." Speech delivered at the Allied Social Science Association Annual Meeting, Chicago, IL: January 5. Available at www.federalreseve.gov/boarddocs/speeches/2007 (Accessed May 15, 2007).

Black, J. 1997. *A Dictionary of Economics*. New York: Oxford University Press.

Bureau of Engraving and Printing. *U.S.Banknotes. Anti-Counterfeiting. Money Facts*. Available at www.moneyfactory.gov (Accessed July 19, 2007).

Burns, A. F. and W. C. Mitchell, 1947. *Measuring Business Cycle*s, New York: National Bureau of Economic Research.

Bussing-Burks, M. 2003. *Influential Economists*. Minneapolis, MN: The Oliver Press, Inc.

———. 2001. *Profit from the Evening News*: *Using Leading Economic Indicators to Make Smart Money Decisions*. Naperville, IL: Sourcebooks, Inc.

———. 2000. *The Young Zillionaire's Guide to Taxation and Government Spending*, New York: The Rosen Publishing Group, Inc.

Butler, B., D. Butler, and A. Issacs, eds. 1997. *A Dictionary of Finance and Banking*, 2nd edition. Oxford: Oxford University Press.

Colander, D. C. 1995. *Macroeconomics*, 2nd edition. Chicago, IL: Irwin.

Congressional Pig Book Summary. 2006. Washington, DC: Citizens against Government Waste. Available at www.cagw.org (Accessed June 23, 2007).

Dobeck, M. F. and E. Elliott. 2007. *Money* (*Greenwood Guides to Business and Economics*). Westport, CT: Greenwood Press.

Downes, J., and J. E. Goodman, eds. 1998. *Dictionary of Finance and Investment Terms*, 5th edition. Hauppauge, NY: Barron's Educational Series, Inc.

Ehrlich, E. and M. De Bruhl, eds. 1996. *The International Thesaurus of Quotations*, 2nd edition. New York: HarperCollins Publishers, Inc.

Federal Reserve Act. 1913. Dispersed throughout 12 USC; ch. 6, 38 Stat. 251, December 23. Available at www.federalreserve.gov (Accessed May 15, 2007).

Federal Reserve Education. *Federal Reserve Education. Fed 101*. Available at www.federalreserveeducation.org (Accessed May 16, 2007).

Federal Reserve statistical release (July 19, 2007), *H.6. Money Stock Measures*, The Federal Reserve Board of Governors. Available at www.federeralreserve.gov (Accessed July 20, 2007).

Financial Audit: Bureau of the Public Debt's Debt Fiscal Years 2006 and 2005 Schedules of Federal Debt. Highlights of GAO-07-127. A Report to the Secretary of the Treasury. U.S. Government Accountability Office, November 2006 (Accessed July 3, 2007).

Fitzhenry, Robert I., ed. 1993. *The Harper Book of Quotations*, 3rd edition. New York: HarperCollins Publishers.

Friedberg, Robert. 1959. *Paper Money of the United States,* 3rd edition. New York: The Coin and Currency Institute, Inc.

Friedman, Milton. 1992. *Money Mischief: Episodes in Monetary History.* New York: Harcourt Brace & Company; reprint, First Harvest, 1994.

Google. *Corporate Information: Google Milestones.* Available at www.google.com (Accessed August 12, 2007).

Gramlich, E. M. "A Stabilization Policy Strategy." Speech delivered at the Wharton Public Policy Forum Series, Philadelphia, PA, April 22, 1999. Available at www.federalreserve.gov/boarddocs/speeches/1999 (Accessed June 25, 2007).

Gressle, S. S. November 8, 1999, updated. *Shutdown on the Federal Government: Causes, Effects, and Process.* Congressional Research Service Report for Congress 98–844. Available at www.ncseonline.org/NLE (Accessed July 3, 2007).

Hailstones, T. J. and F. V. Mastrianna. 1992. *Basic Economics*, 9th edition. Cincinnati, OH: South-Western Publishing Co.

Hall, R. et al. October 21, 2003. *The NBER's Business-Cycle Dating Procedure.* Cambridge, MA: Business Cycle Dating Committee, NBER. Available at www.nber.org (Accessed July 31, 2007).

History at Your Fingertips & Spirit of the Nation. Rev. June 1996. Boston, MA: Public and Community Affairs Department, Federal Reserve Bank of Boston. Available at www.bos.frb.org (Accessed July 19, 2007).

History of Colonial Money. Boston, MA: Public and Community Affairs Department, Federal Reserve Bank of Boston. Available at www.bos.frb.org (Accessed July 19, 2007).

History of Economic Thought Web site. New York: Department of Economics of the New School for Social Research. Available at www.cepa.newschool.edu (Accessed June 1, 2007).

History of the Treasury, Chronology of Events. U.S. Department of the Treasury. Available at www.ustreas.gov/education/ (Accessed November 1, 2007).

Hubbard, R. G. and A. P. O'Brien. 2006. *Microeconomics.* Upper Saddle River, NJ: Pearson Prentice Hall.

Inscoe, D. September 4, 2001. *Milestones in the Collection and Use of Data for Federal Deposit Insurance (1934-2001).* Available at www2.fdic.gov/hsob/milestones.pdf (Accessed August 31, 2007).

Investopedia, Financial Directory. Available at www.investopedia.com (Accessed August 16, 2007).

Johnson, R. T. Rev. 1999. *Historical Beginnings . . . The Federal Reserve.* Boston, MA: Public and Community Affairs Department Federal Reserve Bank of Boston.

Knaup, A. E. May 2005. Survival and Longevity in the Business Employment Dynamics Data, *Monthly Labor Review.* Available at www.bls.gov/opub/mlr/archive.htm (Accessed August 17, 2007).

Kowalski, K. M. 2004. *A Balancing Act: A Look at Checks and Balances.* Minneapolis, MN: Leaner Publications Company.

Krause, C. L. and R. F. Lemke. 1990. *Standard Catalog of U.S. Paper Money.* Iola, WI: Krause Publications.

Kroll, L. and A. Fass, eds. March 8, 2007. *Special Report: The World's Billionaires*. Available at www.Forbes.com (Accessed August 15, 2007).

Meet Jake [Burton]. Burton Company Biography. Available at www.burton.com (Accessed August 14, 2007).

Miller, M. and T. Serafin, eds. September 21, 2006. *Special Report: The 400 Richest Americans*. Available at www.Forbes.com (Accessed August 13, 2007).

Miller, R. L. 2005. *Economics: Today and Tomorrow*. New York: Glencoe/McGraw-Hill.

Mitchell, W. C. 1927. *Business Cycles: The Problem and Its Setting*. New York: National Bureau of Economic Research.

Monthly Statement of the Public Debt of the United States. May 31, 2007. Washington, DC: The Bureau of the Public Debt. Available at www.treasurydirect.gov (Accessed July 3, 2007).

Morris, V. B. and K. M. Morris. 2000. *Dictionary of Financial Terms*. New York: Lightbulb Press, Inc.

News Release: Experian's National Score Index Shows 14 Percent of the U.S. Population Has More than 10 Credit Cards. Experian Global Office. February 15, 2007. Available at www.experian.com (Accessed June 27, 2007).

News Release: Gross Domestic Product. April 27, 2007. Bureau of Economic Analysis, U.S. Department of Commerce (Accessed May 21, 2007).

News Release: U.S. Leading Economic Indicators and Related Composite Indexes for June 2007. The Conference Board U.S. Business Cycle Press Release. July 19, 2007. Available at www.conference-board.org (Accessed July 31, 2007).

O'Sullivan, A. and A. Sheffrin. 2005. *Microeconomics: Principles and Tools*, 4th edition. Upper Saddle River, NJ: Pearson Prentice Hall.

Pennington, R. L. 1999. *Economics*. Austin, TX: Holt, Rinehart, and Winston.

Pierce, D. W, ed. 1992. *The MIT Dictionary of Modern Economics*, 4th edition. Cambridge, MA: The MIT Press.

Pressman, S. 1999. *Fifty Major Economists*. New York: Routledge.

Rich List: Joanne Rowling. 2007. *The Sunday Times*. Available at www.business.timesonline.co.uk/tol/business/specials/rich_list/ (Accessed August 14, 2007).

Riedl, B. M. March 8, 2007. *Federal Spending—By the Numbers*. Washington, DC: The Heritage Foundation. Available at www.heritage.org (Accessed June 12, 2007).

Rowling, J. K. *Biography*, J. K. Rowling Official Site. Available at www.jkrowling.com (Accessed August 15, 2007).

Schiller, B. R. 2006. *The Macro Economy Today*, 10th edition. New York: McGraw-Hill Irwin.

———. 2006. *The Micro Economy Today*, 10th edition. New York: McGraw-Hill Irwin.

Smith, A. 1776. *Wealth of Nations* (Great Mind Series). 10th edition. 1991. New York: Prometheus Books.

Snowboard History. *Vermont Living*. Available at Vtliving.com (Accessed August 14, 2007).

Spencer, M. H. 1993. *Contemporary Economics*, 8th edition. New York: Worth Publishers.

Steve Jobs, CEO Apple, bio press information. Apple Inc. Available at www.apple.com (Accessed August 11, 2007).

Taking Account. July 2007. *Survey of Current Business*. Available at www.bea.gov/scb (Accessed February 20, 2008).

Taylor, G. 1989. *The Federal Reserve System*. New York: Chelsea House Publishers.

The Changing World of Banking: National Banking System Created (1832–1864). Washington, DC: Office of the Comptroller of the Currency. Available at www.occ.treas.gov (Accessed May 19, 2007).

The Federal Reserve System: Purposes and Functions. 1994. 8th edition, Washington, DC: Board of Governors of the Federal Reserve System.

The Story of the Federal Reserve System. 2000. New York: Public Information Department Federal Reserve Bank of New York.

Timeline, Chronology. New York Stock Exchange, NYSE Euronext. Available at www.nyse.com (Accessed November 1, 2007).

U.S. Census Bureau, *Statistical Abstract of the United States: 2007*. 126th edition. Washington, DC, 2006. Available at www.census.gov/compendia/statab (Accessed June 19, 2007).

U.S. Government Accountability Office, GAO-06-929. Credit Cards: Increased Complexity in Rates and Fees Heighten Need for More Effective Disclosures to Consumers. Report to Ranking Minority Member, Permanent Subcommittee on Investigations. Committee on Homeland Security and Governmental Affairs, U.S. Senate. September, 2006. Available at www.gao.gov/new.items/d06929.pdf (Accessed July 1, 2007).

U.S. Savings Bonds. Parkersburg, WV: Bureau of Public Debt. Available at www.treasurydirect.gov (July 3, 2007).

World Economic Outlook Database. April 2007. International Monetary Fund. Available at www.imf.org (May 31, 2007).

PERSONAL INTERVIEWS

Conner, Dawn, Senior Economic Education Specialist at the Federal Reserve Bank of St. Louis; interview by author, June 20, 2007.

Hollenbach, Peter, Director of Public Affairs, Bureau of Public Debt, interview by author, June 18, 2007.

Riedl, Brian M., Grover M. Hermann Fellow in Federal Budgetary Affairs, Heritage Foundation, interview by author, June 11, 2007.

Smith, Shelly, Senior Economist, Bureau of Economic Analysis, interview by author, June 6, 2007.

Spokesperson, Bureau of Engraving and Printing, interview by author, July 19, 2007.

Zerwitz, Donna, Director of Public Information, National Bureau of Economic Research, interview by author, July 31, 2007.

Index

About the Author

MARIE BUSSING-BURKS is a lecturer in economics in the College of Business at the University of Southern Indiana. In addition to teaching economics at the college level for 20 years, Bussing-Burks has taught Junior Achievement business classes in middle school and microeconomics to high school students. She is the author of *The Young Zillionaire's Guide to Taxation and Government Spending, Profit from the Evening News: Using Leading Economic Indicators to Make Smart Money Decisions*, and *Influential Economists*.